Craig Claiborne's Favorites

VOLUME THREE

Books by Craig Claiborne

The New York Times Cook Book
The New York Times Menu Cook Book
Craig Claiborne's Kitchen Primer
Cooking with Herbs and Spices
Classic French Cooking
WITH PIERRE FRANEY
The New York Times International Cook Book
The Chinese Cookbook
WITH VIRGINIA LEE
Craig Claiborne's Favorites Volume One
Craig Claiborne's Favorites Volume Two

Craig Claiborne's Favorites from The New York Times

VOLUME THREE

Times
BOOKS

We are indebted to a number of photographers and artists
whose work is reproduced in this book:
Bill Aller, pages 19, 28, 35, 51, 52, 53, 60, 73, 113, 129, 130, 131, 134, 166, 167, 170, 181, 188,
198, 206, 222, 231, 253, 277, 291, 293, 294, 295, 296
David Scott Brown, page 178
Diana Bryan, page 69
Michael Geiger, page 41
Arthur Grace, page 15
Granger Collection, page 163
James Hamilton, page 119
Cathy Hull, page 49
Leavenworth Jackson, page 110
Tom Koken, page 79
Gene Maggio, pages 84, 156, 212, 213, 234
Eugene Mihaesco, pages 6, 143
Propper/Elman, page 28
Marc Riboud, pages 242, 243
Richard Samperi, pages 94, 227, 228, 229
Sandy Solomon, page 9
George Tames, page 146
Alfred Wegener, page 101
Miriam Wosk, page 237
Tereza Zabala, page 264

Library of Congress Cataloging in Publication Data

Claiborne, Craig.
  Craig Claiborne's Favorites from the New York times.

  Includes indexes.
  1. Cookery.   I. Title: Favorites from the New York times.
TX715.C5743 1975   641.5   75-10599
ISBN 0-8129-0708-6 (v. 3)

For Velma Cannon

Contents

Foreword

It was Samuel Johnson, I believe, who said that the next best thing to eating a great dinner is to read about it. As a food diarist, I can amend that to say that the next most gratifying thing to dining well is to have those meals recorded between the covers of a book. And this volume is a personal diary of feasts and feasting.

In browsing through the records of these feasts, I have savored again a hundred pleasures. They have ranged from a memorable dinner in the small town of Crissier, Switzerland, to a spectacular home-cooked meal produced at the hands of the artist and friend, Ed Giobbi. The first meal embraced dozens of dishes perfumed with the likes of truffles and foie gras and wines of awesome vintage from French vineyards. The second was a complete and delectable meal that Ed conjured out of one large fish head and a pound of pasta, downed with a year-old bottle of wine of his own making.

There was a family feast of mussels gathered one wintry morning on Duxbury Bay in Massachusetts, and a "studious" feast, the recreation of numerous dishes that followed weeks of research at Monticello and in archives in Philadelphia pertinent to food that Thomas Jefferson, America's first and perhaps greatest epicure, might have enjoyed in Washington, Paris and back home in Virginia. That, of course, is but a brief sampling of what this book is all about.

One of the most cherished and highly personal entries in this book is an essay on eating, a subject I had pondered thousands of times over the past twenty years. In this essay I delivered myself of the theory that you can dine well, if you are of sound body, off the fat of the land—butter, eggs, cream and the other good things of life—provided you dine sensibly. Which is to say in moderation. In that essay, I was able to point out the hypocrisy of America's dietary habits and get in my licks about the fright merchants who scare the public out of their wits to peddle wares that promise to keep them eternally slim and young. A few pieces later, I again indulged my enthusiasms and printed a recipe for what I consider the single most elegant creation ever to come out of an oven—a gloriously rich coulibiac of salmon.

Within a twelve-month period, the palate was pampered with a feijoada completa, the national dish of Brazil, a complete herring table, a thorough-going Indian feast, and a venture into the kitchen of a wild boar farm in Nova Scotia. The scope of our feasting ranged from grits and an international assortment of hamburgers to a taste of caviar aboard a yacht en route to Block Island and a marvelously robust Neapolitan aggregation of traditional foods.

I was joined in most of this enterprise by Pierre Franey, and it might be of interest to tell of the beginning of my long-term collaboration with him. More than twenty years ago I had the great good fortune, at the age of 33, to spend a year at a hotel school in Switzerland. It was probably the single most auspicious year of my life. I had literally found myself and knew the direction I wanted my life to take. Prior to that time, I had rarely dined in the great restaurants of America—or the world for that matter. At the hotel school, both the preparation of food and the education in table service and wine was extraordinary. When I came to New York to live I was shocked at what I considered the poor quality of much of the food, particularly in the French restaurants in Manhattan. Table service was even more appalling. I set about in 1959 to write about these conditions. (It must be remembered that this was twenty years ago; to my mind and taste, things have improved immeasurably since that time.)

There was only one restaurant in all of the city with exacting standards and that was the late Le Pavillon. In the course of preparing my article, it was necessary to take a photograph to illustrate the activity in a luxury kitchen. I telephoned Henri Soulé and asked him to let me photograph his chef. He acquiesced and one morning in April I descended to the depths of the kitchen and made the acquaintance of the major domo who conjured up the food that was known internationally and served to the wealthy and fashionable and just plain epicures who had saved up their money. It was, of course, Pierre. We photographed him in his toque blanche standing before a table on which was placed a magnificent striped bass in champagne sauce. I was much impressed with his style and stature as well as his talent. I think he must have been impressed with the photograph and the fact that I had declared him to be the finest chef in the country. Shortly thereafter, Pierre and I held cooking sessions, sometimes once a week, sometimes twice. His contributions to the food columns of *The New York Times* during all the years since that article have been beyond measure. To my great pleasure, Pierre joined *The New York Times* as a member of the food staff in 1976. His contributions in this volume alone are much apparent.

Craig Claiborne's Favorites

VOLUME THREE

January 1976

I N THE COURSE of "news" coverage, there are always certain elements of humor and human interest that do not find their way into print. One of the most unforgettable mornings of my life came about in mid-January when I went to Duxbury, Massachusetts, to interview a gentleman named C. Graham Hurlburt. Now Mr. Hurlburt is, in his professional life, director of administrative services at Harvard University, but I went to visit him to pursue another of his interests, namely the aquaculture of mussels. As I indicated in the article, I am a highly nonathletic type whose major exercise at times seems to be getting in and out of bed. The morning that I met Mr. Hurlburt was bitterly cold but we went to visit his "farm," which was in fact Duxbury bay. He had fortunately insisted that I don heavy rubber boots and other cold weather paraphernalia to reach the boat that would convey us out to the mussel bed. It was necessary to navigate by foot and a prayer through twenty-odd feet of muck. For every step that I took forward, it seemed that I fell back three. With a certain amount of assistance from Mr. Hurlburt and my colleague, Pierre Franey, I tumbled into the boat head first. We spent an hour or longer under leaden skies hauling in a few bushels of mussels that he had cultivated. In those now half-frozen waters my fingers turned blue, the ink in my old-fashioned fountain pen refused to flow, and it turned out to be one of the great endurance contests of my life. All would have been well, however, had it not been for the prospect of renegotiating those dank, soggy and muddy shores. Going back, my feet went up and down in those boots like pistons and, ten feet from the automobile, I lurched forward and fell flat on my face in the mud. Worse, however, my secretarial pad—I am incapable of taking notes on anything else—became mired in the muck. When I returned to my desk, the notes of that morning were either confused or obliterated and it was necessary to reconstruct from memory the details of the interview. But guess what? I'm still mad about mussels!

Specialty Cuts

WITH PIERRE FRANEY

There was a time when specialty cuts of meat—"innards," if you will—were one of the chief bargains of the butcher's trade. Alas, the day may be past, with brains and liver, kidneys and so on, gone the way of the more expensive cuts. There are those, of course, who may view such victuals with loathing and distaste, and a pity it is for these foods can, with proper preparation, be sublime.

Veal Kidneys in Red Wine Sauce

3 tablespoons coarsely chopped shallots
1 cup dry red wine
½ bay leaf
2 sprigs fresh thyme or ½ teaspoon dried
½ teaspoon crushed peppercorns
2 sprigs parsley
4 teaspoons red wine vinegar
1 10¾-ounce can brown beef gravy
Salt and freshly ground pepper
3 veal kidneys, about 1¾ pounds
5 tablespoons butter
½ pound fresh mushrooms, thinly sliced
½ cup heavy cream

1. Combine the shallots, wine, bay leaf, thyme, peppercorns, parsley and one teaspoon of wine vinegar in a saucepan. Bring to the boil and cook about 5 minutes over high heat to reduce.

2. Add the brown beef gravy and simmer 15 minutes. Add salt and pepper to taste.

3. Meanwhile, split the kidneys in half and cut away the white center core. Thinly slice the kidneys crosswise and sprinkle with salt and pepper to taste.

4. Heat 2 tablespoons of butter in a skillet and, when it is very hot and starts to brown, add the kidneys. Cook, shaking the skillet and stirring, over high heat 2 to 3 minutes. No longer. Turn the kidneys into a colander and let stand 10 to 15 minutes to drain thoroughly. Do not wash the skillet but set it aside.

5. To the skillet in which the kidneys cooked add 1 tablespoon of butter and add the mushrooms. Cook over high heat until the mushrooms give up their juices and then until the liquid evaporates.

6. When the sauce is ready, add the remaining vinegar.

7. Add the drained kidneys to the mushrooms. Strain the sauce over all and bring to the boil. Add the heavy cream and when it reaches the boil, swirl in the remaining butter. Add salt and pepper to taste and serve piping hot with baked rice.

Yield: 4 to 6 servings.

Calf's Tripe
Genoa-Style

4   pounds honeycomb tripe
    Salt
2   tablespoons olive oil
½   cup ham fat or fatback
1   cup chopped onion
1   clove garlic, finely minced
1   cup dry white wine
1   hot dried red pepper
2   cups imported canned Italian
    peeled tomatoes
2   cups chicken broth
3   tablespoons chopped parsley
    Freshly ground pepper
    Grated Parmesan cheese

1. Place the tripe in a deep kettle and add water to cover and salt to taste. Bring to the boil and simmer about 30 minutes. Let stand until cool and refrigerate.

2. When ready to cook, drain the tripe and cut it into thin, bite-size strips.

3. Heat the oil in a deep casserole and add the ham fat. Cook about 5 minutes, stirring, and add the onion and garlic. Cook until onions are wilted and add the tripe.

4. Considerable liquid may come from the tripe. Cook this down about 10 minutes and add the wine and red pepper. Cook until almost all the liquid is evaporated. Add the tomatoes, chicken broth, parsley, salt and pepper to taste. Cook, uncovered, stirring occasionally, until quite tender, about 3 hours.

5. Serve with grated Parmesan cheese on the side.

Yield: 10 to 12 servings.

Sautéed Brains

1 *pair calf's brains, about 1 pound*
12 *peppercorns*
   Salt
2 *tablespoons wine vinegar*
1 *bay leaf*
2 *sprigs fresh thyme or ½ teaspoon dried*
   Freshly ground pepper
   Flour for dredging
3 *tablespoons butter*
3 *tablespoons olive oil*
3 *tablespoons lemon juice*
3 *tablespoons water*
1½ *tablespoons finely chopped dill*
2 *tablespoons finely chopped parsley*
½ *teaspoon oregano*
1 *tablespoon capers*

1. The calf's brain consists of a pair of lobes. Place them in a mixing bowl and add cold water to cover. Let them stand several hours, changing the cold water frequently.

2. Drain and pick over the brains to remove the outer membranes, blood and other extraneous matter. Place the brains in a saucepan and add cold water to cover a depth of about ½ inch above the brains. Add the peppercorns, salt to taste, vinegar, bay leaf and thyme. Bring to the boil and simmer about 3 minutes, no longer. Remove from the heat and drain. Run brains under cold water until chilled. They are now ready to cook when patted dry. If the brains are not to be cooked until later, leave them covered with cold water.

3. Season enough flour to coat the brains lightly with salt and pepper.

4. Cut the brains into slices about ¼ inch thick. Dredge in flour. Heat the butter in a skillet and brown the slices on both sides. Add more butter if necessary. Transfer the brains to a serving dish.

5. Combine the olive oil, lemon juice, water, dill, parsley, oregano and capers in a saucepan and bring to the boil. Pour the sauce over the brains and serve lukewarm.

Yield: 6 or more appetizer servings.

Tailored to the Food Processor

If we were to name the greatest food news event of the past year—indeed, the past couple of decades—it would undoubtedly be the phenomenal nationwide acceptance of the French import, the food processor, distributed in this country by Cuisinart. It has been heralded from Boot Head, Maine, Eureka, California, as perhaps the greatest food invention since toothpicks. It is predictable that the current year will see the advent of books on how to use the food processor, and we recently had the pleasure of meeting the first person who, to our knowledge, is offering cooking classes tailored to the machine's employ.

She is Rosemary Manell, a tall, enthusiastic, outgoing woman who has for ten years been an off-and-on helper of Julia Child. We met Rosemary behind the scenes of a television show here while Julia flipped a crepe and Rosemary stood in the wings.

"Julia and Paul and I have known each other for many years, about 30 to be exact. My husband, Abram, was in the Foreign Service with the Childs and we had a home in Marseilles. One time Paul and Julia drove down from Paris with their car trunk loaded with bottles of Pouilly Fumé, the perfect way to begin a friendship, and we've been friends ever since.

"A few years ago Julia came to California to give a benefit demonstration for the San Francisco Museum of Art. I live just across the bridge in Tiburon, so they called one morning and asked if I could give Julia a hand. Of course, I said yes and, ever since, I've been working with Julia whenever she's needed me.

"I was one of the first people in California to buy a food processor and, of course, there's nothing quite like it. I've given cooking lessons for several years, and it became apparent that a lot of people who own the machine seem a bit wary of it. What I teach is that some of the most ordinary things that happen in a kitchen can be done in a food processor and, of course, it has electric blenders beat by a mile.

"Quite honestly, I will never make mayonnaise with the old-fashioned method of using a whisk. That's easy, of course, but when you make it by hand it has a tendency to curdle once the mayonnaise is refrigerated. Made in the food processor, you couldn't shake it into curdling.

"I teach my students all the obvious things, of course—how to slice vegetables, carrots, cucumbers, celery, cabbage; how to chop mushrooms; how to make cream soups and so on. I also teach more advanced things like the preparation of shrimp quenelles.

"The quenelles I make use pâte à choux, which is cream puff pastry, so I

Rosemary Manell teaches students how to make best use of the food processor

make the cream puff mixture in the food processor, scrape it out without washing and then I make the shrimp purée.

"I use the machine for grinding meat, which can be important if you're making something like steak tartare when you want the meat to be ground at the last minute. Or if you want ground pork—a lot of butchers won't grind it unless they have a special machine for grinding pork.

"We make a lot of international foods in the class, tabbouleh, for example, the Lebanese appetizer made with cracked wheat. It calls for chopped parsley, onions and so on, a snap to prepare in the food processor."

The food processor, she noted, is fantastic for almost any pastry making and, of course, "for grating vegetables to be steamed and tossed in olive oil.

"It is excellent for grinding nuts to be used in making tortes and sensational for grinding oatmeal for cookies. It's marvelous for making macaroons.

"One of the most important things to learn in using the machine is to turn the motor on and off to control the kind of texture you need—fine, medium or coarse.

"I also encourage my students to buy a duplicate plastic container for their machine. It saves a lot of steps if you're making several dishes."

Here are several of Rosemary Manell's recipes using the food processor.

Tabbouleh

1   cup fine bulghur wheat (see note)
1   cup loosely packed parsley, preferably Italian parsley
1   cup loosely packed fresh mint leaves or 1 tablespoon dried
1   onion, cut into eighths, about one cup
½   cup coarsely chopped trimmed scallions, green part and all
½   cup fresh lemon juice, more or less to taste
¼   to ½ cup olive oil, more or less to taste
    Salt and freshly ground pepper to taste
3   tomatoes, skinned and cut into wedges for garnish

1. Place the wheat in a bowl and add water to cover, about 2 inches above the top of the wheat. Let soak for several hours or overnight.

2. Drain the wheat and squeeze dry in a clean dish towel. Place in a large bowl.

3. Rinse the parsley and mint and pat dry. They must be well dried, or they will become mush when processed. Place the herbs in the container of the food processor, using the steel blade. Mince but not too finely. Add to the wheat and stir with a fork.

4. Process the onions and scallions, taking care they are not over-blended. Do not crowd the machine, and process, if necessary, in 2 steps. Add to the wheat and stir.

5. Add about half the lemon juice and oil. Add salt and pepper to taste. Add more lemon juice and oil according to taste. Blend well and chill thoroughly, 8 hours or longer. Stir. Taste for seasonings and add more according to taste. Spoon into a low serving bowl and garnish with tomato wedges.

Yield: 6 servings.

Note: Bulghur is available in stores that deal in Middle Eastern foods.

Mushroom and Chicken Liver Pie

1   recipe for chilled pie pastry (see recipe)
½   pound fresh mushrooms, rinsed well and patted dry
2   or 3 shallots, peeled (or use half a small onion)
7   tablespoons butter
2   tablespoons peanut oil
    Salt and freshly ground pepper to taste
½   pound fresh chicken livers, trimmed, cut in half and patted dry
4   eggs, lightly beaten
1⅓ cups light (half and half) cream

1. Roll the pastry into a circle about $^3/_{16}$ of an inch thick. Fit the pastry into a 9- or 10-inch pie dish or quiche pan. Flute the edges. Prick the bottom of the pastry with a fork and chill the shell at least 1 hour.

2. Preheat the oven to 400 degrees. Line the chilled pie shell with wax paper or aluminum foil and fill with raw rice or beans, pressing filling against the sides of the shell. Bake 10 minutes or until pastry is set. Remove the foil and filling and bake 5 minutes longer. The rice or beans may be reserved for a later, similar use. Let the pie shell cool.

3. Reduce the oven heat to 375 degrees.

4. Quarter the mushrooms or cut them into eighths if they are large. Place half of them in the container of a food processor equipped with the steel blade. Blend until finely minced. Scoop them out into a bowl and add the remaining mushrooms to the food processor. Blend well and add these to the bowl.

5. Using the same container, add the shallots and blend. Add these to the mushrooms.

6. Heat 2 tablespoons of butter and half the oil in a skillet. Add the mushroom mixture and cook rapidly over high heat, stirring, until moisture evaporates and mushrooms are quite dry. Sprinkle with salt and pepper to taste. Spoon mixture into a bowl.

7. Add 2 more tablespoons of butter and the remaining oil to the skillet and, when quite hot, add the chicken livers. Cook until livers are nicely browned without but soft and pink within. Season with salt and pepper. Spoon into a dish.

8. Using a plastic spatula, spread the mushrooms over the bottom of the prepared pie shell. Smooth them over. Add the chicken liver pieces and press them into the mushrooms.

9. Combine the eggs and cream and blend well. Add salt and pepper and pour this over the chicken livers and mushrooms. The shell should be filled about a quarter inch from the top. The chicken livers should be covered with the custard. Dot with the remaining butter.

10. Place the pie on the middle rack in the oven and bake 30 to 40 minutes until puffed and nicely browned. Let cool briefly, 10 to 15 minutes before serving.

Yield: 6 to 8 servings.

Pastry dough

1¾ *cups flour*
12 *tablespoons cold butter, cut into thin slices*
2 *tablespoons solid vegetable shortening or lard*
1 *teaspoon salt*
Pinch of sugar
¼ *cup cold water, approximately*

1. Equip the container of a food processor with the steel blade. Combine the flour, butter, shortening, salt and sugar in the container. Blend gradually, turning the motor on and off while blending. Take care not to overblend. With the motor on, add the water gradually until dough begins to ball up. Add more or less water as necessary. Add just enough so that the dough holds together. The dough must not become a sticky mass.

2. Using a rubber or plastic scraper, turn the dough onto a lightly floured surface and knead quickly into a flat cake with the palm of the hand.

Wrap in plastic or wax paper and chill 2 hours or longer, perhaps overnight.

Yield: Pastry for 1 9- or 10-inch pie shell.

Note: You may prefer to remove the butter-flour mixture to a mixing bowl before adding the water. If so, turn the mixture into a mixing bowl and add the water gradually, tossing with a fork. Turn the dough onto a board and knead the dough, small portions at a time, by using the heel of the hand and pushing it away from you to blend the butter and shortening. Then form the dough into a flat cake and wrap and chill as indicated.

Salmon Pâté

2   cups cooked, boneless, skinless
    salmon (see note)
¼   to ½ cup heavy cream
2   tablespoons lemon juice, more
    or less to taste
2   tablespoons capers
1   tablespoon chopped fresh dill
    Salt and freshly ground
    pepper to taste

1. Place the fish in the container of a food processor, using the steel blade. Add about ¼ cup of cream and blend. Gradually add more cream until desired consistency is reached, taking care the mixture does not become too liquid. Stop the blending at intervals and scrape down the sides of the container with a plastic spatula. When properly blended, the mass should be mousselike, holding its shape when picked up with the spatula.

2. Spoon and scrape the mixture into a bowl and add the lemon juice, capers, dill, salt and pepper. Spoon

the pâté into a serving dish such as a small soufflé mold. Cover and chill well, preferably overnight. Garnish, if desired, with chopped dill. Serve with lightly buttered toast.

Yield: 4 to 6 servings.

Note: This pâté is particularly good if made with the leftover morsels of a poached whole salmon, the bits that cling around the main bones of the fish, near and in the head of the fish. These morsels are rich and gelatinous.

Food Processor Mayonnaise

2   egg yolks
    Salt to taste
2   teaspoons imported mustard,
    such as Dijon or Düsseldorf
1¼ cups peanut, vegetable or
    olive oil
    Freshly ground pepper to taste
2   teaspoons or more vinegar or
    lemon juice

1. Place the yolks in the container of the food processor equipped with the steel or plastic blade.

2. Add the salt and mustard and activate the food processor for a split second only. If the yolks are overhomogenized, they may break down. Have the oil in a measuring cup with a pouring spout. Start the motor while simultaneously adding the oil in a thin stream. After half the oil has been added, it can be added more rapidly. Add the remaining ingredients, processing just enough to blend. Spoon into a jar and refrigerate. This will keep a week or longer in the refrigerator.

Yield: About 1½ cups.

Almond Macaroons

½   pound almond paste (see note)
1   cup granulated sugar
2   or 3 egg whites
¼   teaspoon pure almond extract
⅛   teaspoon salt

1. Preheat the oven to 325 degrees.

2. Cut the almond paste into ½-inch pieces and place in the container of a food processor fitted with a steel blade.

3. Add the sugar, 2 egg whites, almond extract and salt. Blend well until smooth and no lumps remain in the almond paste.

4. The mixture should be soft but not loose. If it seems too stiff, add the remaining egg white to a mixing bowl and beat lightly. Add it, a little at a time, to the almond mixture. Blend after each addition.

5. Spoon and scrape the mixture into a bowl and beat with a wooden spoon.

6. Cut a rectangle of brown paper (from a grocery bag) to fit a cooky sheet. Drop the dough by spoonfuls onto the paper, flattening the mounds lightly with the back of a spoon. Place them about 1½ inches apart. If desired, the paste may be squeezed from a pastry bag onto the sheet. Bake 30 minutes or until lightly browned.

7. Cool on a rack. To remove the macaroons, dampen the bottom of the baking paper. Continue dampening slowly and lightly until the macaroons loosen easily.

Yield: 18 or more macaroons, depending on size.

Note: Almond paste is available in cans in fancy food markets and many supermarkets. Do not use almond pastry filling for macaroons.

Mad for Mussels

To a nonathletic type whose sporting blood courses somewhat slowly through his veins, it was a highly unlikely feat on a highly unlikely day. The temperature hovered in the 20's, the sky was overcast and gray and even the Canadian honkers floating on the bay looked desolate and cold. We snuggled more deeply into a quilted ski jacket, wiggled our toes in a pair of borrowed oversize rubber boots and tried to coordinate fingers to pad as C. Graham Hurlburt maneuvered his Land Rover bayside, backing his sixteen-foot fiber glass skiff toward the partly frozen bay.

"First time this bay's frozen over in years," he said, which did little to buoy our spirits or warm the air. "But look out yonder." Out yonder, we observed as we descended from the automobile and sank to our ankles in mud, were vast patches of black, rather large inky islands surrounded by water and ice.

"Everything black there is mussels, millions of them, and that's for lunch." That was a warming thought.

Mr. Hurlburt, who is director of administrative services at Harvard University, is convinced that given rope enough and time—and unpolluted water—America or any nation can do much to alleviate world hunger through commercial cultivation of the common, edible blue mussel, the kind that appears on French menus as moules marinière, moules poulette, moules frites and as the basis for billi-bi, the most delectable of soups.

"Most Americans don't eat mussels. Only the tiniest percentage of the population knows anything about them. The people who really covet them in this country are Europeans of a first or second generation, people who have traveled a great deal in Europe, or people who frequent European restaurants."

Mr. Hurlburt stated that he had eaten mussels all his life, that he has an adventurous appetite and practically nothing that wiggles or squirms in Duxbury or Plymouth Bay was beyond his eating.

His intense and highly serious interest in mussel culture came about two or three years ago.

"My vice president called me in and asked how I'd like a year's leave to pursue any line of work that interested me, much the same as professors on a sabbatical.

"Living around here all my life, I'd always been fascinated with mussels, how good they taste and how easily they proliferate. I also knew that mussels were grown commercially in Spain, France and the Netherlands among other places in Europe, so I decided to take my family, my wife and three of the four children, to investigate the mussel 'farms.' "

In Spain, he noted, they grow 1,000 times more pounds of mussel "meat"

C. Graham Hurlburt believes mussels are the answer to the world's food problems

per acre than we can grow beef in this country. It is possible under the best of circumstances to grow up to 300,000 pounds of mussel meat per acre.

"The astonishing thing to me," he said, "is the nutritional value of the common blue mussel in relation to choice T-bone steaks." He has published a comparison of the two that appears in a Department of Agriculture handbook and it is indeed astonishing. The comparison of three-and-a-half ounces of steak to a comparable amount of mussels found the protein content practically the same. Steak has more than four times more calories than mussels. Beef, the study found, has more than eighteen times more fat than mussels, and mussels have 3.3 grams of carbohydrates. Beef has none. A Department of Agriculture researcher put the cholesterol content of mussels slightly below that of beef.

"The cultivation of mussels is relatively simple. In a natural state, mussels attach themselves to and grow on rocks, on seaweed and themselves. They secrete a liquid that becomes a thread with a 'foot' on the end of it. They attach themselves on any thin solid. Simply put, you can cultivate mussels by using floats with ropes—thousands of them—that hang in the water. The mussels cling to the ropes and a single acre of water can accommodate three to five rafts." In this manner, the gentleman maintains, "in excess of a quarter million pounds of pure meat can be produced annually."

Seafood in this country is diminishing rapidly. "Oysters, clams, scallops, lobsters, they're all becoming scarce. Fishing, if you'll pardon the expression, stinks and most of the fish consumed in America is imported. If mussel cultivation really succeeded here, it would not only be good for mass consumption but would also help unemployment."

Perhaps his dedication to such ideals is inherited. His thirteenth-great-grandfather was Elder William Brewster, the preacher on the Mayflower. His family has lived in Duxbury and the environs of Plymouth Bay ever since.

His experiments have caused a good deal of interest in this country and in Canada. Mr. Hurlburt's enthusiasm extends to the kitchen, where his wife, Sarah, spends many hours each year turning out excellent dishes with mussels as a base, things like steamed mussels, marinated mussels with sour cream, mussel stews and chowders, chafing dish mussels with white wine, casseroles, and so on.

Steamed Mussels

2 *pounds mussels*
2 *shallots, coarsely chopped*
2 *small onions, quartered*
2 *sprigs parsley*
   Salt and freshly ground black pepper to taste
   Pinch of cayenne pepper
1 *cup dry white wine*
½ *bay leaf*
½ *teaspoon thyme*

1. Scrub the mussels well to remove all exterior sand and dirt. Place them in a large kettle with the shallots, onions, parsley, salt, black pepper, cayenne, wine, bay leaf and thyme. Cover and bring to a boil.

2. Simmer 5 to 10 minutes, or until the mussels have opened. Discard any mussels that do not open.

3. Serve the mussels hot in bowls with the liquid or, if desired, strain the mussels and reserve both mussels and liquid. Serve cold, using any desired recipe. Cold mussels in the shell are good with a bland mayonnaise or green mayonnaise.

Yield: 4 servings.

Marinated Mussels with Sour Cream

1 *quart steamed mussels (see recipe)*
2 *tablespoons olive oil*
2 *onions, thinly sliced*
2 *cloves garlic, finely minced*
½ *to 1 cup white vinegar, or according to taste*
1 *cup liquid in which mussels cooked*

1   carrot, scraped and cut into
    rounds
4   whole allspice
4   peppercorns
¼   teaspoon dried tarragon leaves
    or 2 sprigs fresh tarragon
¼   teaspoon dried basil
1   bay leaf
⅛   teaspoon cayenne pepper
    Salt to taste
    Lettuce leaves
1   cup sour cream

1. Drain the mussels, reserving 1 cup of the cooking broth. Let the mussels cool and then remove from the shell. Remove and discard the rubberlike band that surrounds each mussel. There should be about 2 cups.

2. Heat the oil in a kettle and add the onions. Cook, stirring, until wilted. Do not brown. Add the garlic, vinegar, reserved mussel broth, carrot, allspice, peppercorns, tarragon, basil, bay leaf, cayenne pepper and salt to taste. Bring to the boil and immediately remove from the heat. Let cool.

3. Add the 2 cups of mussels and chill overnight or longer.

4. Spoon portions of the mussels with a little of the vegetable and spice marinade on lettuce leaves. Serve with a spoonful of sour cream on top.

Yield: 6 to 12 servings.

Chafing Dish Mussels with White Wine

2   dozen well-scrubbed mussels
1   tablespoon olive oil
3   tablespoons butter

2   tablespoons finely chopped
    onion
¼   cup dry white wine
2   teaspoons finely chopped fresh
    parsley
    Fresh French bread

1. Scrub the mussels and set aside.

2. Heat the oil and butter in a chafing dish and when the butter starts to bubble, add the onion and mussels. Shake the pan and stir the mussels as they cook.

3. As the mussels cook, sprinkle lightly with some of the wine. Continue cooking, adding wine, until the mussels are fully opened, about 5 minutes. Serve immediately with the chafing dish liquid spooned over. Serve with French bread.

Yield: 2 servings.

Mussels for a Beach Picnic

6   quarts fresh mussels
¼   pound melted butter

1. Scrub and clean the mussels, pulling away all the hairy beard and rinsing clean in pure sea water.

2. Place the mussels in a deep, heavy kettle. Do not add water. Cover as closely as possible and place on a hot wood fire. Cook, shaking the kettle to redistribute the mussels top to bottom until they open, about 8 minutes. Serve the mussels in the shell with hot, melted butter. Serve the mussel broth on the side.

Yield: 6 servings.

A Connecticut Cook with Italian Connections

We first heard of Joseph Macaluso a few weeks ago pursuant to a column we wrote on Italian cookery, one that included a recipe for preparing a consummately good vegetable, a leafy green much prized by Italians and those of Italian descent.

In the article we spelled the name of the vegetable as we have always known it, rape (pronounced rah-peh) or rappini. Mr. Macaluso, who is of Italian origin and is himself a sometime food correspondent, wrote that "we have used rabe in our family for many years, and I have never heard it spelled rape or rappini. Even the supermarkets in Stamford spell it *rabe.*"

We have long considered doing missionary work by writing at some length about broccoli di rape or rape in that the sight of it whets our appetite. Another section of Mr. Macaluso's letter whetted our imagination as well, however, when he added:

"I don't consider myself an expert, but I did raise three sons by myself and to me the kitchen is the most fascinating room in the house. My parents insisted that when each of my brothers and sisters reached the age of 13, we be able to cook for the family for one year!"

With some dispatch we wrote the gentleman about our research on the subject, but more than that asked if we might visit him on his home territory to watch him cook.

Of the vegetable, we stated, "The conflict over the name is due, no doubt, to the long-time scarcity of the green in this country. It is, however, becoming increasingly available in supermarkets, which are supplied during the autumn and early winter from markets in New Jersey, throughout the cold months from California.

"One of the few cookbooks we know with recipes for the dish is Ed Giobbi's *Italian Family Cooking,* (Random House, 1971). Both his work and Ada Boni's fabled *Il Talismano della Felicita,* never adequately translated into English, spell the name of the vegetable broccoli di rape, and that is good enough for our own writings and record."

One morning recently we drove to Stamford to greet Joseph Macaluso who, as he stirred a pot of tomato sauce with meat balls, told us that his parents had come to this country from Sicily when they were in their teens.

"They were both fantastic cooks," he added, "and owned a small hotel and restaurant on the Jersey Shore. It was during the Depression and they loved to have company. I think that's important if you like to cook. I still remember Sun-

Joseph Macaluso did all the cooking for his children as a single parent

day mornings, watching my father stand on the doorstep inviting guests in for the midday meal. We often found ourselves dining with total strangers, but it didn't matter.

"Because of those lean times, I guess they wanted to know that all of us could take care of ourselves when we were on our own, and that's why we all had to take a hand at cooking."

Mr. Macaluso, who is 55 years old and a designer of men's sportswear for the Barclay Knitwear Company in Manhattan, said that his wife had died in 1957, and his children at first had gone to live with his parents and relatives. His work in that period kept him away from home for six months and longer each year, taking him to places like Hong Kong, New York, Florida and Italy.

Eventually he decided it would be best if he returned to be with and provide for his children, who range in age from 19 to 25 years old. The two youngest are now attending school at Westminster College in Fulton, Missouri. He has three grandchildren by his oldest son, Randy.

"It wasn't difficult really," he reminisced. "I provided a hot breakfast each morning and a hot dinner each evening. Once in a while we'd go to a restaurant, but my children protested that they'd rather eat at home. Of course, I had a lot of help both from my own family and my mother-in-law."

Mr. Macaluso is active in the Parents without Partners organization. He is the president of the Connecticut Regional Council, which has about 4,000 members and nine chapters. He also writes about food and recipes as a contributing editor to *The Single Parent Magazine*, the organization's publication.

During the school year Mr. Macaluso lives alone in his two-bedroom apartment with a small but well-equipped kitchen. He entertains a good deal, on the average of twice a month.

Today, the gentleman has his two youngest sons at home for school holidays and throughout the summer. He frequently visits his mother and father in Florida where his father tends a small but exceptional garden that produces hot red peppers to be dried or crushed, fennel, eggplant, basil and dandelions. There are also mango and lemon trees.

One speciality of the house down there is pureed fresh lemon pulp for salads. The lemons, fresh from the trees, are peeled. The peel is discarded and the rest, pulp, seeds and all, is blended in a blender. A spoonful or two goes into salad dressing along with oil, salt and pepper. Delicious.

Here are two recipes prepared recently in the Macaluso apartment, including one for broccoli di rape, his style. Delicious.

Broccoli di Rape

1¼ pounds broccoli di rape (also sold as plain rabe or rapi)
    Salt and freshly ground pepper to taste
½   teaspoon hŏt red pepper flakes
¼   cup olive oil
1   clove garlic, finely chopped

1. If the broccoli di rape is bright green, young and tender, it may be simply trimmed at the base and cooked. If it is a bit large and starting to lose its bright green color, it will be necessary to scrape the outside of the stems. The stems, if small, may be left whole. Or they may be cut in smaller pieces.

2. Rinse the broccoli di rape and drain without patting dry. It will steam in the water that clings to the leaves without adding more liquid.

3. Add the broccoli di rape to a heavy kettle with a tight-fitting lid and add the remaining ingredients. Cover closely and simmer over low heat about 5 minutes (see note). Serve immediately and, if desired, with lemon wedges.

Yield: 4 servings.

Note: Actually, Mr. Macaluso cooks his broccoli di rape for 45 minutes, but 5 minutes is more usual.

Chicken and Sausage with Olive and Anchovy Sauce

1½ pounds sweet or hot Italian sausage links
1   3-pound chicken, cut into serving pieces
    Salt and freshly ground pepper to taste
3   tablespoons olive oil
1   cup chopped celery

1   cup chopped onion
½   pound mushrooms, sliced
8   flat fillets of anchovies
½   cup imported black olives,
    preferably in brine and from
    Italy or Greece
1   tablespoon drained capers
¼   cup dry white wine
¼   cup tomato sauce or tomato
    paste

1. Cut the sausage links into 3-inch pieces. Add them to a heavy skillet and cook, turning, until browned all over. Remove, drain and add them to a casserole with a tight-fitting cover. Discard fat.

2. Sprinkle the chicken pieces with salt and pepper to taste. In another skillet, heat the olive oil and brown the chicken pieces lightly on all sides. Add the chicken to the sausage.

3. Meanwhile, add the celery to a saucepan and add water to cover and salt to taste. Bring to the boil and simmer about 5 minutes, or until crisp tender. Drain but reserve both the celery and cooking liquid.

4. To the fat remaining in the skillet after the chicken is cooked, add the onions and mushrooms. Cook, stirring, until onions and mushrooms are wilted. Add the anchovies, olives and capers. Add the drained celery. Add the wine and tomato sauce and simmer about 10 minutes and add this to the chicken and sausage. Add salt and pepper to taste and cover closely. Simmer on top of the stove about 30 minutes, or until chicken is tender. As the dish cooks, if it becomes too dry, add a little of the reserved celery liquid or a bit more tomato sauce.

Yield: 6 to 8 servings.

Mr. Macaluso's recipe for broccoli di rape brought forth a gush of letters relating to the availability or cooking of the vegetable. One lady wrote that her Italian vegetable man says that broccoli di rape is also known as mustard greens, and our advice to her is to change vegetable men or move to another neighborhood. Mary Bonavoglia of the Bronx wrote a note to state that broccoli di rape has been enjoyed in her home since she was an infant. She added that it is delicious when cooked with oil, pepper flakes and garlic and then served with cooked linguine, vermicelli or spaghettini. She recommends the proportion of two pounds of the hot, freshly cooked vegetable, combined with one pound of hot, freshly cooked, drained linguine. "Try it, you'll like it!" We tried it; we like it.

Elizza Montana of Brooklyn recommended yet another way: Fry three strips of bacon until crisp. Remove the bacon from the skillet. Crumble it and set aside. To the remaining fat in the pan, add two or three cloves of chopped garlic. Cook until lightly browned and add about one pound of rinsed, drained broccoli di rape. Cover and cook until wilted. Remove the cover and sprinkle with the crumbled bacon, salt and pepper. If desired, sprinkle with hot, crushed red pepper to taste.

February 1976

I F YOU PURSUE a life dedicated to eating and writing about food, you will inevitably encounter those who will ask if the thought of food does not at times lead to appetite paralysis. The answer is no. In the course of our labors with *The New York Times,* Pierre Franey and I frequently cook twenty or more dishes a day. We entertain regularly on weekends, and most of the conversation revolves around food. There is a certain wonder that after feasting on a five, six, or seven-course meal the appetite is still not satiated, the thirst still not quenched, and there is nothing more frustrating than to go in quest of a culinary idea and to be deprived of the target.

A case in point came about years ago when I traveled to Brazil with one primary aim: to taste the national dish of that country—feijoada, that marvelous, copious and inspired blend of black beans, salted meats, beef and assorted parts of the pig, including spareribs and pig's feet, and those wonderful, savory Portuguese sausages, linguica and paio. In addition, there are fantastic garnishes, including an onion sauce, collard greens, sliced oranges, and faroca, which is manioc flour.

I spent five days in Rio going from restaurant to restaurant searching in vain for a menu that listed the national dish. I learned that it is traditionally served only on Saturday at noon and my time schedule had not permitted my remaining in Brazil over a weekend. My first full experience with a feijoada came about a short while later (and this was nearly twenty years ago) in the home of Doña Dora Vasconcellos. Doña Dora, Brazilian consul-general in New York and a splendid hostess, had an exceptional cook named Noemia Faris. She was a rotund, good-humored lady who had served her specialty to many of the world's celebrities, whose names were duly recorded with appropriate greetings in Noemia's autograph book. One of the guests had been maestro Villa-Lobos, one of South America's most esteemed composers. His tribute was a brief composition titled "A Fugue Without End." The composition was, as I wrote in those days, in four parts, as any good feijoada should be. They were "Farofa," "Meat," "Rice," and "Black Beans."

Since that experience, I seem to have an incurable appetite for feijoada and, fortunately, I have been able to indulge it on numerous occasions in the home of a friend, Dorothea Elman. She makes what may well be the finest feijoada to be found in the United States today. Her recipe is recorded.

À la Mode Mexicaine

WITH PIERRE FRANEY

French chefs, over the years, have had a convenient device for naming dishes. It is the phrase "à la mode," which means "in the style of." Things called "turquoise" mean "à la mode turquoise," or Turkish style; "antiboise," in the style of Antibes; "genoise," Genoa; and so on. It might be thought of as a way of getting off the hook. We take that tack on this page with a menu that might be called "à la mode mexicaine," knowing full well that the dishes are not more authentically Mexican than El Paso. They are simply good dishes using some of the flavors and staples sometimes found in Mexican cooking.

Shrimp Seviche

1¼ pounds raw shrimp in the shell
  Salt
¼ teaspoon red pepper flakes
4 allspice
½ cup finely chopped onion
⅓ cup olive oil
½ cup lime juice
¼ cup chopped fresh coriander (cilantro) or Italian parsley
½ lime shell (squeezed), cut into tiny cubes
2 long hot green or red chilies, cored, seeded and chopped
1 teaspoon finely chopped garlic
1 teaspoon oregano, crushed

1. Cover the shrimp with cold water to cover. Add salt to taste, pepper flakes and allspice. Bring to the boil and simmer 30 seconds. Remove from the heat and let cool. Shell and devein.

2. Put the shrimp in a bowl and add salt to taste and the remaining ingredients. Cover and refrigerate several hours. Serve at room temperature.

Yield: 6 servings.

Chorizo-Stuffed Rump Roast

1 3½-pound rump roast or eye round.
½ pound chorizo sausage or kielbasa (Polish sausage)
  Salt and freshly ground pepper
2 tablespoons peanut, vegetable or corn oil
1 cup chopped onions
¾ cup chopped carrots
1 teaspoon finely minced garlic
½ cup chopped celery
2 tablespoons chili powder
1 tablespoon oregano, crumbled
1 17-ounce can peeled tomatoes with tomato paste, or 2 cups peeled tomatoes plus 2 tablespoons tomato paste
1 cup beef broth

1. Preheat oven to 375 degrees.

2. Make a hole lengthwise through the center of the meat. To do this, run a long, thin, sharp knife through the center. If a sharpening steel is available, this will assist in making the hole.

3. Stuff the opening with lengths of chorizo or other partly cooked sausage.

4. Sprinkle the meat on all sides with salt and pepper to taste.

5. Heat the oil in a heavy dutch oven or casserole and brown the meat all over, turning it frequently, about 10 minutes.

6. Remove the meat and pour off the fat. Return the meat and scatter the onions, carrots, garlic and celery around it. Add the chili powder and oregano and pour the tomatoes over all. Stir in the tomato paste and beef broth. Add salt and pepper to taste and cover. Bring to the boil on top of the stove.

7. Place the meat in the oven and bake 2½ to 3 hours or until the roast is thoroughly cooked and tender. Remove the meat and skim the surface of the sauce to remove all fat. Serve the roast sliced with the sauce.

Yield: 8 or more servings.

Cumin Rice

2   *tablespoons butter*

2   *cups diced green or red sweet peppers*
⅓   *cup chopped onion*
1   *clove garlic, finely minced*
1   *teaspoon cumin*
1½   *cups raw Carolina rice*
1½   *cups hot chicken broth*

1. Preheat oven to 400 degrees.

2. Heat the butter in a casserole and add the peppers and onion. Cook, stirring, until onion is wilted. Add the garlic, cumin and rice. Stir.

3. Add the broth and cover. Bring to the boil on top of the stove and then bake 17 to 20 minutes or until liquid is absorbed and rice is tender.

Yield: 6 to 8 servings.

Oranges Mexicaine

2   *cups orange wedges*
¼   *cup confectioners' sugar*
2   *tablespoons lime juice*
1½   *ounces tequila*
1   *ounce cointreau*

1. Put the orange wedges in a mixing bowl and sprinkle with the sugar and lime juice. Refrigerate.

2. When ready to serve, add the tequila and cointreau. Stir and serve as dessert.

Yield: 6 servings.

Feijoada

King John VI of Portugal, who lived from 1779 to 1826, fled to Brazil with the royal family during the first decade of the nineteenth century and there set up his court. He probably died unaware that he was, in a sense, father of one of the great dishes of the world, Brazil's famed feijoada.

His presence, at least, is credited with the beginnings of the dish in the mind of Dorothea Elman, who makes without question the best and most ambitious feijoada (pronounced fay-joe-ahda) we've ever been privileged to dine on, and we've dined on several including one for which composer Heitor Villa-Lobos scribbled a small, unfinished fugue in the cook's notebook.

"Feijoada is, of course, the national dish of Brazil," Mrs. Elman noted. The handsome young woman, a partner in Propper/Elman, a graphic- and industrial-design consulting firm in Manhattan, added that "beans have always been a staple in my country, the constant diet of the poor. The everyday bean dish is called feijao [pronounced vaguely, fay-jaw], which may be simply a dish of beans flavored and cooked with a bay leaf and a pig's tail."

According to Mrs. Elman, it was King John who imported slaves from Africa into Brazil, and it was the African influence that raised the feijao to its ultimate glory as feijoada.

"The African influence is very much apparent in the extraordinary use of various parts of the pig, which had never made their way to the white table—pig's ears, pig's feet—collard greens and perhaps even mandioca [manioc] flour, which is made with ground cassava root."

A feijoada completa is one of the most festive dishes known to man, and we wholeheartedly agree with Mrs. Elman's long considered appraisal that it is also one of the most sensual.

"There is this extraordinary blending of textures—the coarseness of the manioc flour, the seductive flavor of the beans cooked with meats, the crunchiness of onion and collard greens—the marvelous combination of flavors, tomato and oranges and hot peppers and, of course, the substantial but tender variety of sausages and meats. There's a good bit of voodoo involved in all of this." We have yet to meet the person who, including ourselves, on first being introduced to the dish did not start rhapsodizing in a similar vein.

Although there are more than a score of components to the best feijoada, including the basic bean dish with its meats and the cold garnishes, there are an infinite number of conceivable and acceptable mutations. Almost any of the meats can be eliminated but within reason. The dish calls, for example, for two kinds of Portuguese sausages, which are available at special sources. For these, Polish or other sausages commonly found in supermarkets could be substituted.

Dorothea Elman holds Brazil's national dish, which has more than twenty ingredients

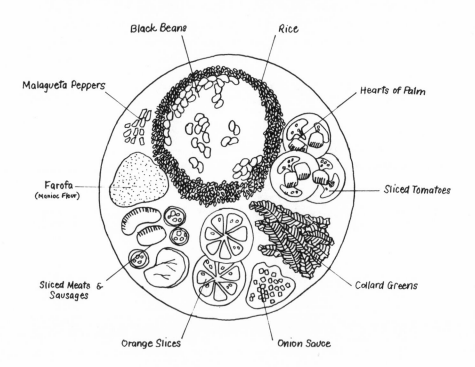

Fresh pork hocks could be substituted for the odd parts of the pig such as the tail, ears and foot. The ears could be eliminated altogether, and so on.

The workings of a proper feijoada are as follows: The meats, including the sausages, are thinly sliced and arranged neatly on platters. The meats with the beans, which have somewhat disintegrated into a fantastic dark sauce, are served hot in a separate dish. So is the rice.

The garnishes, all of which are served separately, include a cold onion sauce, the hot shredded collard greens, a tomato and heart of palm vinaigrette, a cold orange salad, the manioc flour plus hot peppers. The flour is always browned when Mrs. Elman makes a feijoada and blended with olives and eggs. In many homes it is simply served raw.

Before the meal, Mrs. Elman serves an insidiously good (and strong) rum and lemon drink and, as a dessert, a Croesus-rich egg and coconut "pie." You can't get more festive than that.

The ingredients for a feijoada can be obtained in Portuguese and Spanish markets on Ninth Avenue and at the markets on upper Park Avenue between 110th and 116th Streets. One specific source for many of the ingredients, including the salted pig parts, farofa and so on, is Serafim C. Garnecho Grocery Store, a Portuguese-American delicatessen, 323 Bleecker Street.

Feijoada Completa

1 pound black turtle beans (*feijao preto*)
1 clove garlic, peeled
1½ pounds jerked beef (*carne sêca*)
1 1- to 1¼-pound salted pig's foot (*pé*)
½ pound salted pig's tail (*rabo*)
3 pig's ears (*orelha*)
1¼ pounds salted spareribs (*costeleta*)
2 smoked ham hocks (*joelho*)
⅓ pound lean, smoked fat back (*toucinho*)
1 1½-pound fresh pig's foot, split in half (to yield the knuckle plus the bottom of the foot)
1 ¾-pound fresh pig's tail
1½ pounds smoked beef tongue (half a tongue)

1½ pounds lean chuck or bottom round
1 Portuguese sausage of the kind called linguica, about ¾ pound
1 Portuguese sausage of the kind called paio, about 1½ pounds
¼ cup peanut, vegetable or corn oil
1 cup finely chopped onion
2 cloves garlic, finely minced
½ cup chopped fresh parsley

Garnishes

Brazilian rice (see recipe)
Onion sauce (see recipe)
Collard greens (see recipe)
Tomato and heart of palm salad (see recipe)
Orange salad (see recipe)
Farofa (see recipe)
Pickled malagueta, Tabasco or other hot peppers

1. It is important to note that in making this recipe the beans will be reduced to a delicious sauce. Most of the beans will not retain their firm shape. It is also important that the beans be stirred from the bottom often to prevent sticking. The pieces of meat must be turned often so that they will cook evenly.

2. Place the beans in a large bowl and add the peeled garlic clove. Add water to cover to about 1½ inches above the top level of the beans. Let soak overnight.

3. Split the jerked beef in half lengthwise. Place in a separate bowl and add water to cover. Let stand overnight.

4. Combine the salted pig's foot, pig's tail, pig's ears and spareribs. Add water to cover and soak overnight.

5. Add the ham hocks and fat back to another bowl with water to cover and soak overnight.

6. When ready to cook, remove the garlic clove from the beans. Add the beans and their soaking liquid to a large kettle. Add the smoked fat back. An ideal kettle measures about 16 by 5 inches with an 18-quart volume, but this is arbitrary. Any kettle large enough to contain the beans, cooking liquid and meats will do.

7. Add 6½ quarts (26 cups) of water and bring to the boil without adding salt. It should not be necessary to add much more water to the kettle, but add a little more as you deem necessary. Simmer, uncovered, over medium heat.

8. As the beans cook, drain the jerked beef and scrape away all yellow fat that coats the meat. Place the beef in a separate pot, cover well with water and let boil about 2 hours. Add more water as necessary to keep the meat always covered. Drain the meat and add it to the beans.

9. At the same time, drain the smoked ham hocks, salted pig's tail, salted pig's foot, salted spareribs and salted pig's ear. Put them in another pot and cover with water. Bring to the boil and simmer 10 minutes. Drain and add the meats to the beans.

10. Similarly, add the fresh pig's foot and fresh pig's tail to a kettle and add water to cover. Bring to the boil and simmer 10 minutes. Drain and add to the beans.

11. Add the tongue and chuck to the beans and continue cooking. As the meats become tender, remove them and set aside. For example, the pig's tails, ears, both fresh and salted, the spareribs and smoked fat back should be tender after cooking about 1 hour and 20 minutes. The tongue should cook for about 1 hour.

12. When the beans have cooked for about 1½ hours, place the sausages in a kettle and add cold water to cover. Bring to the boil and simmer about 1 minute. Drain and add to the beans. Let the sausages cook about 20 minutes and remove them.

13. Continue cooking the beans for 4 to 4½ hours. At the end of that time the jerked beef, ham hocks, fresh pig's foot and lean beef should be tender and all the meats removed.

14. To finish the dish, heat the oil in a skillet and add the onion and minced garlic. Cook until the onion is wilted. Add the parsley and stir. Add about 1 cup of the beans from the kettle and stir to blend. Spoon and scrape this mixture into the boiling beans.

15. Serve the meats thinly sliced, removing and discarding bones as necessary. Arrange them symmetrically on 1 or 2 large platters. In separate bowls and platters serve the hot beans, rice and all the garnishes. Let guests help themselves. The foods are generally spooned onto and eaten from one single plate per guest.

Yield: 12 to 16 servings.

Brazilian rice

2   cups long-grain rice
3   tablespoons peanut, vegetable or corn oil
¾   cup finely chopped onion
1   clove garlic, finely minced
    Salt to taste
3   cups water

1. Rinse the rice and drain it.

2. Heat the oil in a heavy casserole with a lid. Add the onions and garlic and cook, stirring, until onion is wilted.

3. Add the rice, salt and water and bring to the boil. Cover closely and reduce the heat. Simmer over low heat about 25 minutes or until rice is fully cooked and tender.

Yield: 12 to 16 servings for feijoada.

Onion sauce

4   cups finely chopped onion
1   whole clove garlic
2   cups distilled white vinegar
1   large or 2 small bay leaves
⅔   cup peanut, vegetable or corn oil
4   teaspoons liquid from canned pickled jalapenos or other hot peppers (see note)

2   tablespoons finely chopped jalapenos or other hot chilies (see note)
    Salt to taste
½   teaspoon freshly ground black pepper

Combine all the ingredients and let stand at room temperature several hours. Remove garlic clove before serving.

Yield: About 5 cups.

Note: The traditional hot peppers used in this recipe are malagueta peppers. They are rarely available in America. Jalapenos are available in markets and supermarkets where Mexican ingredients are sold.

Collard greens

3   large bunches collard greens, about 1½ pounds each
1½ cups lean salt pork cut into ¼-inch cubes

1. Rinse the collard greens and shake or pat most of the water from the leaves. Cut off the tough bottom stems. Also, using a sharp knife, cut away and discard the tough part of the stems that go about halfway up into the center of the leaves.

2. Stack the leaves, about 10 at a time, and roll them into a sausage shape. Using a sharp knife, cut the rolled greens into fine shreds. There should be about 14 cups.

3. Heat the salt pork in a large, heavy skillet, stirring. Cook until all fat is rendered and the pieces of salt pork are crisp. Spoon out and reserve the crisp pieces. Leave the fat in the pan

4. Just before serving, heat the fat in the pan. Add the collard greens to the skillet and cook, stirring, quickly. Cook and stir until the greens are piping hot, a bit darker and slightly wilted. Cook about 1 minute and spoon the greens into a serving dish. Scatter the crisp pieces of salt pork over the greens and serve hot.

Yield: 12 to 16 servings for feijoada.

Tomato and heart of palm salad

6   *to 8 red, ripe, firm tomatoes, about 3 pounds*
2   *14-ounce cans heart of palm*
1   *cup salad dressing (see recipe)*

1. Do not peel the tomatoes, but cut away and discard the cores. Cut the tomatoes into slices about ¼ inch thick. Arrange them neatly on a flat serving dish.

2. Drain the hearts of palm and cut the palm into slices about ⅓ inch thick. Arrange the heart of palm over the tomatoes. Spoon the salad dressing over.

Yield: 12 to 16 servings for feijoada.

Salad dressing

¼   *cup red wine vinegar*
¾   *cup olive oil*
1   *teaspoon water*
1   *tablespoon dry mustard*
     Salt and freshly ground pepper to taste
1   *clove garlic*
½   *teaspoon sugar*

Combine the ingredients and shake, beat or blend to blend

thoroughly. Let sit for 2 hours before using. Remove garlic clove.

Yield: About 1 cup.

Orange salad

10   *to 12 very sweet seedless oranges*

1. Peel the oranges, cutting away all the external white pulp from the surface of the oranges.

2. Cut the oranges into slices about ⅓ inch thick. Arrange them symmetrically in a bowl, slices overlapping.

Yield: 12 to 16 servings for feijoada.

Farofa

1½   *pounds farinha de mandioca (manioc flour)*
12   *tablespoons butter*
¼   *pound sliced bacon cut into ½-inch squares*
1   *cup unpitted, imported black or green olives*
4   *hard-cooked eggs, peeled Salt to taste*

1. Preheat the oven to 400 degrees.

2. Place the farinha in a flat, rectangular baking pan. A pan measuring 16 by 9 by 2½ inches is ideal. Place the pan in the oven at 400 degrees and bake 50 minutes, stirring often to prevent burning. When ready, the flour should be sand-colored and uniformly brown. Cut the butter into pieces and add it, stirring, to coat the flour evenly. Continue baking about 10 minutes.

3. Meanwhile, cook the bacon in a skillet until it is crisp. Drain the pieces. Discard the fat.

4. Add the bacon and olives to the flour. Chop the eggs and add them. Add salt to taste. Stir well until all ingredients are blended.

Yield: 12 to 16 serving for feijoada.

Quindin de Yá-yá

(An egg and coconut dessert)

11 *egg yolks*
1   *whole egg*
2   *tablespoons melted butter*
2   *cups dessicated shredded unsweetened coconut, available in health food shops*
2   *cups sugar*

1. Preheat the oven to 375 degrees.

2. Combine the yolks and whole egg in the bowl of an electric mixer. Spoon in the butter. Add the coconut and sugar.

3. Beat, gradually increasing speed, until the ingredients are thoroughly blended.

4. Lightly butter a 9- or 10-inch glass pie plate. Pour and scrape the mixture into the pie plate. Place the plate on a baking dish and pour boiling water around it. Bake 2 hours or until a needle or the point of an ice pick comes out clean when inserted in the middle.

5. Invert the dish, while hot, onto a pie plate. It may be necessary to run a thin sharp knife around the rim of the pie to help it unmold.

Yield: 12 to 16 servings.

Batida

(A daiquiri-like rum drink)

1   *cup fresh lemon juice*
2½ *cups cachaça (see note) or white rum*
¾   *cup sugar*

Combine all the ingredients in the container of an electric blender. Blend until the sugar is melted.

Yield: About 3½ cups.

Note: Cachaça is a white rum spirit, quite inexpensive in Brazil and ideal for this drink.

Specialties of the Landes Region

In the world of gastronomy, nobody in America is outdoing the French when it comes to commemorating the Bicentennial. A few weeks ago the outfit known as Food and Wines from France staged a luncheon presided over by the Count Philippe de Lafayette, a descendant of the French rebel who aided the American cause. The dessert for the occasion was coupe Jefferson.

More recently, La Société des Maîtres Cuisiniers de France, an organization whose membership includes many of the most prestigious French chefs of the world, sponsored a dinner at the Hotel Pierre in Manhattan. The menu included filets de sole Washington, which turned out to be sole fillets with an américaine sauce made with lobster; a granité de la victoire de Yorktown, an ice to be taken between courses to refresh the palate; a main course of roast squab sur canapé Lafayette, and the last course, a surprise glace de bicentennaire or a Bicentennial vanilla and pistachio "bombe."

Perhaps the most interesting part of the dinner was a decidedly un-American but decidedly delicious first course that had been brought to these shores by Jacques Grimaud, one of the leading producers and packers of foie gras in France. The dish in question was slices of fresh foie gras baked in loaves of brioche dough and with aspic added. It was something of a triumph and, Mr. Grimaud explained, something that, if present plans go through, may be found in specialty shops and the luxury restaurants of Manhattan.

The dish, to our knowledge, is unique as an import and its availability depends on an impressive feat, transporting a highly perishable product from France and maintaining a high standard of excellence through an Atlantic crossing. The foie gras as served was marvelously pink, tender and rich as butter. The brioche casing was excellent.

At the dinner, Mr. Grimaud informed us that he accomplishes his feat by packing the produce in a composition plastic such as styrofoam and shipping it to this country within hours of its production.

So impressed were we with Mr. Grimaud's product and his inventiveness, we invited him into our kitchen in East Hampton to cook and tell us more.

Mr. Grimaud, who is 58 years old and weighs 185 pounds, has had professional training as a chef. He arrived about noon with his wife, Yvonne, a pretty Frenchwoman who is also an excellent cook.

The gentleman told us that his family's firm, Le Foie Gras Vieille France, in the small town of Malbourguet in the southwest of France, was started by his father in 1922. His father had been a chef prior to World War I, working in such

Jacques Grimaud is from the region of foie gras, Armagnac, and ortolans

establishments in Paris as the restaurants Fouquet, Prunier and Gaillon. During the war he enlisted in the army and shortly thereafter was the victim of a poison gas attack.

On recovery he was advised to leave the cold of Paris, so he went south and started a goose farm. His professional training had qualified him well for the preparation of foie gras—a technique said to date from the ancient Romans—and because of his friendly relations with the chefs of Paris, he was able to sell his product rather easily. Today they supply many of the best restaurants throughout the nation.

During his stay in East Hampton he prepared, as we had requested, several spécialités landaise, that is to say the foods of the Landes region, which is known for Armagnac, the region's strong and admirable equivalent of cognac; guinea hens; turkeys; chickens; and ortolans or bobolinks, those small birds pan roasted and eaten whole.

Among the dishes he prepared on his visit were roast chicken with piperade, the delectable Basque-flavored specialty that resembles ratatouille, and a tourte landaise, an interesting and easily made anise-flavored cake served with pastry cream.

Mr. Grimaud also made a splendid foie gras salad, which is interesting on a number of counts. This salad consists of Boston lettuce leaves garnished with wafer-thin slices of foie gras and a dressing made with lemon juice, port wine and oil. It is served increasingly in the luxury restaurants of France, and Mr. Grimaud states flatly that it was the culinary invention of his father, André, founder of Le Foie Gras Vieille France.

As he went about his preparations, aided by his wife, the chef told us that he raises 10,000 specially fattened geese each year and 20,000 ducks, which are also fattened. The livers from both birds are processed as foie gras and the meat is turned into a confit or preserved dish, also canned.

Foie gras begins with the fattening of the poultry and this requires from four to five months. The geese or ducks are fed for a short while on bran. The diet is then changed to nettles and cabbage with lots of water. For three months or so they dine on grass and, after four months, on wheat and oats. During the final two weeks they are fed corn that has been cooked in water or milk.

When the geese or ducks have been killed, the livers are soaked in milk and then drained. Before cooking the livers are marinated with salt, a touch of nutmeg, pepper, Armagnac and port wine. The livers are then either pressure cooked or baked. The end result is absolute bliss, even more so if the foie gras is served with a highly chilled, genuine sauternes wine, which is unctuous, sweet and fruity. A curious combination but a marriage made in heaven.

We were fascinated to learn that although more than two million pounds of foie gras are processed in France each year, less than half the livers are from domestic geese. French foie gras producers must necessarily rely on imports, chiefly from Poland, Hungary, Czechoslovakia and Israel. Israel, Mr. Grimaud said, produces and exports to France enormous quantities of the raw livers. Israeli foie gras, he adds, is some of the finest in the world.

Here are some of Mr. Grimaud's specialties.

Poulets Rotis à la Piperade et Sauce Moutarde

(Roast chicken with piperade and mustard sauce)

2	3½-pound chickens
3	tablespoons butter
	Salt and freshly ground pepper to taste
1	cup water
½	cup heavy cream
4	tablespoons imported mustard such as Dijon or Düsseldorf Piperade (see recipe)

1. Preheat the oven to 400 degrees.

2. Rub the chickens all over with butter. Sprinkle them inside and out with salt and pepper. Truss. Arrange the chickens on their sides in a shallow roasting pan.

3. Roast the chickens about 20 minutes and turn them on the other side. Baste often. Continue roasting about 20 minutes and turn the chickens on their backs. Roast 20 minutes or longer or until cavity juices run clear when chickens are lifted so that the juices flow into the pan. Continue roasting, if necessary, until done.

4. Remove the chickens and keep warm. Pour off the fat from the pan. Add the water to the pan, stirring to dissolve the brown particles that cling to the pan. Pour this pan liquid into a saucepan and cook to reduce by half.

5. Add the cream and cook briefly. Add the mustard and cook, stirring, about 30 seconds.

6. Serve the chicken sliced with the mustard sauce and piperade.

Yield: 8 to 12 servings.

Piperade
(A tomato and pepper dish)

5	green peppers, about 1½ pounds
5	large, red, ripe tomatoes, about 2½ pounds
2	or 3 onions, about ¾ pound
1	clove garlic, finely minced Salt and freshly ground pepper to taste
¾	cup plus 1 tablespoon peanut, vegetable or corn oil
⅛	pound thinly sliced prosciutto or other ham, cut into shreds or cubes
1	tablespoon finely minced garlic
2	bay leaves
3	eggs

1. Core and seed the peppers. Cut them into thin strips. There should be about 5 cups. Set aside.

2. Core and peel the tomatoes. Cut them into eighths. There should be about 5 cups. Set aside.

3. Peel the onions and cut them in half. Then cut the onions into very thin slices. There should be about 3 cups. Set aside.

4. Heat ¼ cup of oil in each of 3 skillets. Add the peppers to one skillet, the tomatoes to another and the onions and garlic to the third. Cook the peppers, onions and garlic until they are browned without burning, about 30 minutes. Cook the tomatoes until they are somewhat reduced and saucelike. Add the peppers and onions

to the tomatoes. Add salt and pepper to taste.

5. Heat the remaining tablespoon of oil in a skillet and add the ham. Cook about 30 seconds and add to the tomatoes. Add the garlic and the bay leaves. Cook about 15 minutes.

6. Turn the heat to very low and add the eggs one at a time, stirring constantly. The trick is to incorporate the eggs into the tomato sauce, stirring so as to prevent curdling. The heat must be gentle. After the eggs are added, do not cook further but serve immediately.

Yield: 8 to 12 servings.

Omelette piperade

Prepare the recipe for piperade, but do not add the eggs at the end. Make omelets according to standard recipe and use the tomato and green pepper sauce as a filling.

Salade André Grimaud

(Salad with port wine dressing, foie gras and truffles)

6   cups Boston lettuce leaves, prepared for the salad bowl
     Salt and freshly ground pepper to taste
3   tablespoons lemon juice
3   tablespoons peanut oil
1   tablespoon port wine
3   to 4 wafer-thin slices foie gras (either duck or goose liver) per serving
½   cup slivered black truffles, optional

1. The lettuce should be rinsed well and patted dry or dried in a spin-drier.

2. Add the salt and pepper to a salad bowl. Add the lemon juice and whisk in the oil and port wine.

3. Add the lettuce and toss well to coat. Arrange the salad on individual chilled salad dishes. Arrange 3 or 4 slices of foie gras over the salad. Sprinkle with truffles and serve.

Yield: 8 to 12 servings.

Tourte Landaise "Pastis Bourrit"

(An egg cake from the Landes region of France)

½   pound sweet butter
4¼   cups cake flour
1   tablespoon baking powder
½   teaspoon salt
1   cup plus 2 tablespoons sugar
4   eggs, separated
1   cup milk
2   tablespoons lemon juice
3   tablespoons Pernod, Ricard or other anise-flavored liqueur
     Pastry cream (see recipe)

1. Place the butter in a heavy saucepan and let stand over gentle heat until melted. Let cool, but the butter should remain liquid.

2. Preheat the oven to 325 degrees.

3. Add the flour to a mixing bowl and add the baking powder and salt. Add the sugar and blend well. Make a well in the center of the flour and add the yolks, stirring and mixing. Add the milk alternately with the melted butter and, when blended, beat the batter with the hands. Combine the lemon juice and Pernod and add.

4. Beat the egg whites until stiff and fold them in.

5. Butter 2 6-cup charlotte molds and add half the batter to each. Bake 1 hour and increase the heat to 350 degrees. Bake 10 minutes longer. Use your judgment in baking times and increased temperature. Let stand briefly and then unmold the cakes. Let cool to room temperature. Serve sliced with pastry cream.

Yield: 8 to 12 servings.

Pastry cream

6 *tablespoons flour*

6 *tablespoons confectioners' sugar*
5 *egg yolks*
1½ *cups milk*
½ *teaspoon vanilla*
⅛ *teaspoon salt*

1. Combine the flour and sugar.

2. Add the yolks to a mixing bowl and beat in the flour mixture. Gradually beat in the milk, vanilla and salt.

3. Cook over gentle heat, stirring constantly, until the mixture coats the back of a wooden spoon and has the consistency of heavy cream. The mixture must not boil, or it may curdle. Should the mixture curdle slightly, strain it through a sieve.

Yield: About 2 cups.

Vegetable Variety

WITH PIERRE FRANEY

America, by and large, is not a nation of vegetable eaters and the national techniques for cooking vegetables seem remarkably limited. That may account for the recent spate of books that bear such titles as *Eat Roughage, Live Longer*. All greens, cooked or raw, are indisputably good for the system, and vegetables, of course, can be prepared in an infinite variety of ways. Green beans become a wholly new experience when cooked au gratin; zucchini, a relatively new arrival on the American scene (it was all but unheard of in this country twenty years ago) is capital baked with herbs and cheese; and carrots and celery, perhaps the commonest vegetable staples in the nation's refrigerators, are delectable when creamed—but without using a standard cream sauce made with flour.

Green Beans au Gratin

1¼   *pounds green beans*
1   *pound potatoes*
     Salt
5   *tablespoons butter*
⅛   *teaspoon grated nutmeg*
3   *tablespoons Parmesan cheese*

1. Preheat oven to 450 degrees.

2. Pick over the green beans and cut them into 2-inch lengths. Set aside.

3. Peel the potatoes and cut them into 2-inch pieces. Put the potatoes in a saucepan and add cold water to cover and salt to taste. Bring to the boil and add the green beans. Cook 10 to 15 minutes or until the beans are crisp tender. Do not overcook. Drain.

4. Pour the mixture into the container of a food processor or blender and blend to a fine puree. Add 3 tablespoons butter and salt to taste. Add the nutmeg. Spoon and scrape the mixture into a baking dish and smooth it over. Sprinkle with cheese and dot with remaining butter. Bake 20 minutes.

Yield: 4 to 8 servings.

Zucchini à l'Italienne

(Baked zucchini with herbs and cheese)

3   *or 4 medium-size zucchini, about 1¾ pounds*
     Salt and freshly ground pepper
⅓   *cup plus 2 tablespoons olive oil*
1   *clove garlic*
1   *cup white bread trimmed of crust and cut into 1-inch cubes*
6   *sprigs fresh parsley*
½   *teaspoon rosemary leaves*
⅓   *cup Parmesan cheese, preferably freshly grated*

1. Preheat oven to 400 degrees.

2. Trim off the ends of the zucchini and cut the zucchini on the bias into ½-inch slices.

3. Sprinkle the slices with salt and pepper. Heat ⅓ cup of oil in a skillet and cook the slices until golden brown on one side. Turn and brown on the other. This may take several steps. Arrange the slices slightly overlapping on a baking dish in which they will fit neatly.

4. Blend the garlic, bread, parsley and rosemary in a food processor or blender. Sprinkle this over the zucchini and sprinkle with the cheese. Dribble the remaining oil over all and bake 20 minutes or until bubbling. If desired, run under the broiler to brown further.

Yield: 6 to 8 servings.

Creamed Carrots and Celery

4 *large carrots, about 1 pound*
5 *or 6 ribs celery, about*
   ¾ pound
   Salt
6 *tablespoons butter*
   Freshly ground pepper
¼ *teaspoon grated nutmeg*
½ *cup heavy cream*

1. Trim and scrape the carrots and celery.

2. Cut the carrots into ¼-inch slices lengthwise. Cut each slice into 1½-inch lengths. There should be about 2½ cups.

3. Cut the celery ribs into ¼-inch strips lengthwise and cut the strips into 1½-inch lengths. There should be about 3½ cups.

4. Place the carrot and celery pieces in a saucepan and add water to cover and salt to taste. Bring to the boil and simmer about 10 minutes. Do not overcook. The pieces must remain crisp tender. Drain well.

5. Heat the butter in a heavy saucepan and add the vegetables. Add salt and pepper to taste and nutmeg. Add the heavy cream and cover. Cook, tossing and stirring the vegetables so they cook evenly, about 5 minutes. Serve piping hot.

Yield: 8 to 10 servings.

Eeling It

"Some days you can eel it and eel it and eel it and still come home empty-handed," Bill Lusty was saying, "but this year I've had pretty good luck."

Mr. Lusty, one of a small band of eeling enthusiasts hereabouts, was speaking before a blazing fire in the warmth of his comfortable home. This is eel country, and some of the best hauls come from Three Mile Harbor, a few miles distant.

"Last time I was out, when the harbor was frozen solid, I shipped about fifty-five pounds to New York."

In America, at least, eels are something of a gastronomic curiosity and, with the exception of smoked eels, are rarely found on menus in Manhattan, a regrettable truth, for eels can be a delicacy of excelling goodness. Eels are a commonplace in Japan, where they are grilled and served with a somewhat sweet, dark brown, lacquerlike sauce. The Greeks eat them with gusto stewed or fried or in other olympic preparations. Escoffier lists more than twenty preparations for anguilles, or eels, and one of the most delectable and praised of the "new" appetizers served in the great luxury restaurants of France are pâtés of eel. A pâté of eel is frequently available at the Lutèce Restaurant in Manhattan.

One of the most sublime dishes of the Western world is anguilles au vert, or eels in a green sauce made with a puree of sorrel and other greens. It is on the menus of Le Cirque and Quo Vadis in the city. Many of the luxury restaurants in the city, including La Caravelle, offer smoked eels.

"You don't need much equipment to go eeling," Mr. Lusty observed. "You need a bucket or something to put the eels in and you need a spear." An eel spear resembles a small lyre attached to the end of a sixteen- or seventeen-foot pole made of spruce or white pine. The lyrelike business end consists of a center, rounded blade. On either side of it are two sets of hooks, three to each side. The spear is shoved into the mud or sand and, with luck, an eel is trapped within the hooks. When the spear is lifted, the eel, of course, is hooked. On his expeditions, Mr. Lusty carries two spears in case one breaks.

In winter, eels may be caught either by ice fishing or by going out in a boat. Mr. Lusty, who, like his father before him, has been eeling since he was an infant, prefers the ice. He finds boating in winter a bit too raw and brutal.

"When you go out on the ice, it's got to be firm enough to support a man's weight. Three inches of ice is enough, but the last freeze we had the ice was eight inches deep." In the wintertime the basic equipment includes, in addition to the spear and bucket, an ax of the standard sort found in many households.

"You use the ax to break the ice. You make a hole in the ice about eighteen inches across. You fish there for a while and, if there's no luck, you move on.

Sometimes you fish eight or nine holes with no success, and on the tenth you can pull up eight to ten good eels. The last three holes I cracked I got about thirty pounds of eels."

Mr. Lusty formerly worked in New Jersey as a "detail man" for the Eli Lilly Pharmaceutical Company. He retired in 1969, and he "eels" primarily as a hobby.

In summer when he goes out in a boat, it is generally with one other companion, and they take turns eeling and propelling the boat. "At night in summer we go firelighting, as they say. We take the headlight of a car attached by wires to a storage battery. The headlight is submersible and lights up the bottom of the harbor." In winter when you drop the spear through the ice, it is pretty much a hit-or-miss proposition. "When you go firelighting in summer, you can see the eels squirming around on the bottom."

Mr. Lusty generally throws back into the water any eels that are eight inches or less in length. The eels range from a few inches to sixteen inches, and he prefers those about ten or twelve inches long. These, he claims, are more tender and less fatty.

Mr. Lusty's favorite dish is his wife's barbecued eels. "I cook them," she stated recently, "according to an old Girl Scout recipe for barbecue sauce. It's made with catsup, brown sugar, lemon, bay leaf, dry mustard, mixed spices, vinegar and water." The eels are grilled over charcoal and basted often with the sauce, about thirty minutes.

Here is an assortment of eel recipes, mostly of European inspiration.

Fried Eel

1   or 2 skinned and cleaned eels,
    about 1¼ pounds total weight
    Milk to cover
    Salt and freshly ground
    pepper to taste
¼   teaspoon Tabasco sauce
½   cup flour
    Oil for deep frying
1   large bunch parsley
    Lemon wedges
    Tartar sauce (see recipe)

1. Cut the eels into 3-inch lengths. Place in a mixing bowl and add milk to cover, salt, pepper and Tabasco sauce.

2. Drain well. Dredge the eel pieces in flour seasoned with salt and pepper.

3. Heat the oil in a deep fryer or a skillet and, when it is hot and almost smoking, add the eel pieces. Cook, stirring occasionally and turning the pieces, until golden brown and cooked through. Drain on paper toweling.

4. Trim off and discard the parsley stems. If the parsley is totally clean, do not wash it. If it is rinsed, it must be patted thoroughly dry. Add the parsley and deep fry until crisp. It will darken as it cooks. Drain well and serve with the eel pieces. Serve with lemon wedges and tartar sauce.

Yield: 6 or more servings.

Tartar sauce

1 egg yolk
1 teaspoon wine vinegar
2 tablespoons prepared
    mustard, preferably Dijon or
    Düsseldorf
    A few drops of Tabasco
    Salt and freshly ground
    pepper to taste
1 cup oil, preferably a light olive
    oil or a combination of olive
    oil and peanut, vegetable or
    corn oil
    Lemon juice to taste, optional
¼ cup finely chopped parsley
3 tablespoons finely chopped
    green onion
¼ cup finely chopped cornichons
    or sour pickles
3 tablespoons chopped drained
    capers

1. Place the yolk in a mixing bowl and add the vinegar, mustard, Tabasco, salt and pepper to taste. Beat vigorously for a second or two with a wire whisk or electric beater.

2. Start adding the oil gradually, beating continuously with the whisk or electric beater. Continue beating and adding oil until all of it is used. Add more salt to taste if necessary, and the lemon juice if desired.

3. Add the remaining ingredients and blend well.

Yield: About 1½ cups.

Anguilles au Vert

(Eels in green sauce)

1 bunch watercress
1 pound fresh spinach in bulk or
    1 10-ounce package fresh
    spinach in plastic bag
1 cup loosely packed fresh
    parsley
½ cup coarsely chopped green
    part of green onions
2 fresh sage leaves or ½
    teaspoon dried sage
2 sprigs fresh tarragon or ½
    teaspoon dried
2 sprigs fresh savory or ½
    teaspoon dried
½ cup loosely packed fresh dill,
    optional
1½ to 2 pounds cleaned, skinned
    fresh eels, 1 or 2 eels,
    depending on size
4 tablespoons butter
    Salt and freshly ground
    pepper to taste
1 cup dry white wine
6 egg yolks
2 tablespoons lemon juice

1. Cut off and discard the tough bottoms of the watercress. Place the watercress leaves in the container of an electric blender or food processor. It may be necessary to blend the watercress and other greens in 1 or 2 stages. In any event, start blending to a puree and continue until all the watercress is blended. Spoon and scrape into a saucepan.

2. Rinse and dry the spinach. Blend the spinach with the parsley, onions, sage, tarragon, savory and dill. Do this in 1 or 2 stages until all the greens are a fine puree. There should be about 2 cups. Add to the watercress in the saucepan.

3. Cut the eels into 3-inch lengths. Melt the butter in a large skillet and add the eel pieces. Add salt and pepper to taste. Cook, turning often. When the eels change color, add the wine. Cover closely and simmer 8 to 10 minutes. Spoon the eel pieces into a serving dish or mixing bowl. Let cool.

4. Add the yolks to the pureed greens and bring just to the boil, stirring constantly and vigorously with a wire whisk. Add salt and pepper to taste. Do not boil or the eggs will curdle. Immediately pour the sauce over the eel pieces. Let cool. Serve cold or at room temperature as an appetizer.

Yield: 6 to 10 servings.

Matelote of Eel

2   cleaned, skinned eels, about
    2½ pounds total weight
¼   cup plus 1½ tablespoons flour
    Salt and freshly ground
    pepper to taste
3   tablespoons peanut, vegetable
    or corn oil
1   cup finely chopped onion
2   cloves garlic, chopped
¾   cup finely diced carrots
2½ cups dry red wine
½   teaspoon dried thyme or 2
    sprigs fresh thyme
1   bay leaf
½   pound mushrooms, preferably
    button mushrooms (if the
    mushrooms are large, slice
    them)
3½ tablespoons butter
¼   cup water
1   tablespoon anchovy paste
    Juice of ½ lemon

6   to 8 slices French bread
1   clove garlic, peeled and cut in
    half
    Boiled potatoes

1. Cut each of the eels into 3-inch lengths. Dredge the pieces in ¼ cup flour seasoned with salt and pepper.

2. Heat the oil in a heavy skillet and brown the eel pieces on all sides, turning often, about 5 minutes. Pour off the fat.

3. Scatter the onion, garlic and carrots between the eel pieces and cook about 3 minutes.

4. Add the wine, thyme, bay leaf and simmer about 10 minutes.

5. Meanwhile, combine the mushrooms in a saucepan with 1 tablespoon of the butter, water, anchovy paste, lemon juice, salt and pepper to taste. Bring to the boil and simmer, stirring, about 5 minutes. Add the mushroom liquid to the eel. Set the mushrooms aside. Simmer the eels in the sauce 5 minutes longer

6. Remove the eel pieces and keep warm.

7. Blend the remaining butter with the remaining flour. Add it bit by bit to the sauce, stirring. Strain the sauce through a sieve into another skillet and bring to the boil. Simmer about 5 minutes. Add the eel pieces and mushrooms.

8. Toast the French bread slices and rub on all sides with garlic. Serve the eel and mushrooms hot with the sauce poured over and the toast on top. Serve with boiled potatoes.

Yield: 6 to 8 servings.

Broiled Eel with Mustard Butter

The eel

1   1¼-to-1½-pound skinned eel
    (cleaned weight)
3   tablespoons butter
    Salt and freshly ground
    pepper to taste

The mustard butter

4   tablespoons butter at room
    temperature
    Juice of half a lemon
2   teaspoons imported mustard,
    preferably Dijon or Düsseldorf
3   tablespoons finely chopped
    parsley
¼   teaspoon Worcestershire sauce
    Tabasco sauce to taste
    Salt and freshly ground
    pepper to taste

1. Preheat the broiler to its highest heat.

2. Using a sharp knife, score the eel flesh top and bottom. To do this, make shallow ⅛-inch parallel incisions at ½-inch intervals. Cut the eel into 6-inch lengths.

3. In a baking dish, gently melt the 3 tablespoons butter and add the eel pieces. Sprinkle with salt and pepper and turn the eel pieces in the butter until coated all over.

4. Place the dish of eel about 4 to 6 inches from the source of heat and broil about 1½ to 2 minutes. Turn the pieces and cook about 2 to 3 minutes longer. Pour off all the fat that has accumulated in the pan. Serve immediately with the mustard butter.

5. To make the mustard butter, combine all the ingredients for the butter and beat rapidly with a whisk or wooden spoon until well blended. Spoon equal amounts over the fish sections and serve immediately.

Yield: 6 servings.

Fish Soup with Eel

5   tablespoons olive oil
2   tablespoons finely chopped
     onion
1   tablespoon coarsely chopped
     garlic
1   teaspoon leaf saffron,
     crumbled
¼   cup flour
1   cup dry white wine
4   cups fish broth or use half
     bottled clam broth and half
     water
3½   cups canned Italian peeled
     tomatoes
½   teaspoon thyme or 2 sprigs
     fresh thyme
1   bay leaf
½   teaspoon anise or fennel seed
     Salt and freshly ground
     pepper to taste
1   ¾-to-1-pound eel, cleaned and
     skinned
1½   to 2 pounds fresh fish such as
     cod, striped bass or sea bass,
     preferably with bones
1   pint shucked oysters
1½   pounds fresh scallops
1   cup heavy cream
1   to 2 tablespoons Pernod,
     Ricard or other anise-flavored
     liqueur
2   tablespoons chopped parsley

1. Heat 3 tablespoons of oil in a heavy skillet and add the onion and garlic. Cook briefly until onion is wilted. Add the saffron and sprinkle with flour. Add the wine and broth, stirring rapidly with a whisk.

2. When the mixture boils, add the tomatoes, thyme, bay leaf, anise seed, salt and pepper to taste. Bring to the boil and simmer 30 minutes.

3. Meanwhile, cut the eel into 12 sections of equal length. Set aside.

4. Cut the other fish into 2-inch cubes.

5. Heat the remaining 2 tablespoons oil in a skillet and add the eel. Sprinkle with salt and pepper and cook, turning the pieces, about 3 minutes. Pour off the fat from the skillet.

6. Strain the sauce over the eel, pushing with the back of a wooden spoon to extract as much liquid as possible from the solids. Bring to the boil and simmer 5 minutes. Add the cubed fish and cook 5 minutes longer.

7. Add the oysters and scallops and bring to the boil. Add the cream. Return to the boil. Add the Pernod or Ricard to taste and serve piping hot. Serve sprinkled with chopped parsley.

Yield: 6 or more servings.

Favorite Appetizers

WITH PIERRE FRANEY

Some while ago, when we canvassed a number of restaurants in France in search of a rather expensive and well-publicized dinner for two, we decided on Chez Denis on the rue Gustave Flaubert in Paris. In the course of our research, we visited the restaurant for lunch one Sunday, and not the least of our desires was to sample a first course called chiffonade de homard, or lobster chiffonade. An acquaintance had recently returned from a vist to the restaurant and described the dish with some exultation. "I can't," he told us, "analyze the sauce." We visited the restaurant and were much taken with that dish among others. It is an excellent appetizer made, as we deciphered it, with lobster and a mayonnaise subtly seasoned with cognac and tarragon. The recipe is listed here along with a recipe for another favorite, a raw sliced beef appetizer that is becoming increasingly popular in Manhattan, carpaccio with a shallot mayonnaise.

Chiffonade of Lobster Chez Denis

2   1½-pound live lobsters or 2 cups cubed cooked lobster meat
1   egg yolk
1   tablespoon white wine vinegar
1   tablespoon prepared imported mustard such as Dijon or Düsseldorf
1   tablespoon tomato paste
    Salt and freshly ground pepper
⅛   teaspoon cayenne pepper or Tabasco sauce to taste
1   cup olive oil
    Juice of half a lemon
1   teaspoon chopped fresh tarragon or ½ teaspoon dried, chopped
2   teaspoons cognac
½   cup cubed foie gras, optional
¾   cup cubed, seeded tomatoes
6   to 12 leaves fresh, crisp unblemished romaine lettuce leaves, rinsed and patted dry

1. If live lobsters are used, drop them into vigorously boiling salted water and cover. Cook 10 minutes and remove from the heat. Let stand about 15 minutes. Drain and let cool.

2. When the lobsters are cool enough to handle, crack them and remove the meat from the claws and tail. Reserve and set aside any red coral. There should be about 2 cups of meat and coral. Refrigerate until ready to use.

3. Place the yolk in a mixing bowl and add the vinegar, mustard, tomato paste, salt and pepper to taste, and cayenne. Gradually add the oil, beating vigorously with a wire whisk. Beat in the lemon juice, tarragon and cognac.

4. Add the lobster, foie gras and tomatoes to the mayonnaise and fold them in with a rubber spatula. This may be done in advance and refrigerated for an hour or so.

5. When ready to serve, stack the romaine lettuce leaves and cut them into the finest possible shreds, using a heavy sharp knife. There should be about 2 cups loosely packed shreds. Add this to the salad and fold it in. Serve immediately before the shreds wilt.

Yield: 6 to 8 servings.

Carpaccio

(Sliced raw beef with shallot mayonnaise)

1½ *pounds boneless shell steak,*
     cut into 12 ¼-inch-thick slices

1   *cup shallot mayonnaise (see*
    recipe)
12 *seedless lemon wedges or*
    lemon halves
    Freshly ground pepper

1. Place each slice of meat, one at a time, between 2 sheets of plastic wrap (Baggies split in half are good for this) and pound with a flat mallet or the bottom of a clean, heavy skillet, until the slices are approximately ⅛ inch thick. As the slices are prepared, arrange one on each of 12 chilled appetizer plates. Chill until ready to serve.

2. To serve, spread a little more than 1 tablespoon of the shallot mayonnaise over each slice. Garnish with lemon wedges. Serve a peppermill on the side.

Yield: 6 to 12 servings.

Shallot mayonnaise

1   egg yolk
2   teaspoons imported mustard,
    such as Dijon or Düsseldorf
    (do not use the ball park
    variety)
    Salt and freshly ground
    pepper
2   tablespoons lemon juice
1   cup olive, vegetable or corn oil
2   tablespoons finely chopped
    shallots

1. Place the yolk in a mixing bowl and add the mustard, salt and pepper to taste, and lemon juice.

2. Start beating with a wire whisk or an electric beater. Gradually add the oil until the sauce starts to thicken, beating constantly. When the mixture thickens, the oil may be added rapidly. Add more salt if desired.

3. Place the shallots in cheesecloth and run under cold water. Squeeze to extract most of the moisture. Add the shallots to the mayonnaise.

Yield: About 1 cup.

We had a note from Tony May of Manhattan stating that he, frankly, was not all that taken with our printed version of the carpaccio sauce, that he had sampled "the same dish in five different restaurants . . . prepared in five different ways, and each of the five chefs or restaurant operators feel their version to be the correct and original one. Which is the correct carpaccio? While I believe in my own recipe, I still have to wonder, as I'm sure many of your readers will."

For what it's worth, here is Tony May's recipe, which he called Carpaccio alla Harry, presumably after Harry's Bar in Venice.

Carpaccio alla Harry

12   thin slices raw lean beef
15   fillets of anchovies
1   teaspoon English mustard
2   small gherkins
¼   cup capers
½   cup chopped onion
1   tablespoon Worcestershire
     sauce
     Juice of 2 lemons
1   bunch parsley
     Salt and freshly ground
     pepper to taste
6   ounces olive oil
1   ounce red wine vinegar

1. Have the meat sliced as thinly as possible on an electric slicer. Arrange 2 slices on each of 6 chilled dinner plates.

2. Place the remaining ingredients in a blender and blend to a coarse, creamy consistency.

3. Pour the mixture over the beef slices and serve.

Yield: 6 servings.

Broccoli Soup

26 Dec 77
Very Good

There are basically four sorts of soups in this world: clear soups such as consommés of beef, chicken, fish or game; vegetable soups like minestrone and alphabet (the childish American answer to minestrone); stewlike soups such as a petite marmite or a bouillabaisse, which may serve as meals in themselves; and cream soups, which compete only with consommés as the most elegant of them all.

A hot, silken, artfully made cream soup can, particularly in midwinter, be bliss to the appetite. The preparation of such a soup is simplicitly itself, as the accompanying step photographs set about to prove. This is a quickly made, eminently delicious cream of broccoli soup.

Cream of Broccoli Soup

1	bunch (about 1¼ pounds) fresh, green, unblemished broccoli
4	tablespoons butter
6	tablespoons flour
5	cups chicken broth
	Salt and freshly ground pepper to taste
½	cup heavy cream
½	cup milk
¼	teaspoon grated nutmeg
	Cayenne pepper

1. Trim off enough of the top clusters of the bunch of broccoli to fill a 1-cup measure. This will be used as a garnish for the soup. Cut the rest of the broccoli into 2-inch pieces. Cut the large stems in half or into quarters.

2. Place the larger broccoli pieces—not the garnish—in a deep skillet or saucepan and add water to cover and salt to taste. Cook about 5 minutes or until crisp tender. Do not overcook. Similarly, cook the garnish in boiling salted water about 2 minutes. Drain both batches and set aside.

3. Meanwhile, melt the butter in a saucepan and add the flour, stirring with a wire whisk. When blended, add chicken broth, stirring rapidly with the whisk. Cook, stirring, until thickened and smooth.

4. Add the large broccoli pieces (not the garnish) and simmer, stirring occasionally, about 10 minutes.

5. Ladle the soup, solids and all, into the container of a food processor or electric blender. This will have to be done in 2 or 3 steps. Blend until smooth. Return this mixture to a saucepan and bring to the boil. Add salt and pepper to taste. Add the cooked garnish, heavy cream, milk, nutmeg, and a touch of cayenne pepper.

6. Ladle the soup into individual, heated soup bowls—preferably cream soup dishes—and serve hot.

Yield: 6 to 8 servings.

A Harvest of Scallops

WITH PIERRE FRANEY

This has been a bountiful season for scallops, particularly the bay scallops harvested on the East Coast of America. Somehow they seem plumper and sweeter than usual. Although bay scallops in a frozen state are available throughout the year, the season for them ends in mid-March. The recipes here are designed for bay scallops, although larger ocean scallops may be used, provided they are halved or quartered, depending on size.

Scallops Seviche

2   pounds scallops, preferably bay scallops
3   or 4 fresh limes
1½ tablespoons finely chopped garlic
2   tablespoons chopped fresh coriander
1   or 2 jalapeno peppers, preferably fresh although the canned peppers may be used
3¼ pounds fresh, red, ripe tomatoes
½   teaspoon crushed, dried oregano
¼   cup olive oil
1   avocado, peeled, seeded and cut into ½-inch cubes

1. If bay scallops are used, cut them in half. If ocean scallops are used, quarter them or cut them into smaller pieces. Put the scallops in a mixing bowl.

2. Squeeze enough limes to make ⅓ cup of juice. Add the juice to the scallops. Finely chop ½ of a squeezed lime, pulp and all, and add it to the scallops. Add the garlic and coriander.

3. If desired, remove the seeds from the jalapeno peppers. The dish will be more piquant if the seeds are used. Chop the peppers and add them. Add the remaining ingredients and stir. Serve immediately.

Yield: 6 servings.

Coquilles St. Jacques Dugléré

(Scallops in a cream and tomato sauce)

2   pounds fresh bay scallops
2   tablespoons butter
⅓   cup finely chopped shallots
    Salt and freshly ground pepper
⅓   cup dry white wine
2   cups cored, seeded and cubed tomatoes or 2 cups drained, coarsely chopped canned tomatoes
1½ cups heavy cream
2   egg yolks
    Juice of half a lemon
¼   cup finely chopped parsley

1. If desired, rinse and drain the scallops.

2. Heat the butter in a saucepan or small, fairly deep skillet and add the shallots. Cook briefly and add the scallops, salt and pepper to taste. Cook 1 minute, stirring, and add the wine. Cook, stirring frequently, about 3 minutes. Do not overcook.

3. Using a slotted spoon, scoop out the scallops. Set them aside. Reduce the liquid in the pan or skillet by half. Add the tomatoes, salt and pepper to taste. Cook over brisk heat about 5 minutes and add any liquid that has accumulated around the scallops. Continue cooking the tomatoes briefly until they are thickened but not dry.

4. Add the cream and cook over high heat, stirring often, about 5 minutes.

5. Beat the yolks and spoon about ½ cup of the hot sauce into them, beating constantly. Add this to the sauce, stirring rapidly. When thickened, add the scallops. Sprinkle with lemon juice, stir and add the parsley. Serve immediately in scallop shells or ramekins.

Yield: 6 to 8 servings.

Scallops with Shallot Butter and Pine Nuts

1	*pound fresh bay scallops*
12	*tablespoons butter*
3	*tablespoons finely chopped shallots*
	Salt
2	*tablespoons pine nuts*
1	*tablespoon chopped parsley*
⅓	*cup fine bread crumbs*
1	*tablespoon lemon juice*

1. Preheat oven to 500 degrees.

2. Rinse the scallops and pat them dry.

3. Work the butter with the fingers until it is soft. Add the shallots, salt to taste, pine nuts, parsley, bread crumbs and lemon juice.

4. Add equal amounts of scallops to each of 8 scallop shells or ramekins. Top the scallops with equal portions of the butter. Place on a baking dish and bake 10 minutes or until piping hot and bubbling.

Yield: 8 servings.

March 1976

THIS WAS A memorable month for a couple of alliterative dishes ranging from the high sophistication of herring to what some people call the lowly hamburger. High or low, I can dine on either one with equal measure of pleasure and greed.

A casual acquaintance in East Hampton had invited me early in the year to a small herring feast cooked by an enthusiastic young Swede named Paul Sandblom. It was not an elaborate feast, but that sampling was enough to set my appetite ablaze. A couple of weekends later, Sandblom was kind and accommodating enough to come into my home and prepare a sumptuous herring table and I could state without exaggeration that the herring of his creation could rival that of the famed smorgasbord at the Operakelleren restaurant in Stockholm.

As to those hamburgers, my passion for that all-American specialty is as keen as that of the next hungry Yankee. What we tried to do in my kitchen was to offer them on an international scale—a pizza burger with mozzarella cheese, tomato sauce and oregano; a Swiss burger with a fondue topping; and, what turned out to be a personal favorite, a marvelous Mexican burger seasoned with chili and served with a spicy sauce.

A Well-Made Herring Table

"Speaking of kitchen kitsch," Paul Sandblom said as he thumbed his way through a fat, well-worn volume, a Swedish cookbook titled *Prinsessornas.* "That," he said, "translates as *The Three Princesses Cook Book* and refers to Princess Astrid of Belgium, Princess Martha of Norway, and Princess Margaretha of Denmark. All of them were of Swedish parentage. The book was written by Jenny Akerstrom and published in 1929."

Mr. Sandblom, who is 36 years old and whose reed-slender physique belies an intense, strongly cultivated interest in food and food preparation, was in the midst of preparing an assortment of dishes for a traditional "herring table." The assortment would include a galaxy of herring dishes, about ten or twelve of them, as beguiling and tempting to the eye as to the palate.

The dishes included cold fare that ranged from a cardinal-colored herring salad with sharp sauce to a creamy golden platter of mustard herring flecked with dill; from a multilayered glasmastarsill or "chef's" herring to spicken, an enormously simple pickled herring dish with sour cream and chives. There would also be two baked dishes, rolled herring baked with cream plus that curiously named but irresistible creation, Jansson's temptation.

Paul Sandblom has lived in America, where he is pursuing a doctor of philosophy degree in Fine Arts at New York University, for five years. He is a former curator of art at the National Museum in Stockholm.

His major hobby is cooking—"basic Swedish or French home cooking"—and his vade mecums, his cookbook collection, can almost inevitably be found in his baggage when he travels.

To tell the truth, young Sandblom is considering pursuing his interest in cooking in two directions: He plans to compile a herring cookbook. It is a comforting thought for, to our knowledge, such a volume does not exist in English. He also hopes to branch out into catering.

In addition to the *Three Princesses Cook Book,* which he calls old-fashioned but excellent, he also travels with Tore Wretman's *Svensk Husmankost,* a Swedish home cookbook published in 1967 and to which he gives highest marks, particularly for its herring and smorgasbord dishes.

Wretman, he recounted, is the man often referred to as the father or patron saint of the present day smorgasbord in Sweden. Present legend has it that the traditional smorgasbord in Sweden had fallen to a low level as a result of the deprivations of World War II. Wretman, proprietor of the famed Operakelleren Restaurant in Stockholm, is credited with gathering up the pieces, so to speak, and restoring the Swedish smorgasbord to its earlier glory. Wretman's book has never been translated into English.

Paul Sandblom's herring table includes as many as a dozen herring dishes

Mr. Sandblom's most valuable book, he declares, at least where rarity is concerned, is one that came from his grandmother's kitchen. This is the *Kok-Konsten* or *The Cook Book* by Doktor Hagdahl, published in 1879. Hagdahl in this work gave Swedish cooking an organization it had not had before. He is considered by some to be the Escoffier of Swedish cookery.

The young cooking enthusiast maintains that you can find some of the finest, fattest schmaltz (schmaltz, of course, means fat) herring in the world in New York. He purchased his herring at Russ and Daughters, 179 East Houston Street. (As an aside, let us also heap praise on the herring at Murray's Sturgeon Shop, 2429 Broadway, between 89th and 90th Streets, often referred to as the Tiffany of herring and smoked fish delicacies including smoked salmon, sturgeon and so on.)

"The herring at Russ and Daughters," Mr. Sandblom continues, "is Iceland's finest. The fattest or largest herring is the most expensive, and I use it for the most delicate herring dishes like mustard herring and pickled herring. For blended herring dishes like herring salad, I resort to the smaller, less expensive herrings."

Mr. Sandblom buys his other imported Swedish staples from that Swedish landmark in Manhattan, Nyborg & Nelson, 937 Second Avenue. There he obtains Swedish vinegar, which has a greater strength, that is to say acidity, than commercially available brands in this country. It is also his source for tinned sprats, which resemble canned anchovies but are somewhat different in texture and flavor. Anchovies are frequently substituted for sprats and, in a pinch, will do. Nyborg & Nelson is also an excellent source for Swedish hard breads.

There are several dishes that are essential to a well-made herring table. There should be aquavit (kept in the freezer or placed in the freezer several hours before serving—it will not freeze) and cold beer; boiled potatoes and hard Scandinavian rye breads, widely available in supermarkets and specialty shops dealing in imported foods. There should be five or six cold herring dishes and one or two baked dishes such as Jansson's temptation and baked herring.

Mr. Sandblom pointed out that spicken herring is a traditional luncheon dish and, after having spent five hours and more in the kitchen, added, "I sometimes think I'd be just as happy to make a meal on spicken herring as go through all the work we've been through today." He was only kidding. Getting there was half the fun. Making a herring table isn't work, it's play. Here are the recipes he has adapted from his various Swedish sources. Skol.

How to Fillet Salt (Schmaltz) Herring

Using a pair of scissors, cut off the fins from the herring. Using a sharp knife, slit open the stomach and remove the roe or milch. Discard it or set aside for another use. The roe is sometimes blended, put through a sieve and added to marinades for herring fillets, but not in the recipes printed here.

Turn the herring and, using the knife, slit the fish down the back, cutting off first one fillet, then the other, inserting the knife at the tail end and slicing through as close to the bone as possible. When the fillets have been cut off, skin them by pulling with the fingers, starting with the tail ends. Discard the skins. Rinse the fillets and pat them dry on paper towels or proceed as indicated in individual recipes.

Herring Salad

1   small salt herring
3   potatoes, about 1 pound
    Salt to taste
½   pound pickled beets, canned
    or prepared according to any
    standard recipe, cut into
    ¼-inch cubes

¼ *pound corned beef or a*
    combination of corned beef
    and cooked veal
2   *sour pickles*
1   *onion, about ¼ pound*
2   *firm apples*
1   *tablespoon imported Swedish*
    or German mustard
1   *teaspoon Dijon mustard*
1   *tablespoon sugar*
2   *tablespoons red wine vinegar*
¼ *cup peanut or corn oil*
¼ *cup heavy cream*
2   *hard-cooked eggs, peeled*

1. Soak the herring overnight and fillet it. Cut the herring into ½-inch cubes and put it in a mixing bowl.

2. Rinse the potatoes well and put them in a kettle. Add cold water to cover and salt to taste. If available, put in a few stems from fresh dill. Bring to the boil and cook until tender. Drain. When cool enough to handle, peel the potatoes and cut them into ¼-inch cubes. There should be about 3 cups. Put them in the bowl. Add the pickled beets.

3. Cut the corned beef into small cubes. There should be about 1 cup. Add the meat to the bowl.

4. Cut the pickles into small cubes. There should be about 1¼ cups. Put them in the bowl.

5. Chop the onion finely. There should be about ¾ cup. Put it in the bowl.

6. Peel and core the apples. Cut them into small cubes. There should be about 1½ cups. Put them in the bowl.

7. Add the mustards to another bowl and add the sugar and vinegar. Stir to blend and gradually beat in the oil. Whip the cream and fold it in. Stir this sauce into the herring mixture.

Spoon the salad into a 7- or 8-cup mixing bowl or a mold of equal volume. Pack it in and refrigerate. When ready to serve, unmold the salad onto a serving dish. Garnish with hard-cooked egg whites and yolks, separately sieved. Serve, if desired, with sharp sauce (see recipe).

Yield: 12 or more servings for a herring table.

Sharp sauce

1   *raw egg yolk*
1   *hard-cooked egg yolk, put*
    through a sieve
1   *teaspoon imported Swedish,*
    French or German mustard
2   *teaspoons red wine vinegar*
¼ *teaspoon Worcestershire sauce*
    Salt and freshly ground
    pepper to taste
1   *cup peanut oil*
¾ *cup heavy cream*
2   *tablespoons chopped fresh dill*

1. Put the raw and cooked yolks in a mixing bowl and stir in the mustard, vinegar, Worcestershire sauce, salt and pepper to taste.

2. Start beating with a wire whisk while gradually adding the oil. Continue beating until a mayonnaise forms and all the oil is added.

3. Whip the cream until stiff and fold it into the mayonnaise. Stir in the dill. Serve with herring salad or poached fish.

Yield: About 3 cups.

Herring Rolls

2 large salt herring, soaked
  overnight in cold water
4 whole anchovy sprats (do not
  use smoked Brisling sardines,
  also sold as sprats)
¼ cup chopped red onion
¼ cup finely chopped parsley
2 tablespoons chopped fresh dill
3 tablespoons fine bread crumbs
1 tablespoon butter
⅓ cup heavy cream

1. Preheat the oven to 350 degrees.

2. Fillet the herring or have them filleted.

3. Split the sprats down the stomach and, using the fingers, open them up. Pull off and discard the skin. Pull away and discard the bone. Chop the sprats to a pulp and add the onion, parsley and dill.

4. Place the herring fillets, skin-side down, on a flat surface and cut each fillet in half lengthwise. Spoon equal portions of the sprat mixture in the center of each herring half. Roll up each half to enclose the filling. Arrange the rolls, pleat-side down and close together, on a small baking dish (a round dish about 6 inches in diameter is suitable for this).

5. Sprinkle with the bread crumbs and dot with the butter. Pour the cream over all and bake 15 minutes.

Yield: 12 servings for a herring table.

Spicken Herring

(Simple pickled herring)

2 large salt herring, filleted
1 quart plus 3 tablespoons milk
3 tablespoons sugar
  Boiled potatoes
1 cup sour cream
¼ cup chopped chives

1. Place the 4 herring fillets in a bowl and add 1 quart of milk and the sugar. Refrigerate overnight.

2. Drain the herring and cut into 1-inch pieces. Serve with boiled potatoes and sour cream diluted with the remaining 3 tablespoons of milk. Garnish with chives.

Yield: 12 servings for a herring table.

The following dish is best if it is twice-baked. It may be baked initially an hour or longer before it is given a final baking just before serving.

Jansson's Temptation

6 potatoes, about 1¾ pounds
6 whole anchovy sprats (do not
  use smoked Brisling sardines,
  also sold as sprats)
3 tablespoons butter
1 cup finely chopped onion
1¾ cups light cream or use half
  heavy cream and half milk
¼ cup bread crumbs

1. Preheat the oven to 350 degrees.

2. Peel the potatoes and drop them into cold water to prevent them from discoloring. Using a knife, cut them into slices slightly less than ½ inch thick. Stack the slices and cut them into the shape of French fries, less than ½ inch thick. There should be about 7 cups. Drop into cold water and set aside.

3. Split the sprats down the stomach and, using the fingers, open them up. Pull off and discard the skin. Pull away and discard the bone. Split the sprats in half to make fillets.

4. When ready to assemble the dish, butter a baking dish (an oval baking dish measuring about 8½ by 13½ by 2 inches is a useful size) with 1 tablespoon of butter. Drain the potatoes. Make a single layer of potatoes, the pieces close together. Dot the potatoes with half the sprats broken into pieces using the fingers. Add about half the onions. Add another layer of potatoes, more sprats and more onions. Make a final layer of potatoes. Sprinkle the top with about 2 tablespoons of juice from the can of sprats. Sprinkle the cream evenly over all and sprinkle with bread crumbs. Dot with the remaining butter.

5.. Bake uncovered about 50 minutes and remove from the oven. Let stand. Before serving, bake 30 minutes longer. This dish could, of course, be once-baked, about an hour and a half before serving, until the potatoes are tender.

Yield: 12 or more servings for a herring table.

Mustard Herring

The herring

2   salt herrings, soaked overnight
     in cold water

2   tablespoons white vinegar,
     preferably imported Swedish
     vinegar
½   cup water
1½   tablespoons sugar

The mustard sauce

1   tablespoon mustard,
     preferably imported Swedish
     mustard, or use a dark
     domestic mustard
1   tablespoon Dijon or
     Düsseldorf mustard
2   tablespoons red wine vinegar
¼   teaspoon ground white pepper
½   cup heavy cream
½   cup peanut oil
2   tablespoons finely chopped dill

1. Fillet the herrings or have the herring filleted. Place the fillets in a mixing bowl and add the white vinegar, water and sugar. Stir to dissolve the sugar. Cover and refrigerate 2 hours or longer. Drain and pat dry.

2. Add the 2 mustards to a mixing bowl and stir in the vinegar, using a wire whisk: Add the pepper and cream and gradually stir in the oil. Add the dill.

3. Cut the herring fillets into 1-inch crosswise slices and arrange in 1 layer in a dish. Pour the mustard sauce over and serve.

Yield: 12 servings for a herring table.

Pickled Herring

2   large salt herring, soaked
     overnight in cold water

⅓ cup white vinegar, preferably imported Swedish vinegar
1 cup water
1 small onion, peeled and cut into eighths
2 carrots, scraped and cut into thin rounds
1 red onion, peeled and sliced
1 cup finely chopped white part of leeks
½ cup coarsely chopped parsley
½ cup coarsely chopped fresh dill
1 teaspoon crushed white peppercorns
1 teaspoon crushed whole allspice

1. Skin and fillet the herring and set aside.

2. Bring the vinegar, water and onion to the boil in a saucepan. Let cool.

3. Arrange 2 of the fillets compactly but in 1 layer on the bottom of a deep dish. Add half the carrots, onion rings, leeks, parsley, dill, peppercorns and allspice over the herring.

4. Add the remaining fillets and remaining carrots, onion rings and so on. Strain the vinegar mixture over all. Refrigerate at least 24 hours before serving.

Yield: 12 servings for a herring table.

Glasmastarsill

(Chef's herring)

½ cup white vinegar, preferably imported Swedish vinegar

¾ cup water
½ cup sugar
1 onion, cut into eighths
2 teaspoons white peppercorns, crushed
2 teaspoons whole allspice, crushed
2 teaspoons whole mustard seed
10 cloves
2 bay leaves
2 whole unfilleted salt herring soaked overnight in cold water
1 carrot, scraped and cut into thin rounds
1 cup chopped thinly sliced white part of leeks
2 red onions, peeled and sliced, about 2 cups
1 1-inch piece fresh horseradish, peeled, sliced and cut into ¼-inch cubes
1 ½-inch piece fresh ginger, peeled and coarsely chopped

1. Combine the vinegar, water, sugar and onion in a saucepan. Add half of the spices, i.e., half the peppercorns, allspice, mustard seed, cloves and bay leaves. Bring to the boil. Stir to blend well. Remove from the heat and let cool.

2. Meanwhile, cut off and discard the fins of the herring. If there is any roe, remove and discard it. Do not fillet or skin the fish. Rinse the whole herring well and pat dry. Cut the herring crosswise into 1-inch slices and arrange half of the pieces neatly in a deep bowl. Make layers with the other pieces, the carrots, leeks, sliced red onion, horseradish, ginger and remaining spices. Strain the vinegar solution over all. Cover and refrigerate 4 or 5 days.

Yield: 12 servings for a herring table.

With the exception of three raw egg yolks, the ingredients in this dish are arranged in neat, ever expanding circles. The yolks are placed in the center to represent the "eye" of the sun. Before eating, the ingredients are blended together and served.

"Sun Eye"

8   whole anchovy sprats (do not use smoked Brisling sardines, also sold as sprats)
½   cup finely chopped onion
¼   cup coarsely chopped capers
¾   cup pickled beets, cut into fine cubes
3   raw egg yolks
    Chopped parsley for garnish

1. Split the sprats down the stomach and, using the fingers, open them up. Pull off and discard the skin. Pull away and discard the bone. Chop the sprats to a pulp.

2. Arrange the chopped sprats in a circle in the center of a round dish. Leave an empty space or "well" in the center of the sprats large enough to hold 3 raw egg yolks when added.

3. Neatly arrange the chopped onion in a compact circle around the sprats.

4. Similarly, arrange the capers in a larger circle around the onions. Arrange a circle of chopped beets around the capers.

5. Add the egg yolks to the center and sprinkle with chopped parsley. Place the dish on a herring table. Before serving, blend the ingredients, including the yolks, with a fork.

Yield: 12 servings for a herring table.

Marinated Sprats

(Anchovies)

12   whole anchovy sprats (do not use smoked Brisling sardines, also sold as sprats)
2   tablespoons finely chopped dill
⅓   cup finely chopped red onions
3   tablespoons wine vinegar
¼   teaspoon finely ground black pepper
½   clove garlic, crushed to a puree
½   cup peanut oil

1. Split the sprats down the stomach and, using the fingers, open them up. Pull away and discard the bone, but do not split the sprats in half. Cut off and discard the tail.

2. Arrange the sprats, split-side down, on a flat surface. Blend the dill and onions and spoon equal portions of the mixture onto the center of each sprat. Fold the sprats, head to tail, to enclose the filling. Arrange them neatly on a flat dish in 1 layer. Blend the remaining ingredients and pour over the sprats. Refrigerate an hour or so.

Yield: 12 servings for a herring table.

I am happy to say that in part because of our association, Paul Sandblom opened the Red Herring at 384 Bleecker Street, a very successful herring shop that specializes in takeout delicacies.

In the article on Mr. Sandblom, we noted that he was in the process of compiling a herring cookbook and added that we found this comforting because "to our knowledge, such a volume does not exist in English."

Several readers wrote to inform us that such a volume does exist, and it is titled *Herrings, Bloaters and Kippers* by Ambrose Heath, published by Herbert Jenkins, Ltd., in London, 1954. If anyone cares to buy the book, they may have to travel to England to obtain it. We telephoned Eleanor Lowenstein, proprietor of our favorite source for out-of-print and hard-to-find books on food, The Corner Book Shop, 102 Fourth Avenue (at 11th Street). She added she does not have a single copy on her shelves, and it would take eight weeks to obtain it by mail.

We still look forward eagerly to Mr. Sandblom's book.

One of those who wrote to inform us of Mr. Heath's volume was Samuel Abramson of Manhattan. He added the unhappy thought that "herring is fast vanishing and on the verge of extinction."

"In 1965 Iceland's herring catch was 763,000 tons," Mr. Abramson informed us. "It has dropped to about 50,000 tons, and is going down steadily. This has been caused by modern fishing factory vessels, particularly the Soviet fishing fleet, which sweep across the seas like vacuum cleaners, sucking up everything that swims. This has been reflected in the high price of herring today. I remember when the best schmaltz herring on the market cost ten cents. Today, in New York, the price for a prime Iceland schmaltz ranges from $1.50 to $2.00 (large) at Russ & Daughters on Houston Street; $1.69 at Scotty's on Essex Street and $1.78 at Zabar's on Broadway.

"The day is fast coming when the herring will be gone forever. A world without herring is a prospect too horrible to contemplate. The moment has arrived to preserve the herring for future generations. Herring lovers of the world arise and insist that the fishing fleets of the world go back to the old methods when fish were caught in nets. This gave young fish a fighting chance and did not leave the seas barren. The cod and haddock are also endangered species. By saving the herring their future, too, will be assured."

A Complete Indian Meal

WITH PIERRE FRANEY

One of the best Indian cooks in Manhattan is Ismail Merchant, a 36-year-old, Bombay-born movie producer whose credits include such critically acclaimed and rewarding films as *Shakespeare Wallah* and *Savages*. (He is currently involved in the production of *Train to Pakistan* and an adaptation of Henry James's novel, *The Europeans*.)

In the kitchen, Ismail offers working proof that there are scores of dishes from his homeland that are not in the least difficult to prepare. A complete Indian menu is offered here—an easily made first course, shrimp with dill; an excellent, delectable, multiflavored pan-roast of lamb as a main course; hot green beans with a tangy and tantalizing sauce of mustard; dal, the traditional lentil dish, this one made special with lemon; and a seductive milk, almond and saffron dessert, sheer (milk) khorma (nuts and things). Of the dal, Ismail states, "It is a rich man's, poor man's dish and every household has its own version. It is a must with any meal, and if you don't offer it, something is wrong."

Dahi Shrimp

(Shrimp with dill)

2   *pounds raw shrimp*
1   *cup yogurt*
2   *teaspoons cayenne pepper (use less if you wish the dish less spicy)*
2   *cloves finely chopped garlic*
1   *teaspoon caraway seeds*
¼   *teaspoon ground turmeric*
    Salt
4   *tablespoons oil, preferably mustard oil (see note)*
¾   *cup finely chopped fresh dill*

1. Peel and devein the shrimp. Rinse well and drain. Pat dry and set aside.

2. Combine the yogurt, cayenne, garlic, caraway, turmeric and salt to taste. Add the shrimp and blend well.

Cover and refrigerate until ready to use.

3. Heat the oil in a deep skillet or casserole and add the shrimp. Cook, stirring gently, and cover. Cook until the shrimp change color. Sprinkle with dill and serve hot. The pan juices will be quite liquid.

Yield: 8 to 12 servings.

Note: Mustard oil is available at Kalustyan Orient Expert Trading Corporation, 123 Lexington Avenue, (between 28th & 29th Streets).

Bhuna Ghost

(Pan-roasted lamb)

1   *4¼-pound lean, skinless, boneless leg of lamb (about 7 pounds before boning)*

2 tablespoons finely chopped
  fresh ginger
3 hot green chilies, chopped,
  with seeds
1 tablespoon finely chopped
  garlic
1½ tablespoons chopped fresh
  coriander leaves
  Juice of 1 lemon
  Salt to taste
1 teaspoon freshly ground black
  pepper
1 tablespoon peanut, vegetable
  or corn oil

1. Cut the lamb or have it cut into 1½-inch cubes.

2. Place the lamb in a bowl and add the remaining ingredients. Set aside until ready to cook, 1 hour or longer.

3. Preheat oven to 350 degrees.

4. Spoon the lamb into a shallow roasting pan. A recommended size is about 16 by 9½ by 2½ inches. Smooth the lamb over and place the pan in the oven, uncovered. Bake 1 hour and

15 minutes without stirring. The lamb should be quite tender and the pan juices will be quite liquid. Serve with rice.

Yield: 12 servings.

26 Dec 77
Excellent

Green Beans with Mustard Sauce

2 pounds green beans
1 tablespoon imported mustard
  such as Dijon or Düsseldorf
  Salt and freshly ground
  pepper
  Juice of one lemon
⅓ cup olive oil

1. Cut or snap off the ends of the beans, but leave the beans whole. Let stand in cold water until ready to use.

2. Drain the beans and, preferably, steam them in a vegetable steamer about 5 minutes. Or cook them briefly in a large quantity of boiling water about the same length of time. The important thing is not to overcook them. They must remain crisp tender.

3. As the beans cook, spoon the mustard into a small bowl and add the salt, pepper and lemon juice. Stir to blend and whisk in the oil.

4. Drain the beans. Add the mustard sauce to the beans and toss to coat well. Serve piping hot in a hot serving dish.

Yield: 12 servings.

Limbo Dal

(Lemon lentils)

1¼ cups peanut, vegetable or corn oil
2 onions, halved and thinly sliced, about 1½ cups
4 2-inch pieces of cinnamon stick
2 pounds red lentils (see note)
1 tablespoon chopped fresh ginger root
5 cups chicken broth
5 cups water
   Salt
1 teaspoon cayenne pepper
   Juice of 1 lemon
   The squeezed, seeded shell of 1 lemon including skin and pulp
½ cup chopped onion
1 clove garlic, finely minced
1 hot green chili, chopped, with seeds
4 bay leaves
½ cup chopped fresh coriander leaves

1. Heat ¾ cup of the oil in a large saucepan and add the sliced onions.

Cook to wilt and add the cinnamon pieces and lentils. Add the ginger and cook, stirring often, about 10 minutes. Add the broth and water, salt to taste and cayenne pepper. Bring to the boil and simmer about 10 minutes.

2. Add the lemon juice and lemon shell and cook about 50 minutes longer, stirring often.

3. Heat the remaining ½ cup of oil and add the onion, garlic, chili and bay leaves. Cook, stirring, until onion is browned. Add this mixture including the oil to the lentils. Sprinkle with chopped coriander leaves and serve hot.

Yield: 12 or more servings.

Note: Red lentils are available at Kalustyan Orient Expert Trading Corporation, 123 Lexington Avenue (between 28th and 29th Streets).

Sheer Khorma

(A north Indian dessert)

1½ cups shelled pistachios
¾ cup almonds, shelled but with the skin on
⅛ pound Indian vermicelli (see note)
8 tablespoons butter
5 cups milk
¾ cup heavy cream
½ teaspoon saffron
5 tablespoons sugar

1. Place the pistachios and almonds in a mixing bowl and add cold water to cover. Let stand overnight. Drain and rub off the skins.

2. Place the nuts in the container of a food processor or electric blender

and blend. Do not blend to a puree. The texture should be coarse-fine. Set aside.

3. Break the vermicelli sticks in half. Heat the butter in a large saucepan and add the vermicelli. Cook, stirring, until vermicelli is nicely browned without burning. Add the milk and cream and bring to the boil.

Add the pistachio mixture, saffron and sugar. Cook, stirring often, about 15 minutes.

Yield: 12 or more servings.

Note: Indian vermicelli is available at Kalustyan Orient Expert Trading Corporation, 123 Lexington Avenue (between 28th and 29th Streets).

Hamburgers with Class

There is a moment in Noel Coward's play, *Private Lives*, in which a couple, divorced, meet by chance on a terrace in the south of France. It is a moment charged with old-fashioned sentiment, heightened abruptly by the sound of a piano off-stage playing "I'll See You Again." Amanda, the lady in the case, remarks, "Extraordinary how potent cheap music is."

That's the way we feel about hamburgers, if you happen to think that hamburgers are trashy and banal, if not to say vulgar—to use the word in context of meaning popular. To put it one way, we infinitely prefer a well-made hamburger to an overcooked filet mignon or an ill-seasoned porterhouse.

Although the name is of German extraction, a hamburger is as quintessentially American as pasta is Italian or paprika dishes Hungarian. It would seem, after a considerable amount of random research that has spanned a couple of decades, that there is no concretely documented evidence of the precise moment the first hamburger came into evidence.

Evan Jones in his recently published *American Food* (E. P. Dutton, $19.95) offers a most reasonable explanation for the name. The patty itself was originally "a nineteenth-century import from Germany, a meat dish of chopped beef," first known in this country "as a Hamburg steak after the . . . port on the Elbe River." Rombauer–Becker's well-known *Joy of Cooking* (Bobbs-Merrill, $10) reprints the most commonly accepted conjecture as to the hamburger's origin. It was, the book notes, at "the St. Louis World's Fair in 1904 that broiled, bunned beef was introduced to the rest of the world by the Germans of South St. Louis."

It is not the patty itself that makes the hamburger so typically American. It is, rather, the patty-cum-bun or sandwich factor that puts it in league with apple pie (only more so; it has been estimated that Americans consume more than forty billion hamburgers a year, and if there is any other dish that exceeds that figure, we'll eat those words). Ground meat in various shapes, patties and otherwise, occurred in the world's cuisines years, perhaps centuries, before the St. Louis exposition. There are polpette di carne of Italy; the frikadeller of Sweden; the boulettes de viande of France; the albondigas of Mexico and the koftas of India, to offer a brief sample of cooked, shaped ground-meat dishes. But a broiled or grilled meat patty in a bun you can waltz around with smacks of the stars and stripes forever.

We have long held a theory that the simplest dishes in the world are frequently the most difficult to cook. It is, in truth, we feel, more difficult to scramble an egg than make a good soufflé; it is far more difficult to make a succulent and splendid roast chicken than a platter of coq au vin. The same is true of hamburgers. It takes talent to turn out a hamburger with class. We offer

here an assortment of hamburgers that have pleased us recently in our home kitchen. There is a basic and elegant hamburger on toast with butter and parsley plus a few "gimmick burgers," if you wish to call them that—a pizza burger, a Swiss burger, a Mexican burger, and so on.

How to Cook Hamburgers

Shape ground beef, preferably round steak or sirloin (the ground tail of porterhouse or T-bone makes excellent hamburgers) into round flat patties.

There are two recommended methods for cooking hamburgers in a skillet. In the first, sprinkle a light layer of salt in the bottom of a heavy skillet such as a black iron skillet. Heat the skillet thoroughly and add the hamburgers. If the heat is hot enough under the skillet, they will not stick. When cooked on one side, use a

pancake turner and, with a quick motion, scoop under the hamburgers, turning them in the skillet. Reduce the heat and continue cooking the hamburgers to the desired degree of doneness. Add a touch of butter, salt and pepper to taste.

The more conventional method of skillet cookery is to melt for each hamburger about half a teaspoon of butter in a heavy skillet and when it is hot but not browning, add the hamburger or hamburgers. Cook until browned on one side, turn and continue cooking to the desired degree of doneness. Sprinkle with salt and pepper and serve with the pan juices.

The preferred method for cooking hamburgers is on a grill fired with charcoal or gas-fired coals. The grill should be very hot when the hamburgers are added. Cook until nicely grilled on one side, turn and cook to the desired degree of doneness. Add a touch of butter, salt and pepper to taste.

Hamburger Deluxe

¼ pound ground round steak or
    sirloin
    Salt
2   teaspoons butter
2   or 3 dashes Tabasco sauce
3   or 4 dashes Worcestershire
    sauce
½   teaspoon lemon juice
1   slice trimmed, buttered toast
    or one split, toasted
    hamburger bun
    Freshly ground pepper to taste
1   tablespoon finely chopped
    parsley

1. Shape the meat into a round patty, handling it as little as possible.

2. Sprinkle the bottom of a heavy skillet with a light layer of salt and heat the skillet until quite hot. Add the hamburger and sear well on one side. If the skillet is hot enough, it will not be necessary to add any fat to the skillet. Quickly slip a pancake turner under the meat and turn it. Reduce the heat and continue cooking to the desired degree of doneness.

3. As the meat cooks, melt the butter and add the Tabasco, Worcestershire sauce and lemon juice. Transfer the hamburger to the toast or bun and sprinkle with salt and pepper to taste. Pour the butter sauce over it. Sprinkle with parsley and serve immediately.

Yield: 1 serving.

Pizza Burger

2   pounds ground round steak or
    sirloin
4   tablespoons plus 6 teaspoons
    grated Parmesan cheese
2   tablespoons cold butter, cut
    into small pieces
    Salt and freshly ground
    pepper to taste
    Marinara sauce (see recipe)
6   ¼-inch thick slices mozzarella
    cheese, cut into small cubes
6   toasted hamburger buns

1. Place the meat in a bowl and add 4 tablespoons Parmesan cheese, butter, salt and pepper to taste. Blend well and shape into 6 patties of equal size. Grill or cook in a skillet as indicated above.

2. Arrange the hamburgers on a baking sheet. Spoon 1 tablespoon or more of the marinara sauce on each hamburger patty. Sprinkle with remaining Parmesan cheese. Top with equal amounts of mozzarella and broil until cheese melts. Transfer the hamburgers onto toasted hamburger bun bottoms. Serve immediately with the toasted tops on the side.

Yield: 6 pizza burgers.

Marinara sauce

3   cups canned Italian plum
    tomatoes
1   tablespoon olive oil
1   teaspoon finely chopped garlic
2   teaspoons dried oregano
3   tablespoons chopped parsley
    Salt and freshly ground
    pepper to taste

1. Place the tomatoes in a saucepan and cook until reduced by half. Stir often to prevent sticking.

2. Heat the oil in another saucepan and add the garlic. Cook briefly and add the tomatoes, oregano, parsley, salt and pepper to taste.

Yield: About 1½ cups.

Mexican Burgers

1   pound ground round steak or
    sirloin
1   teaspoon finely chopped garlic
1   tablespoon chili powder
    Salt and freshly ground
    pepper to taste
4   toasted hamburger buns
    Brown chili sauce (see recipe)

1. Place the meat in a bowl and add the garlic, chili powder, salt and pepper to taste. Work with the hands to blend the ingredients. Shape the mixture into 4 ¼-pound patties and grill or cook in a skillet as indicated above.

2. Place 1 patty on each of 4 toasted bun bottoms. Spoon the chili sauce over the hamburgers and serve with the toasted tops on the side.

Yield: 4 Mexican burgers.

Brown chili sauce

2   pounds chicken necks and
    wings chopped into 1-inch
    lengths
2   tablespoons flour
2   teaspoons ground cumin
1   tablespoon chopped garlic
3   or more tablespoons chili
    powder

1   tablespoon dried oregano
2   tablespoons tomato paste
1   cup fresh or canned beef broth
2   cups water

1. Add the chicken pieces to a heavy saucepan and cook, stirring often, until browned. It is not necessary to add fat, but the pieces must be stirred to prevent sticking.

2. Pour off the fat from the saucepan and sprinkle the chicken pieces with flour, cumin, garlic, chili powder and oregano. Stir and add the tomato paste. Stir once more and add the broth and water. Stir constantly until the sauce boils. Cook about 40 minutes, stirring often from the bottom to prevent sticking.

3. Strain the sauce, discarding the solids, and serve hot. This is a general-purpose sauce and is good with tacos, enchiladas, chili burgers and so on.

Yield: About 2 cups.

Hamburgers à la Holstein

1   pound ground round steak or
    sirloin
4   toasted hamburger bun
    bottoms or rounds of toast
4   eggs
2   tablespoons peanut, corn or
    vegetable oil
12 flat fillets or rolled, caper-
    stuffed anchovies
4   tablespoons butter

1. Shape the meat into 4 patties and cook in a skillet or grill as indicated above.

2. Place 1 patty on each of 4 toasted bun bottoms.

3. Meanwhile, fry the eggs sunny-side-up in oil, taking care that the eggs do not touch each other and stick together as they fry. Remove with a pancake turner and place 1 fried egg on each hamburger. Garnish each egg with 3 flat achovy fillets or rolled anchovies. Heat the butter in a skillet until it is hazelnut brown (beurre noisette) and pour equal amounts of it over the hamburgers topped with eggs and anchovies.

Yield: 4 servings.

Swiss Fondue Burgers

1   or more hamburgers
    Toasted buns or toast
    Swiss fondue (see recipe)

1. Cook the hamburgers according to taste. Arrange on bottom half of a toasted bun.

2. Spoon hot, freshly made Swiss fondue over the hamburger and serve the other half of the bun on the side.

Yield: 1 or more hamburgers.

Swiss fondue

¾   pound pure, unprocessed
    Gruyère or Swiss
    (Emmenthaler) cheese (see
    note)
1   teaspoon cornstarch
5   or 6 tablespoons dry white
    wine
½   teaspoon chopped garlic
    Salt and freshly ground
    pepper to taste
1   tablespoon kirschwasser,
    optional

1. Cut the cheese into ½-inch cubes and place in a mixing bowl. Add the cornstarch and toss to coat.

2. Add the cheese and wine to a saucepan and cook, stirring constantly with a wooden spoon, until the mass is smoothly blended. Add the remaining ingredients and serve while hot and bubbling.

Yield: About 2 cups.

Note: Pure Gruyère cheese has approximately the same texture as Swiss (Emmenthaler) cheese, but it has a slightly stronger flavor. It is not to be confused with the processed, gummy, wedge-shaped bits of cheese made from Gruyère. Two 6-ounce slices of Muenster of Tilsiter cheese, available in supermarkets, can be substituted for the Gruyère.

Welsh Rabbit Burgers

1   pound ground round steak or
    sirloin
4   slices trimmed, toasted bread
    or 4 split hamburger buns,
    toasted
2   to 2½ cups piping hot Welsh
    rabbit (see recipe)
    Freshly ground pepper to taste

1. Prepare and cook the hamburgers as indicated.

2. Arrange each hamburger on 1 slice of toast or half a bun.

3. Spoon the Welsh rabbit over and serve sprinkled with pepper.

Yield: 4 servings.

Welsh rabbit

¾ *pound aged Cheddar cheese
(see note)*
2 *teaspoons dry mustard*
1 *teaspoon paprika*
½ *cup beer*
½ *to 1 teaspoon Worcestershire
sauce
Salt to taste*
2 *egg yolks, lightly beaten
Freshly ground pepper to taste*

1. Cut the cheese into small cubes about ½ inch thick.

2. Blend the mustard and paprika in a small bowl and add a little beer, stirring to make a paste and prevent lumping. Continue adding beer gradually, stirring. Add the Worcestershire sauce and set aside.

3. Add the cheese to a heavy saucepan and add the beer mixture. Cook over low heat, stirring constantly. It is best to start stirring with a wooden spoon until cheese is almost melted, then shift to a rubber or plastic spatula so the mixture can be stirred uniformly around the bottom and sides of the pan. Continue stirring rapidly until the mixture is hot, blended and smooth. Add salt to taste.

4. Add about 4 tablespoons of the mixture to the yolks and return this to the saucepan. Cook briefly without boiling or the egg yolks might curdle. Serve piping hot with toast points or on hamburgers. Serve sprinkled with pepper.

Yield: About 2 cups.

Note: Almost every traditional recipe for Welsh rabbit specifies "unprocessed American cheese at least 1 year old." This is the yellow cheese once called rat-cheese in America. Unprocessed American cheese is rarely found thus labeled in supermarkets and grocery stores today. Use a good grade of yellow Cheddar.

The Infinite Variety of Chicken Dishes

WITH PIERRE FRANEY

It may seem odd to link Cleopatra and chicken in the same paragraph. But we don't feel in the least profane in twisting a phrase from Shakespeare, turning it to our own good purpose in saying that, to our taste, time cannot wither nor custom stale the infinite variety of chicken dishes. Chicken is almost without question the most versatile of basic main course ingredients known to man, surpassing beef, pork, lamb, fish, game and all other barnyard fowl in its uses. It can be earthy or elegant, and it adapts marvelously well to a multitude of flavors, simple or complex as demonstrated here.

Chicken Sauté with Pecans

2   2½-to-3-pound chickens, cut
    into serving pieces
    Salt and freshly ground
    pepper
4   tablespoons butter
½   cup finely chopped onion
½   cup finely chopped celery
1   bay leaf
½   teaspoon dried thyme or 2
    sprigs fresh thyme
¼   teaspoon grated nutmeg
2   whole cloves
1   bottle (3 cups) dry red wine
½   cup heavy cream
½   cup chopped pecans

1. Sprinkle the chicken pieces with salt and pepper to taste.

2. Heat the butter in a heavy skillet and brown the chicken pieces all over. Scatter the onion, celery, bay leaf and thyme around the pieces.

Sprinkle with nutmeg. Add the cloves and wine, salt and pepper to taste.

3. Cover and simmer 30 minutes or until the chicken is tender.

4. Remove the chicken pieces and keep warm. Skim off the fat from the surface of the sauce. Reduce the sauce to about 2 cups. Add the cream. Return the chicken pieces and return to the boil. Add the pecans and serve hot.

Yield: 6 to 8 servings.

Chicken with Olives Mexican-Style

1   3½-pound chicken, cut into
    serving pieces
    Salt and freshly ground
    pepper
2   tablespoons olive oil
1   cup finely chopped onion
2   cloves garlic, finely minced

¼ cup dry sherry
1 tablespoon chili powder
1 teaspoon ground cumin
1 teaspoon oregano, crushed
2 tablespoons flour
2½ cups chopped fresh tomatoes
   or 1 17-ounce can Italian
   peeled tomatoes
20 pitted green olives

1. Sprinkle the chicken pieces with salt and pepper to taste.

2. Heat the olive oil in a heavy skillet and when it is hot but not smoking add the chicken pieces skin-side down. Cook until golden brown on one side and turn the pieces. Cook until golden on the other side. Transfer the pieces to a heavy casserole.

3. To the fat in the skillet, add the onion and cook, stirring, until wilted. Add the garlic and stir. Add half the sherry and let cook until most of the liquid evaporates. Sprinkle with chili powder, cumin, oregano and flour. Stir with a wooden spoon until the ingredients are well blended.

4. Add the tomatoes and stir until thickened. Add salt and pepper to taste. Cook, stirring, about 10 minutes and spoon the sauce over the chicken. Cover tightly and cook over low to moderate heat about 30 minutes or until the chicken is tender. Add the olives. Stir in the remaining sherry, bring to the boil and serve with rice.

Yield: 4 to 6 servings.

Chicken in Mexican Green Tomato Sauce

1 3½-pound chicken
  Chicken broth or water to
  cover
  Salt

½ cup chopped onion
2 serrano chilies (see note)
16 blanched almonds
1 cup shredded romaine lettuce
1 clove garlic
½ cup loosely packed fresh
   coriander leaves
1 12-ounce can Mexican or
   Spanish green tomatoes
   (tomatillos enteros or tomatitos
   verdes)
3 tablespoons butter
   Freshly ground pepper

1. Place the chicken in a large saucepan or small kettle and add the chicken broth or water. Add salt to taste and bring to the boil. Simmer, partly covered, about 20 minutes. Remove from the heat and let stand about ½ hour.

2. Remove the meat from the bones. Pull away the skin. Discard the bones and skin or return them to the kettle and continue cooking the broth.

3. Cube or shred the chicken. Set aside.

4. Combine the onion, chilies, almonds, lettuce, garlic and coriander in the container of an electric blender or food processor. Add ¼ cup of broth. Reserve the remaining broth for another use.

5. Drain the tomatoes well and add them. Blend the mixture to a puree.

6. Heat the butter in a skillet and add the tomato mixture. Add salt and pepper to taste and cook, stirring, three minutes or longer. Add the chicken and stir gently until chicken is coated. Serve hot with hot fresh tortillas or rice.

Yield: 4 servings.

Note: Serrano chilies and Mexican green or Spanish tomatoes (tomatillos) can be purchased in cans in Spanish-speaking markets including Casa Moneo, 210 West 14th Street, as well as in many supermarkets in the metropolitan area. The green tomatoes in this recipe are not the garden-variety green tomatoes found in America. They are rarely found in a fresh state in this country.

This recipe is freely adapted from a veal recipe in Elizabeth Lambert Ortiz's *The Complete Book of Mexican Cooking* (Bantam Books).

April 1976

T HE WORD AMATEUR should not have a pejorative connotation. It stems from amare, meaning, of course, to love. It is a fine and flattering thing to be called an amateur in French, to indicate that you have a special enthusiasm toward one pursuit or another. It is inevitable that in any profession one is notably influenced by amateurs. One of my most prized acquaintances is Ed Giobbi, who is a true amateur of the kitchen in the finest sense of the word. It is not an exaggeration to say that he is a creative genius, particularly in the cuisine of his family and ancestry. Ed, as anyone probably knows who has read my columns over the years, is a successful artist, but he is also the author of an excellent cookbook called *Italian Family Cooking*. There have been times when dining in Ed's home I have eaten such food as to make me think he surely can't surpass himself. But he certainly did in my own kitchen in the spring of 1976. He was spending the weekend with his family and, when he arrived, the trunk of his car was laden as usual with a vast array of good things from his garden, local market or kitchen—things like his incredible home-canned tuna in olive oil (one of his annual rituals is "putting up" tuna in his summer home in Provincetown), dried basil, pigeons of his own raising, and homemade pasta. On this particular spring weekend, he also arrived with an enormous fish head from his local merchant. While I went about my chores in the morning, Ed proceeded to convert that single fish head into one of the damnedest and most gratifyingly delicious meals I've ever eaten. Served with pasta cooked in the broth made from the head, it was ample for four. On my next visit to his home in Katonah, I encouraged him to reproduce that dish and others for the pleasure, if not to say profit, of *The New York Times* readers.

Pasta, Economy-Style

The notion that the more you spend for ingredients the better a dish will be is nonsense, Ed Giobbi was saying. It was approaching noon and his kitchen, one of the most comfortable and stylish in these environs, was rampant with the good odors of tomatoes, garlic, parsley and freshly chopped basil. Ed's kitchen is one of those places we always visit with bounding enthusiasm and keen appetite, for although he is a painter and sculptor by profession, he is a splendid cook who goes about his hobby with the cool dexterity of a croupier shuffling cards.

On the morning in question he was demonstrating for his own amusement and ours the proof of his premise that good food can come from a modest base.

"This fish head," he stated, "I got for free from my fish market, Conte's in Mount Kisco. You cook the head with water and salt and after it's done take the meat off the head. You heat a little olive oil—olive oil is one thing you should never stint on—and add a little garlic and parsley. You add the meat from the head, a bit of red pepper flakes and toss it with a pound of freshly cooked pasta. Fantastic. And it serves four easily."

Other "economy" dishes we have dined on from Ed's stove include noodles tossed with a quarter pound of lightly cooked smoked salmon and cream ("serves four"), tripe florentine-style with pasta and broccoli ("the tripe cost $1.33 and with a pound of pasta serves eight"); and tomatoes and onions with pasta ("pennies and it serves four or more").

Ed Giobbi, we have reflected for several years, comes as close to being a polymath as anyone we know who indulges his passion. He spends many hours each week with a paint brush, and yet last year he made 200 bottles of red wine, perhaps the best and most sophisticated homemade wine we've ever sampled; he has an extensive and well-tended garden and more than half the produce consumed in his home is homegrown (he finds fresh basil and fresh Italian parsley indispensable in his cooking, and he grows both, the small-leaf, Genoa-style basil from seeds he purchased in Rome last year, in clay pots throughout the winter months); he raises geese, chickens, a special breed of squab, a pair of which he brought from Florida some years ago, and rabbits.

We first met Ed years ago when we learned that he made an annual practice of putting up his own tuna each summer in Provincetown. Over a glass of his homemade wine, we inquired recently if he continued the practice, and he told us that he had to skip last summer.

"We got to Provincetown too late for the season, but it didn't really matter. The year before I had come across a 400-pound tuna, which I processed in jars. That's a lot of tuna, enough to last me two years running."

Ed's kitchen is a match for his talents. It boasts a professional six-burner

Ed Giobbi teaches artists how to survive and eat well

Garland range, the best stove there is to our way of thinking. It is equipped with an overhead "salamander," a broiler-type unit whose function is to glaze dishes—au gratin dishes, for example—and is not used, as people often ask, for grilling meats. Next to the kitchen is a splendid sitting room, hung with his own art, and equipped with a fireplace. It is also a sort of greenhouse where his basil, parsley and bay or laurel plant thrive. Come to think of it, Ed is the only person we know who has a continuing supply of fresh bay leaves. It is a difficult plant to grow.

Giobbi and his wife, Elinor, are the parents of three children, Gina, 16, Lisa, 14, and Cham, 13. All of the offspring are artists (they illustrated Ed's cookbook, *Italian Family Cooking*, Random House, 1971) and Lisa, in particular, is rather emotional when it comes to eating the homegrown animals.

Recently, Ed skinned and cleaned one of the rabbits and turned it into a fine cacciatore dish.

"O.K., Dad, who is it?" Lisa demanded without a touch of guile.

Ed, who has eaten well throughout his life, thanks to a mother who is a splendid cook, grew up nonetheless in a household where money was scarce. His cash-flow did not start until he was several years outside art school in Italy. It has long been his contention that what young artists need most is a course in survival during that transitional period between leaving school and becoming established in whatever profitable direction their careers may take. Thus he is planning a series of lessons in "Survival," which will include instructions in cooking, at the Art Students League, 215 West 57th Street.

"Most kids," he states, "don't know how to live economically in a healthy way. It's easy to live on very little if you know when, where and how to shop. Take my spaghetti with fish heads. It costs pennies if you know your way around."

Here is an assortment of Ed's pasta dishes, economy-style.

Fish Head Pasta

1   or 2 very fresh fish heads, gills
    removed (see note)
    Salt to taste
3   ribs celery, quartered
6   sprigs fresh parsley
3   carrots, scraped and cut into
    2-inch lengths
1   bay leaf
1   onion, peeled and quartered
16 peppercorns, crushed
1   pound linguine, lingue di
    passeri or spaghetti
5   tablespoons olive oil
1   tablespoon chopped garlic
½   to 1 teaspoon red pepper
    flakes, according to taste
⅔   cup finely chopped parsley

1. Place the fish heads in a kettle and add water to cover, salt, celery, parsley sprigs, carrots, bay leaf, onion and peppercorns. Bring to the boil and reduce the heat. Simmer 20 minutes, skimming the surface as necessary. Strain and reserve the broth. Let fish heads cool.

2. When fish heads are cool enough to handle, pick over them to remove all bits of meat. Discard skin and bones. Set meat aside.

3. Bring the fish broth to the boil. Add the linguine and cook, stirring, to the desired degree of doneness.

4. When the linguine is almost done, heat 3 tablespoons of oil in a deep skillet or casserole. Add the garlic and when it starts to brown, quickly drain the linguine and add it. Add the flaked fish, pepper flakes, chopped parsley and remaining oil. Toss and serve piping hot in hot bowls.

Yield: 4 servings.

Note: Cod heads are especially good in this dish, although any white-flesh, non-oily fish will do. One large head—2 to 3 pounds—is preferable to 2 small ones.

Pasta with Tomato and Onion Sauce

4   cups thinly sliced onions
3   tablespoons butter
3   tablespoons olive oil
3   cups imported tomatoes put
    through a sieve or a food
    processor
¾   cup hot milk
¼   cup chopped parsley
    Salt and freshly ground
    pepper to taste
1   pound spaghetti, spaghettini
    or linguine
¾   cup grated Parmesan cheese

1. Prepare the onions and set them aside.

2. Heat the butter and oil in a deep skillet and add the onions. Cook, stirring, until wilted, about 5 minutes. Add the tomatoes and cook, stirring, about 5 minutes. Add the hot milk. When added, the milk may appear curdled. Pay it no mind. Add parsley, salt and pepper.

3. Meanwhile, drop the pasta into boiling salted water and cook until half done, about 5 minutes for spaghettini, slightly longer for spaghetti or linguine. Drain the pasta quickly and add it to the sauce. Turn the heat to high and continue cooking, turning the pasta constantly in the sauce.

4. Cook the pasta to the desired degree of doneness and add half the cheese. Stir until blended and serve piping hot with remaining cheese on the side.

Yield: 4 to 6 servings.

Egg Noodles with Smoked Salmon

¼ *pound thinly sliced smoked salmon*
   Salt to taste
½ *pound egg noodles, preferably imported tagliarini*
3 *tablespoons butter*
2 *tablespoons cognac*
½ *cup warm cream*
   Freshly ground pepper to taste
⅓ *cup freshly grated Parmesan cheese*

1. It is important in the preparation of this recipe that all the ingredients be prepared and ready to cook. The dish must be assembled, cooked quickly and served immediately and piping hot. It would be helpful if the serving plates such as soup bowls were also heated in advance.

2. Cut the salmon into 1½-inch squares. Set aside.

3. Bring 3 quarts of water to a rolling boil and add salt to taste. Add the egg noodles and stir to prevent sticking. The cooking time for these noodles will vary. Store-bought domestic noodles should cook about 3 to 5 minutes. Imported egg noodles will take a bit longer, perhaps 5 to 7 minutes. Do not overcook.

4. When the noodles are almost done, heat the butter in a deep skillet and when it is very hot but not brown, add the salmon, stirring gently and quickly. Do not overcook or the pieces will become dry. They should just lose the bright pink color. Immediately add the cognac and, if desired, ignite it, shaking the skillet. Add the cream and bring to the boil.

5. When the cream is added, drain the noodles fairly well. Add them to the sauce. Add salt and pepper to taste. Add the cheese, toss quickly and serve piping hot.

Yield: 4 appetizer servings or 2 main courses.

Pasta with Broccoli

½ *pound fresh broccoli (see note)*
½ *pound spaghettini or linguine*
5 *tablespoons olive oil*
2 *to 3 cloves fresh garlic, finely chopped*
½ *teaspoon hot red pepper flakes, approximately*

2   cups water, approximately
    Salt to taste
    Freshly grated Parmesan
    cheese for garnish

1. This recipe is incredibly easy to make, but there are a couple of pitfalls that must be guarded against. When the pasta and vegetables are cooked, the pasta must be stirred often to keep the strands from sticking to themselves and to the bottom of the pan. It is best to stir gently but often with a plastic spatula to prevent this.

2. Trim off and reserve the bud clusters at the top of the broccoli stems. Leave part of the stem attached to the base of each cluster. If the clusters are very large, cut them in half. Reserve the stems as well.

3. Unless the broccoli is very young and tender, pare or peel off the outer skin of the stems. If the stems are large, slice them in half lengthwise. In any event, cut the stem sections into 2-inch lengths. Combine and set aside the prepared broccoli pieces.

4. Break the pasta into 2- or 3-inch lengths. Set aside.

5. Heat the oil in a heavy, not too large skillet or casserole, about 9 or 10 inches in diameter. Add the garlic and cook briefly. Add the hot pepper flakes, pasta and broccoli. Add 1 cup of water and, when it boils, stir the ingredients to make certain the pasta does not stick to itself or the bottom of the pan.

6. Cover the pan and continue cooking but stirring often and adding water as it is absorbed, about ¼ cup at a time. Add salt to taste. When this dish is ready, the pasta will be cooked, the broccoli crisp-tender and

most of the liquid will be absorbed. The "sauce" that clings to the pasta will be minimal. The total cooking time is about 10 to 12 minutes. Do not overcook or the pasta will become mushy.

7. Serve immediately in hot soup plates with Parmesan cheese on the side.

Yield: 4 appetizer servings or 2 main dishes.

Note: Broccoli di rape, a tender, delicious and somewhat bitter Italian green, which is becoming more available in America, may be substituted for the broccoli.

Pasta con Asparagi

(Pasta with asparagus)

1½   pounds fresh asparagus
3   tablespoons butter
      Salt and freshly ground
      pepper to taste
2½   tablespoons olive oil
2   whole cloves garlic
2   cups canned Italian plum
      tomatoes put through a sieve
1   tablespoon finely chopped
      parsley
1   teaspoon dried basil or 1
      tablespoon finely chopped
      fresh basil
¾   pound penne, rigatoni or other
      tubular pasta
2   eggs plus 1 egg yolk, beaten
      well with a fork
½   cup grated Parmesan cheese

1. Have all the ingredients for this recipe prepared and ready to cook before starting to cook. Bring about 3 cups of water to the boil and have it ready for the pasta.

2. Cut the asparagus into lengths about 2 inches long. If the stalks are thick, cut them in half or quarter them. Leave the tips intact. Heat the butter in a skillet and add the asparagus pieces, salt and pepper to taste. Cook 4 to 5 minutes or until crisp-tender and lightly browned. Remove from the heat.

3. Heat the oil in a deep skillet and add the garlic. Cook until lightly browned and remove and discard the garlic. Add the tomatoes, parsley, basil, salt and pepper to taste. Cook, stirring, about 10 minutes.

4. Meanwhile, add the pasta and salt to the water and, when it returns to the boil, cook about 7 minutes or until tender. Do not overcook.

5. Just before the pasta is done, turn off the heat under the tomatoes and add the beaten eggs, stirring vigorously so that they blend in the sauce without curdling. Do not boil the sauce after the eggs are added.

6. Add the asparagus to the tomato sauce and stir to blend.

7. Drain the pasta immediately. Add the tomato sauce and asparagus, toss with half the cheese. Serve piping hot with the remaining cheese on the side.

Yield: 8 or more servings.

Penne or Rigatoni Modo Mio

(Tubular pasta with cauliflower and ham)

2   *tablespoons butter*
2   *tablespoons olive oil*
2   *cups thinly sliced onions*
1   *teaspoon finely chopped garlic*
1½ *cups boiled ham cut into ½-inch cubes*
2   *tablespoons chopped fresh basil or half the amount dried*
2   *tablespoons chopped fresh parsley*
1   *cup dry white wine*
    Salt and freshly ground pepper to taste
½   *pound penne or rigatoni*
2   *cups peeled, raw potatoes cut into ½-inch cubes*
4   *cups cauliflower (1 small) broken or cut into "flowerettes"*
½   *cup grated Parmesan cheese*

1. Have all the ingredients cut, chopped, measured and ready to cook before starting this dish. Have a kettle of water at the boil for the pasta.

2. Heat the butter and oil in a skillet and add the onions. Cook, stirring, until golden. Add the garlic, ham, basil, parsley, wine, salt and pepper to taste and continue cooking.

3. Simultaneously, as soon as the onions start to cook, add the penne or rigatoni and potatoes to the boiling water. Add salt and pepper to taste. Let return to the boil, stirring often so that the pasta does not stick. Let cook about 4 minutes.

4. Add the cauliflower and continue cooking 4 to 5 minutes or until the pasta is just cooked. Do not overcook. When done, drain immediately and add the pasta mixture to the ham mixture. Toss with half the grated Parmesan cheese. Serve with the remaining cheese on the side.

Yield: 8 servings.

Pasta e Broccoli con Trippa

(Penne or rigatoni and broccoli with tripe)

Tripe florentine-style (see recipe)
Salt to taste
1 pound penne or rigatoni
½ pound broccoli, cut or broken into bite-size chunks
½ cup grated Parmesan cheese

1. Prepare the tripe and have it hot and ready.

2. Bring about 3 quarts of water to the boil and add salt to taste. Add the penne or rigatoni and cook, stirring to make certain the pasta does not stick.

3. Cook the pasta about 5 minutes and add the broccoli. Cook about 2 to 4 minutes longer or until the pasta is just tender. Do not overcook. Drain and add to the tripe. Toss well and serve piping hot with grated Parmesan cheese on the side.

Yield: 8 to 10 servings.

Tripe Florentine-Style

1½ pounds honeycomb tripe
4 tablespoons olive oil
1 tablespoon butter
1 cup finely chopped onion
1 cup thinly sliced mushrooms
1 teaspoon finely chopped garlic
1 sprig fresh rosemary or 1 teaspoon chopped dried
1 cup dry white wine
1 bay leaf
2 tablespoons finely chopped parsley
¾ cup chopped carrots
1 cup chicken broth
2 cups canned Italian plum tomatoes blended or put through a food mill
Salt and freshly ground pepper to taste

1. Put the tripe in a kettle and add water to cover, about 3 quarts. Bring to the boil and cook about ½ hour.

2. Drain the tripe and let cool. Cut the tripe into strips about ¼ inch wide and 2 to 3 inches long.

3. Heat the oil and butter in a deep skillet and add the tripe. Cook over moderate heat, stirring constantly. Cook 6 to 7 minutes or until tripe starts sticking to the bottom of the skillet. Add the onions, mushrooms and garlic. Cover and cook until onions wilt. Add the remaining ingredients and cover. Bring to the boil.

4. Meanwhile, preheat the oven to 350 degrees. Place the tripe in the oven and cook, covered, about 2 hours.

Yield: 8 or more servings.

Dinners-in-a-Pot

WITH PIERRE FRANEY

Although the foods of our puritan forefathers may be lacking in lusty flavors, one finds on occasion a traditional dish that smacks of that early heritage and yet, withal, has a good deal of subtle appeal, perhaps because of its very simplicity and humble nature. One of these is that Yankee specialty, the New England boiled dinner with its corned beef and winter vegetables including potatoes, turnips, cabbage and beets. These are things that remain with us during the present season. Along with a recipe for that dinner-in-a-pot, we offer a delectable and equally simple European boiled dinner—boiled beef with caper sauce.

New England Boiled Dinner

1	6½-pound corned beef
6	quarts water
5	or 6 carrots, about 1 pound
8	to 12 small white turnips or 1 rutabaga, about ¾ pound
8	small, whole white onions, about ¾ pound
1	or 2 young heads of cabbage, about 4 pounds
10	potatoes, about 1¾ pounds
10	young beets, about 1 pound
	Salt
¼	pound butter
	Horseradish, preferably freshly grated
	Mustard

1. Place the corned beef in a large kettle or Dutch oven and add the water. The water should cover the top of the beef by about 2 inches. Cover and cook about 2 hours, or until the corned beef is almost tender. Do not add salt.

2. Meanwhile, trim the carrots and cut them in half widthwise. Cut each half into quarters. Set aside.

3. Peel the turnips and set aside.

4. Peel the onions and set aside.

5. If 2 cabbages are used, quarter them. If 1 head is used, cut it into eighths. Pull away any tough outer leaves and cut away part of the core of each section. Set aside.

6. Peel the potatoes and drop them into cold water to prevent discoloration. Set aside.

7. Peel the beets and set aside.

8. After approximately 2 hours when the meat is almost tender, add all the vegetables except the beets. Taste the cooking liquid. It should not need salt. If it does, add it to taste.

9. Put the beets in a saucepan and add water to cover and salt to taste and cook until tender.

10. Cook the meat and remaining vegetables in water to cover and salt to taste until tender.

11. Remove the meat and slice it thin.

12. Arrange the drained vegetables symmetrically on a hot platter. Melt the butter and pour it over the vegetables. Serve the dinner with horseradish and mustard on the side.

Yield: About 10 servings.

Boiled Beef with Caper Sauce

The beef

1   6½-pound untrimmed brisket of beef or one 5½-pound trimmed brisket of beef
1   ¾-pound green cabbage, cored
16   cups water, approximately
    Salt
10   peppercorns, crushed
2   cloves garlic, peeled and left whole
1   bay leaf
8   small or 4 large leeks
2   sprigs fresh thyme or 1 teaspoon dried
6   sprigs fresh parsley
6   to 8 small white turnips, about 1½ pounds, peeled
4   carrots, about ¾ pound, trimmed and scraped
1   small heart of celery (outer ribs removed), tied with a string
1   onion stuck with 2, cloves
4   parsnips, about ½ pound, trimmed

The garnishes

Caper sauce (see recipe)
Assorted imported mustards
Imported French sour pickles
(cornichons)
Grated horseradish, fresh or bottled
Coarse salt
Mustard fruit, packed in syrup and available in jars from shops that specialize in fine imported Italian delicacies

1. If the brisket is not trimmed of excess fat, trim off most of the fat, leaving a thin layer. Or have this done by the butcher.

2. Place the brisket in a kettle or deep casserole and add water to cover. Bring to the boil. Meanwhile, tie the cabbage in cheesecloth and add it. When the water boils, let both the meat and cabbage simmer about 5 minutes. Drain and run the meat under cold water. Reserve the cabbage.

3. Return the meat to the kettle and add cold water to cover, about 16 cups. Add salt to taste, peppercorns, garlic and bay leaf. Bring to the boil and simmer, partly covered, about 1 hour.

4. Meanwhile, trim off the ends of the leeks. Split the leeks almost but not down to the root end. Rinse thoroughly between the leaves and drain. Tie the leeks in a bundle with the thyme and parsley.

5. Prepare the remaining vegetables. When the meat has cooked 1 hour, add the cabbage and remaining vegetables to the kettle. Test the vegetables with a fork or knife. As they become tender, remove them and set aside. Let the meat continue cooking. The total cooking time for the meat is about 2 hours.

6. When ready to serve, return the vegetables briefly to the kettle just to heat them thoroughly. Serve the meat sliced and hot. Cut the assorted vegetables including the leeks into serving portions. Serve with the caper sauce and recommended garnishes according to choice.

Yield: 8 or more servings.

English caper sauce

9   *tablespoons butter at room temperature*
3   *tablespoons flour*
2   *cups beef broth from the boiled beef*
⅓   *cup chopped drained capers Juice of ½ lemon or more according to taste*
Salt and freshly ground pepper

1. Melt 3 tablespoons of butter in a saucepan and add the flour, stirring with a wire whisk. When blended, add the beef broth, stirring rapidly with the whisk. When the mixture is thickened and smooth, cook, stirring occasionally about 5 minutes.

2. Add the capers, lemon juice, salt and pepper to taste. Bring to the boil and remove from the heat. Immediately whisk in the remaining butter, about 2 tablespoons at a time.

Yield: About 2½ cups.

Sweetbreads

WITH PIERRE FRANEY

There is no more "reason" why sweetbreads are the basis for some of the most elegant dishes in the world than there is in why people climb mountains or take to the air in ascension baloons. Sweetbread dishes are simply a "natural" thread in the fabric of fine dining and have been for centuries. Sweetbreads, the tender thymus glands of calves, adapt well to many kinds of treatment and often serve interchangeably between first courses and main dishes. A trio of sweetbread dishes appears here.

Ris de Veau et Champignons à la Creme

(Sweetbreads and mushrooms in cream sauce)

2	pounds fresh sweetbreads
	Salt
¼	pound fresh mushrooms
2	tablespoons butter
1	tablespoon finely chopped shallots
	Freshly ground pepper
1	tablespoon flour
½	cup milk
½	cup heavy cream
⅛	teaspoon grated nutmeg
	Tabasco sauce
4	to 6 slices buttered toast

1. Place the sweetbreads in a mixing bowl and add cold water to cover. Soak for several hours but change the water frequently. The soaking will make the sweetbreads white.

2. When the sweetbreads are ready, drain them. Use a paring knife and cut away the arteries and so on.

3. Place the sweetbreads in a saucepan and add cold water to cover and salt to taste. Bring to the boil and simmer 5 minutes. Drain immediately, then run under cold water until well chilled.

4. Place a cake rack in a dish and cover with a clean towel. Add the sweetbreads in one layer and cover with the towel. Add a heavy weight (we used a flour crock filled with flour) and let stand several hours.

5. If the mushrooms are very small, leave them whole. Otherwise, quarter or slice them.

6. Melt 1 tablespoon of the butter in a small skillet and add the shallots and mushrooms. Cook, stirring, about 3 minutes and add the sweetbreads, salt and pepper to taste. Cook, stirring frequently, about 10 minutes.

7. In a small saucepan, heat the remaining butter and add the flour, stirring with a wire whisk. When blended, add the milk and cream, stirring rapidly with the whisk. Add the

nutmeg and Tabasco. Add the sweet-breads and mushroom mixture and blend. Simmer 25 minutes. Serve on buttered toast.

Yield: 4 to 6 servings.

Curried Sweetbreads with Mushrooms

2   to 4 pair sweetbreads, about
    3½ pounds
6   tablespoons butter
1   cup finely chopped onion
3   tablespoons curry powder
1   cup finely chopped apple
½   cup finely chopped banana
2   tablespoons tomato paste

2   cups chicken broth
    Salt
½   pound mushrooms, quartered
    if small, or cut into eighths if
    large (about 3½ to 4 cups)
    Freshly ground pepper
½   cup dry white wine

1. Place the sweetbreads in a bowl and add cold water to cover. Soak overnight or for several hours in the refrigerator, changing the water occasionally. Drain.

2. Place the sweetbreads in a large saucepan and add cold water to cover. Bring to the boil and simmer 5 minutes. Drain immediately. Run under cold water and let stand in the water until thoroughly chilled. Drain.

3. Place the sweetbreads in a flat

pan and cover with another flat pan of the same size. Cover with a heavy weight and let stand 6 hours or more.

4. Remove the uppermost pan. Cut the sweetbreads into 1-inch cubes, cutting, trimming or pulling off and discarding connecting tissues and so forth as necessary. Set aside.

5. Heat 2 tablespoons of butter in a saucepan or skillet and add the onion. Cook until wilted and sprinkle with curry powder. Cook briefly, stirring, and add the apple and banana. Add the tomato paste, stirring, and add the chicken broth. Continue stirring until well blended. Add salt to taste. Pour the sauce into the container of a food processor or electric blender and blend until smooth. Set aside.

6. Meanwhile, heat the remaining butter in a large, heavy skillet or casserole and add the sweetbreads. Cook, stirring and shaking the skillet about 5 minutes. Add the mushrooms and salt and pepper to taste. Cook, stirring often, about 10 minutes and add the wine. Cook until most of the wine is evaporated. Add the sauce. Cook, stirring occasionally, about 15 or 20 minutes. Serve with rice, in puff pastry shells or on toast.

Yield: 6 to 8 servings.

Ris de Veau à l'Anglaise

(Breaded sweetbreads)

1 *pound sweetbreads*
  Salt
½ *cup flour*
1 *egg*
2 *tablespoons water*

2 *tablespoons plus 1 teaspoon peanut, vegetable or corn oil*
  Freshly ground pepper
1¼ *cups fresh bread crumbs*
7 *tablespoons butter*
  Lemon slices for garnish

1. Put the sweetbreads in a saucepan and add cold water to cover and salt to taste. Bring to the boil and simmer 5 minutes, no longer. Drain and cover with cold water.

2. When the sweetbreads are cool, drain them. Place them on a cake rack. Cover with another rack and weight them down. For this we have used everything from meat pounders to saucepans filled with stones. Weight the sweetbreads for about 2 hours.

3. Pick over the sweetbreads and remove any odd membranes, filaments or tendons. Cut the sweetbreads into 8 flat pieces.

4. Dredge the pieces on all sides in flour.

5. Beat the egg and stir in the water, 1 teaspoon of oil, salt and pepper to taste. Dip the sweetbreads first in the egg mixture, then in the bread crumbs. When well coated, tap lightly to help the crumbs adhere.

6. In a large skillet, heat 3 tablespoons of butter and remaining 2 tablespoons of oil. Add the sweetbreads. Cook until golden on one side. Turn and cook until golden on the other side.

7. Remove the sweetbreads to a warm platter. Wipe out the skillet and add the remaining butter. Cook until the foam subsides and the butter is hazelnut brown. Pour the butter over the sweetbreads. Garnish with lemon slices and serve immediately.

Yield: 4 servings.

People frequently ask why sweetbreads must be soaked and weighted. The answer is that they, like fresh fish bones and heads, are likely to contain a certain amount of residual blood, which will turn dark on cooking (blood also clouds broths such as fish broth). The soaking aids in getting rid of much of this. Sweetbreads are weighted down after cooking because it gives them a firmer, more appetizing texture. If they are not weighted, they have a spongy texture that may be acceptable, but it is not preferable.

The Reuben Sandwich

We would give much to learn the origin of the Reuben sandwich but no amount of research has turned up any clues of indisputable nature. It is said, of course, that the Reuben sandwich began in the now defunct but once great New York restaurant known as Reubens on 59th Street and famous for its many layered sandwiches. We can only surmise that whoever created the Reuben initially gave it a name intended to be Reuben-style.

We had a note from Psyche Frederick of West Gloucester, Massachusetts, stating she'd heard us "extolling the marvels of the Reuben sandwich. As I did not hear it all, I would dearly love it if you would send me your recipe. I cannot find it in any cookbook and would appreciate it no end if you would do this for me."

This is our version of the sandwich.

Reuben Sandwich

¾   cup cooked sauerkraut,
      preferably heated (see note)
4   slices rye bread
3   to 4 tablespoons butter, melted
4   to 12 slices thinly sliced
      cooked corned beef (the
      amount will depend on the
      size and thickness of the
      slices)
4   to 8 thin slices Gruyère,
      Swiss or Muenster cheese

1. Preheat the oven to 400 degrees.

2. Drain the sauerkraut well.

3. Use half the butter and butter the slices of rye bread on one side only. Place 2 of the slices buttered-side down on a flat surface and add a layer of corned beef on top of these slices. Top the corned beef with equal amounts of sauerkraut. Cover each serving with half the cheese slices. Cover with the remaining slices of rye bread, buttered-side up.

4. Pour the remaining butter into a heavy, ovenproof skillet, preferably a heavy iron skillet. Smear it around and add the sandwiches in one layer. Heat the skillet and cook the sandwiches on one side, sliding them around in the skillet. When nicely browned on one side, turn them carefully and gently, using a pancake turner. Place the skillet in the oven and bake until the sandwich fillings are piping hot throughout and the cheese is melted. Serve immediately with garlic or dill pickle strips.

Yield: 2 servings.

Note: If leftover sauerkraut is not available, empty the contents of an 8-ounce can of sauerkraut into a saucepan. Drain. Add ¼ cup each chicken broth and dry white wine and a finely chopped clove of garlic. Cover and cook about 30 minutes. Drain and serve.

Sometimes, Russian dressing is served with this sandwich. This is made with mayonnaise and a little ketchup plus real or imitation caviar to taste. Or use capers. Smear the dressing over the corned beef before adding the sauerkraut.

Our wish to learn the origins of the Reuben sandwich provided us with an abundance of letters, most of them pinpointing 1956 as the year the sandwich gained national prominence. We have traced the history to the sponsors of the National Sandwich Contest held in that year. The following treatise, from the National Kraut Packers Association, explains all and includes the original winning recipe for the sandwich:

"The Reuben sandwich, submitted by a waitress, Miss Fern Snider of Omaha, Nebraska, took first place honors in the 1956 National Sandwich Contest. Since that year, the sandwich has steadily grown to its now acclaimed popularity. Today, practically every restaurant, club and diner in the country features a version of the Reuben.

"The idea originated with one of Miss Snider's employers, the Schimmel family, who has operated the Blackstone Hotel in Omaha for years. During 1920–1935, Bernard Schimmel's father belonged to a weekly poker group. Fixing their own sandwiches became the most enjoyed weekly 'feast' on these poker nights. One player, a wholesale grocer named Reuben Kay, devised the combination of kraut, corned beef and Swiss on rye. Thus, in honor of its 'founder,' the Reuben was named.

"Bernard Schimmel, a retired European-trained chef, says the secret of the Reuben is in its bread. It should be fresh pumpernickel, preferably the sourdough kind. The sauerkraut should be crisp, chilled and well drained. At the Blackstone, he explains, only the best ingredients are selected—that is, rich homemade Russian dressing, Emmenthaler Swiss cheese and kosher-styled corned beef that has been trimmed well and sliced very thin.

"Assembling the Reuben is an 'art,' too. Schimmel puts corned beef on one slice of pumpernickel, Swiss cheese on the other. Next, he tops one side of the sandwich with a thick layer of kraut mixed with dressing. Then he either butters and quickly grills it, or serves it cold without the butter. If grilled, he believes the sandwich should be hot on the outside, cold on the inside. The perfect garnishes are chilled, half-cured dill pickles."

Reuben Sandwich

2¼   cups drained sauerkraut
¼   cup chopped sweet onion
3   tablespoons chopped parsley
     Creamy Russian dressing (see note)
16   slices rye bread
¾   pound sliced corned beef
¾   pound sliced Swiss cheese
     Butter or margarine, softened

1. Combine the sauerkraut, onion and parsley. Toss until well mixed.

2. Spread Russian dressing on each slice of bread. Top 8 slices of bread with corned beef, cheese and sauerkraut. Top with remaining bread.

3. Lightly butter both sides of the sandwiches. Grill slowly until cheese melts and bread browns.

Yield: 8 sandwiches.

Note: To make creamy Russian dressing, blend ½ cup mayonnaise with ¼ cup chili sauce.

Although we are persuaded that the above is the true origin of the Reuben sandwich that we have indulged in on many occasions and the sandwich we had in mind when we pondered its origins, we are also in possession of a letter from Patricia R. Taylor of Manhattan who claims that her father, the late Arnold Reuben, was the originator of ALL Reuben sandwiches. Arnold Reuben was, of course, the proprietor for many years of the now-defunct and well-remembered Reuben restaurant on 59th Street.

We feel obliged in all fairness to reprint portions of Mrs. Taylor's letter:

"I am prompted to write after reading of your search for the original Reuben sandwich. Your search is over, here I am, the daughter of the horse's mouth.

"My father . . . for over forty odd years made his restaurant an institution in New York. To quote Damon Runyon, 'Reuben has always been famous for his sandwiches, which are regular productions, not just slabs of bread with things between them. For years it has been Arnold's custom to apply to these masterpieces of the sandwich architect's skill the names of persons of more or less notoriety in our fair city.'

"I would like to share with you the story of the first Reuben's Special and what went into it.

"The year was 1914. Late one evening a leading lady of Charlie Chaplin's came into the restaurant and said, 'Reuben, make me a sandwich, make it a combination, I'm so hungry I could eat a brick.' He took a loaf of rye bread, cut two slices on the bias and stacked one piece with sliced baked Virginia ham, sliced roast turkey, sliced imported Swiss cheese, topped it off with cole slaw and lots of Reuben's special Russian dressing and the second slice of bread. (The bias cut bread made his sandwiches a sandwich and a half.)

"He served it to the lady who said, 'Gee, Reuben, this is the best sandwich I ever ate, you ought to call it an Annette Seelos Special.' To which he replied, 'Like hell I will, I'll call it a Reuben's Special.' "

Let us compromise and say that Arnold Reuben, the sandwich genius, produced a forerunner of what is now served coast to coast as the Reuben sandwich named by coincidence for Reuben Kay, the wholesale grocer in Omaha.

Sarah's Challah

We know of a man of unimpeachable taste, a distinguished figure in medicine, who exercises restraint in his spoken enthusiasms. But when he speaks of Sarah Schecht's challah, he rhapsodizes with undiminished vigor. "Her challah," he claims, "has a texture to rival that of the finest spongecakes. It is airborne, light as a zephyr, delicate as eider-down." The last time she dispatched a challah to his home he wrote, "My dear Sarah, you are a better cook than I am a doctor."

We arranged to meet Mrs. Schecht in her kitchen in Brooklyn to discover, if we might, the secret of her sorcery in making the braided, yeast-leavened egg bread traditionally served by Jews for special and ceremonial occasions or simply for the sheer pleasure of dining.

Mrs. Schecht, who is 73 years old, and who came to America from Poland more than half a century ago, told us that she knew no secret in her baking technique, "the dish just turns out that way." She agreed to let us watch her make the dish and she started about 10:30 in the morning under the watchful, admiring eye of her husband, Al, who was born in Russia and is also 73 years old.

"We've been married 52 years," she told us proudly, "and we have four children and seven grandchildren." Al, now retired, told us that his wife had never cooked before they were married, and she gave him an impish look.

"That's not true," she declared, "I learned from the wife of one of your cousins." Al, however, has fairly good credentials in food preparation. His father was a baker in Russia.

"I worked for years for Max's Stage Delicatessen on Seventh Avenue back in the days of the big band era, and I've worked parties for some of the biggest actors and actresses in America. I catered the first party for Frank Sinatra, it was backstage after he opened at the Paramount theater. I've catered parties for the Marx Brothers at the old Roxy and at the Capital for Xavier Cugat. Back in those days we fed them all."

Mrs. Schecht had several dishes on her mind and stove that morning, including family-style sweet and sour stuffed cabbage and kreplach plus the braided loaf. The couple cook together often with a minor skirmish here and there as things progress. "When he starts dirtying the dishes, I have to get him out of the way." Getting out of the way generally means sitting in a chair at kibitzing distance.

"You start with six cups of flour," Mrs. Schecht said as she emptied the flour into a large mixing bowl. "You add a couple of packages of yeast and a cup of lukewarm water and stir with a fork." She stirred with a fork incorporating only about a quarter of the flour into the yeast mixture. She placed the bowl, un-

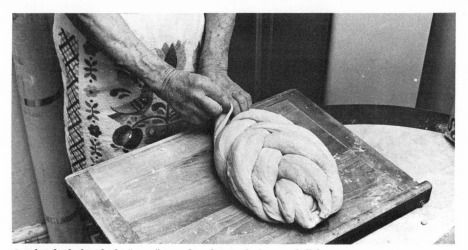

Sarah Schecht braids the "ropes" in making her justly famous challah

covered, on a warm spot on the back of the stove and left it uncovered with the fork still in.

Why do you leave the fork in, we asked?

"Take it out, leave it in, what's the difference. You have to stir it later anyway after the yeast starts working." Good logic.

As the yeast worked, Al busied himself with measuring out the meat for the cabbage with an ice cream scoop, leveling off as he went about his work. "For each cabbage roll you need two ounces of meat. Each leveled-off scoop weighs two ounces. For the cabbage use skirt steak, which I buy at a kosher butcher. Kosher meat is more expensive than other meat."

The Schechts' cooking is not strictly kosher although much of it is. The challah, for example, would be made with margarine rather than butter.

When the yeast had worked, Mrs. Schecht used the fork to incorporate the rest of the flour. Then she turned it out on a board and kneaded it. She is a diminutive woman, but her appearance belies the strength of her fingers, apparent as she kneads the dough.

The cooking liquid was made ready for the cabbage, tomato sauce and dried fruits; the parboiled cabbage leaves were stuffed, skewered with toothpicks and added to the kettle, and the challah dough was kneaded again. Kreplach, the delectable Jewish version of won ton, were made with ground cooked meat and chicken livers and the challah, after one more kneading, was given its final preparation, the braiding.

The dough was cut into eight equal portions and rolled with open palms into eight "ropes." These were gathered at the top and pinched together and then the ropes were braided, left rope to right, right rope to left and so on until a neatly styled tress, gathered at the bottom and pinched to seal, was formed. It was transferred to a large, rectangular baking pan and left to rise once more. After an hour or so the braided loaf had swollen to twice its size and filled the pan. It was brushed with egg, sprinkled with poppy seeds and plumped into the oven. Oh, how it swoll and became golden and gossamer, just like the doctor had said.

Here is a detailed recipe for the challah as well as for the sweet and sour stuffed cabbage and kreplach. Plus a recipe for seductively rich, easily made European cookies, rugelah.

Challah

(A sweet leavened bread)

8½ to 9 cups sifted, unbleached
flour plus additional flour for
kneading
2   packages dry yeast
2½ cups lukewarm water
½   teaspoon baking powder
½   teaspoon cinnamon
1   tablespoon salt
1   teaspoon vanilla
4   large eggs
¾   cup corn oil
¾   cup plus ⅛ teaspoon sugar
1   tablespoon poppy seeds or
sesame seeds

1. Place 6 cups of the flour in a large mixing bowl and make a well in the center. Blend the yeast with 1 cup of the water and stir to dissolve. Add this to the well in the flour. Using a fork, start stirring around the well, gradually incorporating ¼ of the flour—no more—into the yeast mixture. When approximately that amount of flour is blended into the yeast mixture, stop stirring. There is no need to remove the fork. It will be used for further stirring. Set the bowl in a warm, not too hot place, and let stand about 45 or 50 minutes.

2. Sprinkle the baking powder, cinnamon and salt over all. Add the vanilla, 3 of the eggs, the oil and ¾ cup of sugar. Add the remaining water and blend again, first using the fork and then the hands. Add 2 cups of flour, kneading and, if the mixture is still too sticky, add an additional cup of flour.

3. Work the mixture well with a wooden spoon to make a very stiff dough. If necessary, add more flour. Work with the hands about 10 min-

utes. When the dough doesn't stick to the hands, it is ready. Shape the mixture into a rather coarse ball and cover. Let stand about 20 minutes and turn it out onto a lightly floured board. Knead well, adding a little more flour to the board as necessary to prevent sticking. The kneading, which must be thorough and brisk, should take about 5 minutes. Flour a bowl well and add the ball, turning the dough to coat lightly with flour. Cover again and let stand about 30 minutes.

4. Turn the dough onto a flat surface once more and knead briefly. Using a knife, slash off about ⅛ of the dough at a time. As each portion is cut off, knead quickly and shape into a ball. Flour lightly. Return each piece as it is kneaded to a bowl to rest briefly. Continue until all 8 pieces are shaped and floured.

5. Take one piece of dough at a time and place it on a flat surface, rolling briskly with the hands to make a "rope" about 12 to 15 inches in length. Continue until all the balls are shaped thusly.

6. Align the ropes vertically side by side and touching. Start working at the top of the ropes. Gather the tops of the ropes together, one at a time, pinching down to seal well. Separate the rope down the center, 4 ropes to a side. Braid the ropes as follows: Bring the extreme outer right rope over toward the center next to the inside rope on the left. Bring the extreme outer left rope over toward the center next to the inside rope on the right. Continue with this procedure until the loaf is braided and each rope has been brought to the center. As the last ropes are brought over, it will be necessary to pull and stretch them a bit to get them to fit.

7. When the braiding is finished, gather the bottom ends of the ropes together and pinch them together just as at the top.

8. Meanwhile, generously oil (or butter) the bottom and sides of a rectangular baking pan measuring about 15½ by 10½ by 2½ inches. Carefully gather up the braided loaf, using the hands and arms to help sustain the shape.

9. During the next step, preheat the oven to 325 degrees.

10. Cover with a towel and let stand in a warm spot for 1 hour or slightly longer or until the loaf is well puffed and about twice the original volume.

11. Beat the remaining egg with the ⅛ teaspoon of sugar and, using a pastry brush, brush the loaf all over with the egg wash and sprinkle evenly with poppy or sesame seeds.

12. Place the loaf in the oven and bake approximately 1 hour until well puffed, cooked through and golden.

Yield: 1 large loaf.

Family-Style
Sweet and Sour
Stuffed Cabbage

1	2-to-2¼-pound green cabbage
	Salt to taste
½	cup golden seedless raisins
2	tablespoons raw rice
3	marrow bones, split into 3 pieces
2	cups tomato puree
3¼	cups water
1¼	pounds skirt steak or chuck, ground 3 times

12	dried apricots, cut into small pieces
12	dried pitted dates, cut into small pieces
1	cup finely diced golden Delicious apple
1	cup finely chopped onion
⅔	cup finely chopped freshly cooked or canned beets
5	tablespoons cooking liquid (beet juice) from freshly cooked or canned beets
2	tablespoons orange marmalade
2	tablespoons tomato ketchup
1	egg white
1	cup fresh or canned tomato sauce
2	tablespoons lemon juice
2	tablespoons maple syrup
3	tablespoons dark honey
1	tablespoon flour

1. Peel off and discard the tough outer leaves from the cabbage. Carve out and discard the center core of the cabbage. Drop the cabbage into boiling water to cover with salt to taste. Cover and cook about 15 minutes. Drain well.

2. Pull off and set aside 14 of the largest leaves from the cabbage. Set aside remaining cabbage.

3. Place the raisins in a bowl and add hot water to cover. Let stand.

4. Rinse the rice well and set aside.

5. Place the bones in a saucepan with cold water to cover. Bring to the boil and simmer about 1 minute. Drain and rinse under cold water.

6. Place the tomato puree, 3 cups of water and the bones in a kettle. It must be large enough to hold the sauce plus 12 or 14 pieces of stuffed cabbage when added. Cover and bring to the boil. Let simmer.

7. Place the meat in a mixing bowl. Add half the raisins, drained, half the apricots, half the dates, half the apple, half the onion, half the chopped beets, 2 tablespoons beet liquid, the orange marmalade, ketchup, egg white and remaining ¼ cup water. Add salt to taste. Add the rice. Blend well with the fingers and set aside.

8. To the kettle with the bones, add the remaining raisins, apricots, dates, apple, onion, beets, beet liquid and salt to taste. Stir and continue cooking.

9. Using about ⅓ cup of the meat mixture at a time, stuff the large reserved leaves. As each leaf is filled fold the sides over, envelope fashion, to enclose the meat. Seal with toothpicks. Continue until all the leaves are stuffed.

10. Finely shred all the cabbage that remains and add it to the kettle. Add the cabbage rolls, distributing them neatly over the shredded cabbage and sauce. Cover and cook 45 minutes.

11. Uncover and add the tomato sauce, lemon juice and maple syrup. Cook 45 minutes longer and add the honey. Stir. Sprinkle the top with flour and stir gently so that the flour gets into the sauce. Cook about 30 minutes and uncover. Cook about 45 minutes longer. This dish improves on standing and is best when reheated the second day.

Yield: 12 to 14 pieces.

Kreplach

1   recipe for kreplach pastry (see recipe)
1   pound raw lean chuck, trimmed of all fat
2   cups coarsely chopped onions
1   teaspoon paprika
    Salt to taste
½   pound chicken livers, picked over
⅓   cup corn oil
1   egg yolk

1. Prepare the pastry and roll it in wax paper. Refrigerate until ready to use.

2. Place the meat in a saucepan and add water to cover. Add half the onion, paprika and salt. Cover and bring to the boil. Cook until the meat shreds easily and most of the liquid has evaporated. If necessary, add a bit more water as the meat cooks to prevent burning. Let cool.

3. Meanwhile, add the chicken livers to a saucepan and add cold water to cover. Bring to the boil and drain immediately. Chill under cold water. Drain.

4. Heat the oil and add the remaining onion. Cook until onion starts to become golden brown, stirring often. Add the livers and cook, stirring and turning them until they lose their red color and are just cooked through, about 5 minutes.

5. Meanwhile, slice the cooked meat and cut it into cubes. There should be about 2 cups. Add this to the liver mixture. Cook, stirring, about 5 minutes. Add this mixture to a food grinder equipped with a fine blade. Put the mixture through the grinder twice. Add salt and the egg yolk. Blend well.

6. Roll out about half the pastry at a time on a lightly floured board. It should be about ⅛ of an inch thick. Cut it into circles about 2½ inches in diameter. Scraps of dough may be gathered together and rolled again.

7. Fill the center of each circle with 1 tablespoon or so of the meat mixture and fold over like crescent-shaped turnovers. Press the edges to seal well. Bring the pointed sides of the crescents together and pinch to seal. Continue until all the meat is used. There should be about 36 kreplach.

8. Drop the kreplach into boiling water and simmer 10 minutes, stirring gently with a wooden spoon so that they cook evenly. Do not cover as they cook. Drain. Serve in bowls in piping hot chicken broth. Leftover kreplach are also good when browned lightly under a broiler.

Yield: About 36 kreplach.

Kreplach pastry

2¼   to 2½ cups flour, plus flour
       for rolling out dough
2   eggs
⅛   teaspoon salt
5   to 6 tablespoons warm water,
       approximately

1. Place 2¼ cups of flour on a flat surface and make a well in the center. Break the eggs into the well and add the salt. Gradually stir from the center incorporating the flour into the eggs. Add a little more flour if necessary. Add just enough water so that the dough holds together. Knead well.

2. When ready to roll out the dough, cut it in half and roll it out one half at a time. Roll into a circle and turn. Continue rolling and turning until the dough is about ⅛ of an inch thick.

Yield: Pastry for 36 kreplach.

Rugelah

(A sweet crisp cooky)

½   cup confectioners' sugar
2   cups sifted, unbleached flour
½   pound margarine (or butter)
½   teaspoon vanilla
1   egg yolk

1. Preheat the oven to 325 degrees.

2. Combine all the ingredients in a mixing bowl and work with the fingers until well blended.

3. Pull off pieces of dough—about 36 in all—and roll them into small balls the size of small walnuts. Flatten and roll out like a finger. Shape the dough with the fingers into V-shapes, U-shapes, crescents or any desired form. Arrange the shaped dough on a baking sheet.

4. Place the baking sheet in the oven and bake 20 to 30 minutes or until the cookies are crisp and lightly browned. It may be necessary to turn the baking sheet so that the cookies bake evenly.

Yield: About 36 rugelah.

Everyone seemed to like Sarah's rugelah, as well as her challah, but we received numerous letters from readers telling us that, while the pastry we printed delivered excellent results, it most certainly was not the pastry known as rugelah or rogalach. Almost every letter spelled the word differently.

One came from Rose Ehrlich of Roselle, New Jersey, who enclosed her recipe for rugelach, or butter horns, and it is excellent.

Rugelach
(Butter horns)

Cream cheese pastry (see recipe)
½ *pound light raisins*
¼ *pound walnuts*
2 *cups granulated sugar*
1 *teaspoon cinnamon*
½ *cup melted butter, approximately*

1. Prepare the dough and let it chill. Preheat the oven to 375 degrees.

2. Chop the raisins and the walnuts and combine in a mixing bowl. Add the sugar and cinnamon and blend well. Set aside.

3. Divide the dough into 6 equal portions. Roll out one portion at a time into a circle. Brush each circle as it is rolled with a little butter and sprinkle with part of the walnut mixture. Cut the circles into 8 or more pie-shaped wedges and roll. Start rolling from the large side of each wedge toward the tip to enclose the filling (a little of it may fall out). Bend these rolls to make a crescent shape. As they are rolled arrange them on a buttered baking sheet. An alternate method of folding rugelach is as follows: Roll each portion of dough as thinly as possible and cut with a diamond-shaped cooky cutter. Fill the center of the diamonds with the walnut mixture and bring the 3 points of each diamond to the center to enclose the filling. Pinch the points together and brush with butter before baking. When all the crescents are made, brush with butter.

4. Place the butter horns in the oven and bake 15 to 30 minutes, or until nicely browned and cooked through.

Yield: 3 to 6 dozen butter horns, depending on size.

Cream cheese pastry

½ *pound butter*
½ *pound cream cheese*
2 *eggs*
½ *teaspoon salt*
2½ *to 3 cups flour*

1. Combine the butter and cream cheese in the bowl of an electric mixer and beat until creamy. Add the eggs and beat in one at a time. Beat in the salt.

2. Remove the bowl and add the flour gradually, folding it in. When the dough can be worked with the hands, continue adding the flour, kneading with the hands until it can be rolled out. Add only as much flour as needed to make a workable dough. Shape into a ball and chill overnight or at least 2 hours.

3. Use the dough as necessary, rolling it on a floured board.

Yield: About 2 pounds.

May 1976

I T WAS MY GREAT fortune last year to be invited to join a friend on an automobile trip through Nova Scotia. My part of the voyage began in the small resort community of Chamberlain, Maine, where I stopped en route to visit Roger Fessaguet, the distinguished chef of New York's La Caravelle restaurant, and his endearing wife, Annick. We dined on the rocks in front of his home, with the ocean water lapping at our feet, on a simple but elaborate clambake for four. There were freshly harvested lobsters and clams, chicken and corn on the cob. The next evening, I took the ferry overnight from Portland to Yarmouth. We journeyed by car through the province, stopping en route according to whim to dine out of picnic baskets with appropriate wines (it was the first time, incidentally, I had ever dined on crisp potato chips sprinkled with vinegar, an unlikely but highly appealing snack). The food in the restaurants throughout the trip was astonishingly good: fantastic chowders and, of course, fresh fish out of those cold, cold waters. By the way, if you happen to visit the Gaspé Peninsula, as we did, by all means visit the dining room of the Auberge du Gargantua in the artists' colony of Percé. If the food is as it was on my visit, it is exceptional. We returned to Halifax and dined as noted here on fascinating fare in two restaurants, notably the Five Fishermen and Fat Frank's. They, too, will be well worth your while if the standards remain.

Delightful Fare from Halifax

WITH PIERRE FRANEY

If we had always thought of Halifax, Nova Scotia, as a frozen outpost somewhere to the north, we discovered to our considerable delight on a recent visit that it is a quite admirably habitable place and, with equal delight, it is the haven for two restaurants whose kitchens (and décor) deserve enthusiastic applause. The establishments are the Five Fishermen, whose fare included an excellent "fish soup à l'Acadian" and Fat Frank's, where a first-rate oyster and spinach bisque is served. We print here two recipes inspired by the dishes we dined on. Our feeling is that the Acadian soup really had its origins in the Provençal region of France.

Oyster and Spinach Bisque

1   pint shucked oysters with their liquor
4   tablespoons butter
½   cup finely chopped onion
8   tablespoons flour
4   cups fish broth (see recipe)
1   cup dry white wine
     Salt and freshly ground pepper
1   pound spinach in bulk or 1 10-ounce package
1¼   cups heavy cream
½   cup sour cream

1. Do not drain the oysters, but pick them over to remove any bits of shell. If the muscles of the oysters seem thick and tough, cut away and discard. Otherwise leave them whole.

2. Heat the butter in a small kettle and add the onion. Cook to wilt and add the flour, stirring to blend with a wire whisk. When blended, add the broth, stirring rapidly with the whisk. When blended and smooth, add the wine. Cover and cook 10 minutes. Add salt and pepper to taste.

3. Add the spinach and oysters and bring to the boil. Simmer 5 minutes.

4. Pour the mixture into the container of a food processor or an electric blender. This may have to be done in 2 steps. Blend thoroughly and return to a saucepan. Add 1 cup of the heavy cream and bring to the boil.

5. Blend the remaining heavy cream, sour cream and salt to taste. Serve a spoonful or so on top of each serving.

Yield: 6 to 8 servings.

LEAVENWORTH JACKSON '76

Fish broth

3   pounds fish bones, preferably
    including the head or heads,
    but with gill or gills removed
2   tablespoons butter
3   quarts water
2   bay leaves
4   sprigs fresh thyme or 1 tea-
    spoon dried
2   unpeeled cloves garlic
2   ribs celery with leaves
1½ cups peeled and quartered or
    chopped onions
    Salt
10 peppercorns

1. Place the bones in a kettle and let cold running water run over them until it runs clear. Drain.

2. Add the butter and stir the bones in the butter briefly. Add the remaining ingredients and simmer about 30 minutes. Strain through fine cloth and use as needed. Leftover fish broth may be frozen.

Yield: About 3 quarts.

Provençal Fish Soup

¼   cup olive oil
1   cup chopped leeks
¾   cup chopped onion
½   cup chopped celery
3   cloves garlic, finely chopped
1   tablespoon hot or mild paprika
1   tablespoon loosely packed
    saffron stems
2   pounds meaty fish bones from
    any white-fleshed, nonoily fish
    such as cod, striped bass and
    so on
4   cups fish broth (see recipe)
4   tablespoons tomato paste
1   bay leaf
2   sprigs fresh thyme or ½
    teaspoon dried
1   cup dry white wine
1½ pounds boneless, skinless fish
    such as cod, striped bass
1   cup cold aioli (see recipe)

1. Heat the oil in a casserole and add the leeks, onion, celery and garlic and cook until onion is wilted. Add the paprika, saffron, fish bones and stir about 5 minutes. Add the fish broth, tomato paste, bay leaf, thyme and wine. Bring to the boil and simmer 20 minutes.

2. Put the soup through a sieve, pushing through as much of the solids as possible. Return the soup to a saucepan and bring to the boil.

3. Meanwhile, cut the fish fillets into 1-inch cubes and add to the boiling soup. Bring just to the boil and cook as briefly as possible, just until the fish is cooked, about 1 minute. Serve in hot soup bowls with the aioli on the side to be added at will by each guest and stirred into the soup.

Yield: 8 servings.

Quick aioli

1 cup mayonnaise (see recipe)
1 tablespoon finely chopped garlic
Salt and freshly ground pepper

Place the ingredients in a mixing bowl and blend thoroughly.

Yield: About 1 cup.

Mayonnaise

2 egg yolks
2 teaspoons wine vinegar
1 tablespoon imported mustard, preferably Dijon or Düsseldorf Salt and freshly ground pepper
2 cups peanut, vegetable, corn or olive oil
1 tablespoon or more lemon juice

1. Place the yolks in a mixing bowl or the bowl of an electric mixer.

2. Add the vinegar, mustard, salt and pepper to taste.

3. Start beating while gradually adding the oil. Beat until quite thick and all the oil is added. Add lemon juice and more salt to taste.

Yield: About 2 cups.

Charcuterie Plus

Although New York City boasts with considerable reason that it is one of the world's greatest resources for gastronomic treasures, there has, nonetheless, been a conspicuous lack in one area. An enigma we have pondered for many years is the absence of a fine charcuterie. We have found this a painful lack.

What is charcuterie? It is one of the chief, delectable arts of the French kitchen, and the word derives, as Jane Grigson so happily points out in her excellent work, *The Art of Charcuterie* (Alfred A. Knopf, 1968), from chair cuit meaning cooked meat, principally, if not exclusively, of the pig. She adds that the trade of the charcutier goes back "at least as far as the time of classical Rome, where a variety of sausages could be bought, as well as the famous hams from Gaul." The world of charcuterie embraces, in addition to hams, such delicacies as terrines and pâtés, white sausages, blood sausages and, of course, andouilles and andouillettes.

It will be a year next month that what is perhaps the best and most enduring shop for charcuterie opened with small fanfare in Greenwich Village. More recently, a second shop opened on 62nd Street. They are called Les Trois Petits Cochons, or The Three Little Pigs, and are the enterprise of two young Frenchmen who gave New York this gift almost by accident. At least their ambitions lay in other directions.

The young chefs are Jean Pierre Pradie, 31, a native of Bordeaux, and Alain Sinturel, 28, of Paris.

"What we really had in mind," Mr. Pradie said recently, as he sliced into a most engaging bit of charcuterie of his own invention, a terrine Normande made with pork and apples and calvados, "was to open a restaurant. Trouble is, we didn't have the funds."

"We met in London," his partner added, as he chopped a bit of aspic to garnish a platter that included a duck pâté with Grand Marnier and another duck pâté scented with cognac and flavored with truffles. "I'd never worked as a professional chef before, although I had graduated from the hotel school in Lausanne, Switzerland. After that I'd joined the sales department of a hotel chain in Paris—they owned places like the Lotti and the Scribe. As things turned out Jean Pierre and I took a long tour of Africa, north and south, east and west, and we spoke often of going into the restaurant business together.

"When we met again in New York, we discussed it, but capital was scarce. So we decided it would take far fewer funds to open a small place that didn't require a large overhead and a large staff. Or that's what we thought at the time."

Neither Jean Pierre nor Alain had vast experience in the art of pâtés and terrines, but they did painstaking, voluminous research in all the pertinent manuals

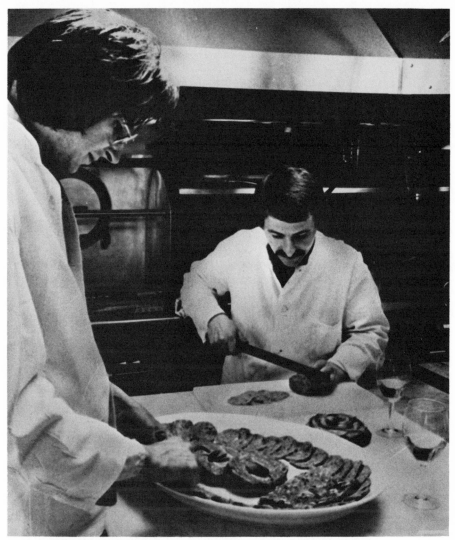

Alain Sinturel garnishes a duck pâté while Jean Pierre Pradie slices a terrine

they could get their hands on and accepted the advice of friends in the local world of chefdom. To this day, particularly with two establishments in operation, a sixteen-hour work day is not uncommon.

Although we have long admired the products turned out in their ovens (we celebrated last New Year's Eve at an extensive bash where their terrines, white sausages and grilled boudins were the talk of the party) we had never met them before they came to our house to demonstrate their talents by making such diverse items as an elegant cream of avocado soup; an engaging platter of hot mussels broiled on the half shell with a sort of snail butter; a fine, piping hot dish of crepes filled with seafood and baked in a lobster sauce; a cumin-flavored and compelling ragout of mutton, Moroccan-style, made from a recipe they'd sampled in their travels about Africa; a first-rate chocolate mousse. Plus, of course, an introduction to the meal consisting of their assorted and choice charcuterie.

We were much amused when, as the assembled company ate their various pâtés, Jean Pierre practiced abstinence. "For the past year I have been surrounded by nothing but ground meat, cognac and truffles. I haven't touched a pâté for the pleasure of dining in the past six months," he confided.

Les Trois Petits Cochons is located in Greenwich Village at 17 East 13th Street (telephone 255-4844) and uptown at 308 East 62nd Street (telephone 826-7048). The shop sells, in addition to charcuterie, an elaborate assortment of take-out foods ranging from striped bass Dugléré, and coulibiac of salmon with a sauce Smitane, to medallions of veal Orloff, to duck à l'orange.

Here are several dishes recently prepared by the young chefs in our East Hampton kitchen.

Creme d'avocats
(Cream of avocado soup)

2   *tablespoons corn oil*
2   *tablespoons finely chopped onion*
2   *ripe, unblemished avocados*
1   *teaspoon lemon juice*
5   *cups rich chicken broth*
3   *cups heavy cream*
1   *egg yolk*
    Salt and freshly ground pepper to taste
2   *tablespoons port wine*

1. Heat the oil in a saucepan and add the onion. Cook, stirring, until wilted.

2. Meanwhile, peel the avocados and remove the pits. Finely dice enough of the flesh to make ½ cup. Add the lemon juice to the diced avocado to prevent discoloration.

3. Blend the remaining avocado flesh in a blender or food processor. There should be about 2 cups.

4. Add the pureed avocado to the saucepan along with the chicken broth and stir with a wire whisk. Add the cream and blend well. Let simmer over low heat about 20 minutes.

5. Beat the egg yolk and add a little of the hot soup. Return this to the saucepan and cook briefly. Add salt and pepper to taste. Put the mixture through a fine sieve and reheat in a saucepan. Add the port wine and the reserved diced avocado. Serve hot.

Yield: 12 servings.

Moules Farcies

3   *pounds mussels*
¼   *teaspoon anise seeds*
    Freshly ground pepper to taste
½   *pound butter at room temperature*
¼   *cup chopped parsley*
2   *teaspoons finely chopped shallots*
1   *teaspoon finely chopped garlic*
    Salt to taste
1   *teaspoon Ricard, Pernod or another anise-flavored liqueur*
2   *tablespoons bread crumbs*

1. Scrub the mussels well and place them in a heavy kettle with a tight-fitting cover. Add the anise seeds and pepper. Do not add liquid.

Cover and let them steam 5 minutes or just until all the mussels are open. Shake the kettle as the mussels cook. Set aside briefly to cool.

2. Drain and reserve for another use or discard the cooking liquid.

3. Preheat the broiler to high.

4. Remove the mussels from the shell and reserve half the shells for stuffing. Pull away and discard the tough, rubbery band that surrounds each mussel. Replace 1 mussel in each shell and arrange on a baking dish.

5. Melt the butter and add all the remaining ingredients except the bread crumbs. Spoon equal amounts of the butter mixture over each mussel. Sprinkle the mussels with bread crumbs. Run under the broiler until the butter is bubbling and the mussels are piping hot.

Yield: 6 to 8 servings.

Crepes aux Fruits de Mer Nantua

(Seafood-filled crepes with lobster sauce)

18 *to 20 crepes aux herbes (see recipe)*
1 *1¼-pound lobster*
6 *tablespoons butter*
½ *cup finely chopped shallots*
¼ *cup plus 1 tablespoon cognac*
1 *clove garlic, finely minced*
2½ *tablespoons tomato paste*
¾ *cup dry white wine*
3 *cups fish stock or use fresh or bottled clam juice*
1 *tablespoon finely chopped fresh parsley*
1 *bay leaf*

½ *teaspoon dried thyme*
 Salt and freshly ground pepper to taste
¼ *cup flour*
1 *cup heavy cream*
1 *cup finely chopped fresh mushrooms*
¾ *pound small scallops, cut into small pieces*
¾ *pound squid, cut into small pieces, optional*
¾ *pound shrimp, shelled, deveined, cut into pieces*

1. Prepare the crepes, stack them and keep covered.

2. Split the lobster in half. Break off the claws and crack them. Remove and discard the tough sac near the eyes of the lobster. Remove the coral and liver from the carcass and set aside.

3. Heat half the butter in a heavy skillet and add the lobster tail, the claws and the carcass pieces. Sprinkle with shallots and cook over high heat, stirring, until lobster shell turns bright red. Add the ¼ cup cognac and flame it. Add the garlic and tomato paste, stirring. Add the wine, fish stock, parsley, bay leaf, thyme, salt and pepper to taste. Cook about 10 minutes, stirring occasionally.

4. Preheat the oven to 400 degrees.

5. Remove the lobster pieces and, when cool enough to handle, remove the meat from the tail and claws and set aside. Chop the lobster shell coarsely and add it to a food processor or put it through the coarse blade of a meat grinder. Blend or grind coarsely. Return this to the sauce and cook about 5 minutes longer.

6. Blend the coral and liver with 2 tablespoons of butter and the flour.

Stir this, bit by bit, into the sauce. Add the cream and bring to the boil. Sprinkle with salt and pepper and put the mixture through a fine sieve.

7. Cut the lobster meat into small pieces.

8. Heat the remaining tablespoon butter and add the mushrooms. Cook briefly and add the scallops and squid. Cook about 30 seconds, stirring, and add the shrimp. Cook until shrimp turn pink. Cover and cook 5 minutes. Uncover and reduce briefly. Add the remaining tablespoon of cognac. Stir in about ⅓ cup of the lobster sauce and heat. Add the lobster and stir.

9. Fill the crepes, one at a time, with equal portions of the mixture and fold the crepes over to enclose the filling. Arrange the crepes symmetrically in an oven-proof baking dish large enough to hold them. Spoon the remaining sauce over. Cover with foil and bake 10 or 15 minutes or until piping hot. Serve on hot plates.

Yield: 8 or more servings.

Crepes aux herbes

1   cup flour
1   large egg
1¼ to 1½ cups milk
    Salt to taste
3   tablespoons melted butter
1½ teaspoons chopped parsley
1½ teaspoons chopped chives

1. Place the flour in a mixing bowl and make a well in the center. Add the egg. Start stirring with a wire whisk while gradually adding the milk. When ready the batter should have the consistency of heavy cream. Continue stirring and beating until well blended and the proper consistency.

2. Strain the batter through a sieve into another bowl. Add the remaining ingredients. Ladle as much of the mixture as necessary to cover the bottom of a 7-inch crepe pan, swirling it around. Cook briefly until lightly browned and turn. Cook briefly and turn out. Continue making crepes until all the batter is used.

Yield: 18 to 20 7-inch crepes.

Ragout de Mouton Marocaine

(Mutton stew in the style of Morocco)

5   to 6 pounds mutton (see note), preferably lean meat plus some bony parts such as breast or neck, all of it cut or chopped into 1½-inch cubes
     Salt and freshly ground pepper to taste
⅔   cup olive oil
2   carrots, scraped and trimmed
3   green peppers, cored and seeded
4   cups onions cut into 1½-inch cubes
2½   tablespoons ras el hanout powder, available in markets that sell oriental spices (see note), or use an equal amount of cumin powder
4   zucchini, about 1¾ pounds, trimmed
2   red, ripe tomatoes, about 1¼ pounds, cut into 1-inch cubes
½   bay leaf
½   teaspoon dried thyme
2   teaspoons finely chopped garlic
½   dried, hot, red pepper

1. Sprinkle the meat with salt and pepper.

2. Heat half the oil in a skillet and add the meat, browning well on all sides. Drain off the fat. Quarter the carrots lengthwise and cut the strips into 1½-inch lengths. Add this to the meat. Cut the green peppers into 1½-inch pieces and add to the meat.

3. Heat the remaining oil in a casserole and add the onions. Cook to brown. Add the meat and vegetables and sprinkle with the ras el hanout or cumin powder. Cut the zucchini into 2-inch pieces and add it. Add the remaining ingredients.

4. Cover closely and cook 2 hours, stirring occasionally. If the stew becomes too dry, add a little water, about 1 cup at a time. It should not be necessary to add more than 2 cups maximum.

Yield: 8 servings.

Note: Mutton may be obtained on special order from numerous butchers in Manhattan. One source is the Maryland Market, 1072 First Avenue (between 58th and 59th Streets).

Ras el hanout is a blend of many spices, but the pronounced flavor is that of cumin.

Mousse au Chocolat

⅓ pound dark or bittersweet chocolate, preferably imported

3 tablespoons butter
3 tablespoons dark rum
6 large eggs
12 tablespoons sugar
¼ teaspoon vanilla
1 cup heavy cream

1. Break or cut the chocolate into pieces and add them to a heavy saucepan. Add the butter and rum and place over low heat, stirring often until chocolate melts and the mixture is blended.

2. Meanwhile, separate the eggs and add 3 yolks to a mixing bowl. Place the whites in another bowl in the refrigerator. Set the remaining yolks aside for another use.

3. Add 6 tablespoons of sugar to the yolks and place the bowl over lightly simmering water. Beat vigorously with a wire whisk until the yolks are thickened and pale yellow in color. Add the vanilla. Stir this mixture into the chocolate, blending well.

4. Beat the egg whites with 3 tablespoons of sugar. Beat until the whites stand in stiff peaks. Fold the chocolate mixture into the whites, using a rubber spatula.

5. Beat the cream until stiff with the remaining sugar. Fold this into the mousse. Spoon and scrape the mousse into a crystal bowl and refrigerate.

Yield: 8 to 10 servings.

Master Plan for Chinese Meals

It is as basic as chopsticks to say that the greatest obstacle in the preparation of a Chinese dinner is the ability to organize dishes to be served of an evening in a manner that permits the home cook to join guests at table while maintaining a cool presence and an outward appearance, at least, of calm.

In fact, one of the questions most often asked of those with more than a casual involvement in Chinese cookery is how to plan a menu without panic and how to execute the cooking without repeated and frantic dashes to and from a hot wok.

It is a subject we have explored many times over the years with our friend and colleague, the elegant and learned Virginia Lee.

The basic menu planning techniques we have agreed on are these: Make the menu in a family-style pattern. This consists generally of four to six dishes, when there are to be four to six people at table. Add an additional dish for each two additional persons.

Prepare several dishes in advance. For example, a few cold appetizers, a hot soup and one or two casseroles or long-simmered dishes. Keep the stir-fried dishes or dishes that must be made at the last moment to one or two, and have all the ingredients for these dishes sliced, chopped, ground and assembled, ready to toss into the wok on a second's notice.

Several dishes for a menu organized along these lines are indicated here. There are two excellent cold dishes, a spicy jellied chicken appetizer and another made with shrimp and cucumber. There is a delectable corn and crab meat soup that can be made in advance, although you may want to add the crab at a late moment. There is a celestial pine nut meatball recipe of a casserole sort, which can be made hours in advance and is sumptuous enough to stand almost on its own with only one or two more dishes. Then there are two stir-fried dishes— one, a sesame seed fish, the other, a Szechuan-style chicken with asparagus and abalone mushroom dish. These foods, of course, should be served with rice.

Pine Nut Meatballs with Dark Sauce

30   to 40 large mushrooms, about
     2½ pounds

8   large leeks (or use 1 bunch of
    scallions)
1¼ cups pine nuts
2   pounds fat and lean pork,
    preferably uncured, unsalted
    bacon
3   whole eggs

Virginia Lee serves only one or two stir-fried dishes at a Chinese dinner

2 tablespoons cornstarch
3 tablespoons black soy sauce
2 tablespoons shao hsing or dry sherry
Salt to taste
2 teaspoons plus 1½ tablespoons sugar
2 tablespoons finely minced ginger
6 to 8 tablespoons cold water
4 cups peanut, vegetable or corn oil
4 scallions
4 ¼-inch thick slices peeled, fresh ginger
3½ cups fresh or canned chicken broth

1. Trim off the mushrooms level with the bottoms of the caps. Drop into a basin of cold water and set aside. Discard the stems.

2. Trim off the ends of the leeks about 1 inch from the bottom. Discard the ends or use for soups. Split the leeks halfway to the middle and rinse well under cold water to remove sand. Drop into cold water and set aside.

3. Chop the pine nuts until fine. Set aside.

4. Place the meat in a bowl and add 2 eggs, the cornstarch, soy sauce, wine, salt, 2 teaspoons sugar, minced ginger, 6 tablespoons of cold water and the nuts. Work briskly with the fingers in a circular motion. The more you work the meat the better. Work the mixture for a minimum of 10 minutes. Shape the meat into 6 large balls of equal size.

5. Beat the remaining egg and dip the fingers into it. The fingers and palms should be coated with the egg. Pick up 1 meatball at a time and toss it back and forth from one hand to another until it is smooth and coated and somewhat flat like a thick hamburger rather than round.

6. Heat the 4 cups of oil in a wok or skillet and add half the meatballs. Ladle the hot oil over the exposed portions of the balls. Cook 2 to 3 minutes and turn. Cook about 2 minutes longer and drain. They should be golden brown. Drain on a plate. Cook the remaining meatballs in the same way. Remove. Leave the oil in the wok. Transfer the meatballs to a casserole so that they fit snugly in one layer. Tie each of the 4 scallions into loops and add them. Add the sliced ginger.

7. Add the chicken broth and remaining sugar and bring to the boil. Cover and simmer 2 hours.

8. Meanwhile, heat the oil in the wok and add half the mushrooms cap-side down. Cook, stirring, about 5 minutes, turning once. Drain. Add remaining mushrooms to the wok and cook in the same way. Add the leeks and cook, turning occasionally so that they cook evenly. Cook about 6 minutes, until wilted but not brown. Drain and add to mushrooms.

9. Carefully garnish the tops of the meatball casserole with the leeks and mushrooms. Do not add the liquid that drained from them. Cover and continue cooking until the leeks

are tender, about ½ hour or longer. Serve half a meatball per guest.

Yield: 12 banquet servings.

Spicy Jellied Chicken

½ pound pork rind
1 4-pound chicken
1 meaty, bony chicken back
4 chicken necks or wings
3 pieces star anise (see note)
1 2-inch piece cinnamon
½ cup black soy sauce
¼ cup shao hsing or dry sherry
4 cups water
2½ tablespoons sugar
    Salt to taste
3 whole scallions
2 ½-inch pieces unpeeled
    ginger, crushed
    Fresh coriander sprigs for
    garnish (see note)

1. Place the pork rind in a saucepan or small kettle, add cold water to cover and simmer 10 minutes. Drain and run under cold running water. Drain and slice away the fat from the rind. Discard the fat and reserve the rind.

2. Drop the chicken into boiling water and turn it occasionally about 3 minutes. Drain. Rinse well under cold water inside and out. Drain.

3. Place the chicken in a kettle and add the pork rind and all remaining ingredients except coriander sprigs. Cover and cook over low heat about 1½ hours. Turn the chicken and uncover. Continue cooking, basting often, about ½ hour longer.

4. Remove the chicken and drain the inside into the kettle. Continue cooking the liquid with the bony parts

about 45 minutes. Strain and skim off all fat. Discard the solids. If more than 2 cups of liquid remain, return it to the kettle and continue cooking until reduced to 2 cups.

5. When the chicken is cool enough to handle, pull away and discard the bones, large and small. Do not skin the chicken, but cut or pull away all excess or peripheral fat and discard it.

6. Arrange the chicken pieces compactly in a bowl such as a souffle dish measuring about 7½ inches wide and 3 inches deep. Pour the sauce over the chicken and let cool. Chill until firm.

7. Unmold the dish onto a flat surface. Cut the mold into thirds. Cut each portion into slices about ½ inch thick. Arrange neatly on a serving dish and garnish with sprigs of fresh coriander.

Yield: 12 banquet servings.

Note: Star anise and fresh coriander are available at United Supermarket, 84 Mulberry Street, and other grocery stores in Chinatown.

Shrimp, Cucumber and Tree Ears with Sweet and Sour Sauce

¾ pound raw, unpeeled shrimp, about 20
  Salt to taste
⅓ cup tree ears (see note)
2 firm, unblemished cucumbers, about ½ pound each
12 small or 3 large hot, dried, red peppers

2 tablespoons Szechuan peppercorns (see note)
¼ cup sesame oil
1 tablespoon corn oil
½ cup red wine vinegar
¾ cup sugar

1. Place the shrimp in a bowl and add water to cover and salt to taste. Let stand about ½ hour. Drain. Drop the shrimp into boiling water to cover. When the water returns to the boil, drain and run under cold water to chill. Peel the shrimp and slice in half. Rinse once more to remove the intestinal vein. Pat dry and refrigerate.

2. Pour boiling water over the tree ears and let stand about ½ hour. Drain. Drop the tree ears into boiling water to cover. When the water returns to the boil, drain and chill under cold running water. Drain and pat dry.

3. Trim off and discard the ends of the cucumbers. Do not peel the cucumbers. Split them in half lengthwise and scoop out the seeds with a melon ball cutter or spoon. Split each half in two widthwise. Slice the cucumbers quite thinly and set aside. There should be about 3 cups.

4. Combine in a saucepan the dried peppers, peppercorns, sesame oil and corn oil. Heat thoroughly and cook, stirring, about 4 minutes. Cook until the red peppers start to turn black-red. The mixture may smoke slightly. Remove from the heat and drain off the hot seasoned oil. Discard the spices.

5. Wipe out the saucepan and add the seasoned oil. Blend the vinegar and sugar and add it. Add salt to taste. Bring to the boil and let bubble up, stirring, about 3 minutes. Pour the mixture into a cup or saucepan and let cool.

6. Arrange the cucumbers on the bottom of a round serving dish. Add a layer of tree ears, then the shrimp. Cover with plastic wrap and chill until ready to serve.

7. Uncover the salad and pour the sauce over. Serve cold.

Yield: 12 banquet servings.

Note: Tree ears and Szechuan peppercorns are available at United Supermarket, 84 Mulberry Street, and other grocery stores in Chinatown.

Szechuan-Style Stir-Fried Chicken with Asparagus and Abalone Mushrooms

1	*pound skinless, boneless, halved chicken breasts (2 whole breasts split in half)*
1	*tablespoon cornstarch*
1	*tablespoon sesame oil*
	Salt to taste
1	*egg white*
½	*teaspoon sugar*
1	*pound asparagus, trimmed and scraped*
1	*10-ounce can Chinese abalone mushrooms or 1 15-ounce can straw mushrooms (see note)*
5	*or 6 small, fresh, hot, red or green peppers, optional*
¼	*cup hoisin sauce (see note)*
2	*tablespoons chili paste with garlic (see note)*
1	*tablespoon shao hsing or dry sherry*
1	*to 1½ tablespoons coarsely chopped garlic*
1½	*cups peanut, vegetable or corn oil*

1. Place the breast halves, skinned side down, on a flat surface. Tap in a diamond pattern this way and that with the edge of a cleaver or knife. Do not cut or chop into the meat. Cut the meat into ¾-inch strips. Cut the strips into ¾-inch cubes.

2. Place the chicken meat in a bowl and add the cornstarch, sesame oil, salt, egg white, sugar and blend well with the fingers. Chill.

3. Cut the asparagus on the bias into 1-inch lengths. Discard the tough ends. There should be about 2 cups of sliced asparagus. Set aside. Drain the mushrooms and set aside. Trim off the stem ends of the hot peppers and set aside.

4. Blend in a small bowl the hoisin sauce, chili paste with garlic, wine and the chopped garlic.

5. Heat the oil briefly in a wok or skillet and add the chicken, stirring it constantly to separate the pieces. Cook the chicken about 3 minutes or just until it changes color. Remember it will cook a second time. Do not overcook. Scoop the chicken out and drain it but leave the oil in the wok.

6. Add the asparagus and abalone mushrooms to the wok and cook briefly, about 1 minute. Drain well, pouring out the oil in the wok. The oil may be reserved for another use.

7. Return about 2 tablespoons of the oil to the wok. Add the mushrooms and hot peppers and cook briefly, stirring. Add the chili paste mixture and cook, stirring, about 30 seconds. Add the chicken and asparagus and cook, stirring, about 1 minute. Scoop onto a serving dish and serve immediately.

Yield: 12 banquet servings.

Note: The Chinese ingredients for

this recipe are available at United Supermarket, 84 Mulberry Street, and other grocery stores in Chinatown.

Sesame Seed Fish

¾   pound fish fillets, preferably
     flounder or fluke
1½ tablespoons shao hsing or dry
     sherry
     Salt to taste
1¾ teaspoons sugar
¾   teaspoon ground white pepper
2   egg whites
4   tablespoons cornstarch
½   cup (1 2¾-ounce bottle)
     sesame seeds
½   cup fine fresh bread crumbs
6   or more sprigs fresh coriander
     for garnish, optional (see note)
½   cup finely shredded ginger
1   tablespoon red wine vinegar
6   cups peanut, vegetable or corn
     oil

1. Place the fish on a flat surface and cut it into 2-inch pieces. Place fish in a bowl and add the wine, salt, ¾ teaspoon sugar and pepper. Stir to coat the fish well and set aside.

2. Blend the egg whites with the cornstarch and salt to taste.

3. Blend the sesame seeds and bread crumbs.

4. Dip one piece of fish at a time in the egg white mixture to coat all over. Dip into the sesame seed mixture to coat and arrange on a plate. Continue this until all the pieces are coated. If necessary, use more sesame seeds and crumbs.

5. Drop the coriander leaves into cold water and let stand. Drain and pat dry.

6. Combine the ginger, vinegar, remaining 1 teaspoon sugar and salt and stir to blend. Let stand until ready to use and then drain the ginger. Discard the marinade.

7. When ready to cook, heat the oil in a wok or skillet and add the fish pieces. Turn off the heat. This will prevent the sesame seeds from exploding. Turn on the heat and continue cooking the fish until nicely browned and crisp, turning as necessary in the oil. Drain.

8. Arrange the fish on a platter. Garnish one end of the platter with coriander leaves and the other with the drained ginger.

Yield: 12 banquet servings.

Note: Fresh coriander is available at United Supermarket, 84 Mulberry Street, and other grocery stores in Chinatown.

Chinese Vegetable Casserole

14 dried mushrooms (see note)
1   2½-to-3-pound Chinese
     cabbage
1   cup peanut, vegetable or corn
     oil
     Salt to taste
1   teaspoon sugar
3   fat pads fresh bean curd (see
     note)
1   large piece chicken fat or
     melted chicken fat or corn oil

1. Place the mushrooms in a bowl and add boiling water to cover. Let stand ½ hour or longer. Drain and cut off and discard the tough stems. Set the whole mushrooms aside.

2. Pull off and discard a few of the large outer leaves of the cabbage. Pull off the remaining leaves and stack them 2 at a time on a flat surface. Neatly trim the leaves into rectangles, trimming away the tops, bottoms and sides of the leaves. Cut the leaves into long strips about 1 inch wide.

3. Heat half of the oil in a large wok or skillet and add the cabbage strips. Cook over high heat, stirring and turning the cabbage, about 5 minutes. Add the salt and sugar and cook briefly, stirring, about 1 minute longer. The cabbage should remain crisp tender. Transfer the pieces of cabbage to a casserole, arranging them neatly. Add the cabbage juices.

4. Wipe out the wok and add the remaining oil.

5. Cut each bean curd pad into 4 slices.

6. Heat the oil until quite hot and add the bean curd slices. Cook about 5 minutes over high heat until golden brown on one side (it will look like pale French toast or a slightly over-cooked omelet). Turn the slices and drain.

7. Arrange the bean curd slices, edges slightly overlapping, around the rim of the cabbage. Arrange the mushrooms in a layer and piled in the center of the bean curd. If a piece of chicken fat is available, place it over the mushrooms to prevent them from drying out. Or brush with melted chicken fat or oil. Cover closely and let simmer about 50 minutes.

Yield: 12 banquet servings.

Note: Dried mushrooms and bean curd are available at United Supermarket, 84 Mulberry Street, and other grocery stores in Chinatown.

Corn and Crab Meat Soup

½ *small, boned, skinned chicken breast*
5 *cups fresh or canned chicken broth*
2 *cups canned cream-style corn*
2 *tablespoons cornstarch*
¼ *cup cold water*
    Salt to taste
1½ *cups fresh lump or backfin crab meat*

1. Cut the chicken breast into cubes and add it to the container of a food processor or electric blender. Add 1 cup of chicken broth and blend until smooth and soupy. Set aside.

2. Bring the remaining chicken broth to the boil and add the corn, stirring. When blended, add some of the hot liquid to the chicken mixture. Add the chicken mixture to the soup and stir.

3. Add the cornstarch mixed with the water, stirring constantly until thickened. Add salt to taste and the crab meat. Stir until blended. Serve piping hot.

Yield: 12 banquet servings.

Gratifyingly Greek

WITH PIERRE FRANEY

All things considered—ease of preparation, versatility and taste—we can scarcely think of a more gratifying dish than the shrimp and tomato dish of Greek origin outlined here. It is a toothsome, simply made concoction with feta cheese and, optionally, ouzo, that spirited Hellenic drink that smacks of anise. Although the dish, garides mi feta, makes a consummately good first course, it would serve quite nicely as a main luncheon dish with a crisp salad and a crusty loaf.

Garides mi Feta

(Shrimp baked with feta cheese, Greek-style)

3   cups imported canned Italian plum tomatoes
1   pound shrimp, about 24
¼   cup olive oil
1   teaspoon finely chopped garlic
¼   cup fresh fish broth or bottled clam juice
1   teaspoon crushed dried oregano
1   teaspoon dried red pepper flakes
2   tablespoons drained capers
    Salt and freshly ground pepper
3   tablespoons butter
¼   pound feta cheese
¼   cup ouzo, a Greek anise-flavored liqueur widely available in wine and spirits shops, optional

1. Preheat oven to 350 degrees.

2. Put the tomatoes in a saucepan and cook until reduced to about 2 cups. Stir often to prevent burning and sticking.

3. Shell and devein the shrimp and set aside.

4. Heat the olive oil in another saucepan or deep skillet and add the garlic, stirring. Add the tomatoes, using a rubber spatula to scrape them out.

5. Add the fish broth, oregano, pepper flakes, capers and salt and pepper to taste.

6. Heat the butter in a heavy saucepan or skillet and add the shrimp. Cook briefly, less than 1 minute, stirring and turning the shrimp until they turn pink.

7. Spoon equal portions of half the sauce in 4 individual baking dishes and arrange 6 shrimp plus equal amounts of the butter in which they cooked in each dish. Spoon remaining sauce over the shrimp.

8. Crumble the cheese and scatter it over all. Place the dishes in the oven and bake 10 to 15 minutes or until bubbling hot.

9. Remove the dishes from the oven and sprinkle each dish with 1 tablespoon ouzo and, if desired, ignite it. Serve immediately.

Yield: 4 servings.

June 1976

THERE IS A certain amount of serendipity in any profession and there is an agreeable amount to be found in mine. One of the most memorable outings of my life came about in the month of June when I traveled with an assortment of chefs and restaurant owners, their wives and children to a 700-acre wild boar farm in Nova Scotia. I had met by some happy circumstances an engaging and hospitable Italian nobleman, now a Canadian citizen who lives in New York but who maintains a splendid home on Roberts Island in Nova Scotia. Carlo Amato, the gentleman, raises wild boar there for breeding purposes and to furnish numerous fine restaurants with boar meat both in Canada and in the United States. The principals at the outing included Carlo Amato; Pierre Franey; Jean Vergnes and Sirio Maccioni, owners of the immensely popular Le Cirque restaurant in New York; and Luigi Nanni, the chef-patron of both Nanni's restaurant and Il Viletto in Manhattan. Also in the party was Egi Maccioni. The serendipity came about because I frankly don't know the butt of a gun from the muzzle, and quite honestly I could not kill a squirrel or any other animal. I had been told by Sirio that his wife, Egi, was one of the great pizza makers of all times. As a consequence, while the rest of the crew went out for the chase, I stayed home with Egi and watched the yeast dough rise. A few hours later, we sat around the dining table and feasted on those crisp-bottomed pies, some topped with tomatoes and mozzarella and others with mushrooms, both cultivated (fresh) and wild (dried). It was, to use a recent idiom, super. Later in the year, I interviewed Egi in her home about pizza making and that column appears in this book.

On a more intellectual plane, I was able to indulge myself in a wholly different passion in June. For years, I have had a deep and abiding interest in Thomas Jefferson, not only as a human being and statesman, but as a man with an incredibly sensitive palate and appreciation of fine food. To pursue this interest, I spent a good deal of time at Monticello (which he chose to pronounce, by the way, Montichello, Italian-style). I discovered a great deal of information about his astonishing interest in both food and wines, and subsequently reproduced numerous dishes from the French repertory that he is known to have enjoyed.

Quenelles Made Easy

There is one anecdote that invariably comes to mind whenever we dine on quenelles of pike, shrimp or whatever. Quenelles are, of course, one of the greatest inventions of French chefdom—gossamer, lighter-than-air ovals of fish or seafood, delicately seasoned, poached briefly and served with any of a number of seafood sauces.

The story dates back several years to the days when Le Pavillon was the ultimate French restaurant in America and Henri Soulé was in charge. His maître d'hôtel and second in command was Martin Decré.

One summer Claude Terrail, owner of the well-known Tour d'Argent, came to New York and was lavishly entertained in numerous private homes up and down Park and Fifth Avenues. The night of his arrival he dined sumptuously and well at a meal that began with quenelles de brochet, or pike quenelles. He was impressed. The next evening in another private home, the waiter arrived with a steaming platter of quenelles de brochet. The dish was duplicated the third evening as well. On the fourth night he was invited to dine at Le Pavillon, and as the menus were distributed around the table, Martin Decré leaned over and whispered in Mr. Terrail's ear, "Monsieur Terrail, I particularly recommend our quenelles de brochet." Terrail frowned. "Martin," he said, "what is this? Are quenelles starting to replace the hamburger as America's favorite food?" It had all come about, of course, because all the hostesses of the previous evenings had had their meals produced in Le Pavillon's kitchen.

In years past, quenelles of any sort have been enormously tedious to prepare. With a food processor they are quite simple, as shown here. An electric blender may also be used, but the process will require more time and patience.

Quenelles de Crevettes

(Shrimp quenelles)

1. Shell and devein ¾ pound raw shrimp. Reserve the shells to be used in making a shrimp sauce for the quenelles (see recipe). Cut half a pound of filleted fresh fish such as flounder, fluke, striped bass and so on into cubes. Add the shrimp and fish to the container of a food processor or

Step 1. Add shrimp to food processor.

electric blender. If a blender is used, this will have to be done in at least 2 steps.

2. Blend the mixture briefly and add salt and pepper to taste, a pinch each of cayenne pepper and ground nutmeg. Add 1 egg yolk and blend.

3. While blending, add gradually 1½ cups of heavy cream.

4. Butter a heatproof dish, one that is large enough to hold the quenelles when they are shaped. There

Step 4. Shape the quenelles with 2 large spoons.

will be 18 or 20 oval-shaped quenelles of equal size. To shape the quenelles, use 2 large soup spoons. Have ready a bowl filled with hot water. Pick up a heaping spoonful of the shrimp mixture with 1 spoon.

5. Dip the second spoon into the hot water and run it around under the

Step 5. Turn the second spoon inside the first spoon.

shrimp mixture, starting on top of the mixture and turning the second spoon inside the first spoon as shown. This should produce a smooth, neat, oval quenelle.

6. As the quenelles are shaped, transfer them to the buttered dish. Arrange them close together and in a neat pattern.

Step 6. Arrange the quenelles in a buttered dish.

7. Cut a sheet of wax paper into a pattern that will fit neatly over the quenelles. Butter it and place it buttered-side down over the quenelles.

Step 7. Place wax paper over quenelles.

8. Meanwhile, bring a large quantity of water to the boil and add salt to taste. Gently ladle water over the wax paper so that it will flow gradually into the dish. Continue adding water until the quenelles are barely covered.

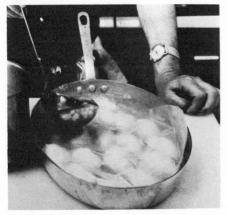

Step 8. Ladle water over wax paper.

9. Bring to the boil on top of the stove and simmer as gently as possible for from 5 to 10 minutes or until the quenelles are piping hot. Do not overcook.

10. Remove the quenelles carefully and quickly, using a slotted spoon, and drain them briefly on absorbent toweling. Serve immediately with piping hot shrimp sauce spooned over.

Step 10. Serve with hot shrimp sauce.

Sauce aux crevettes
(Shrimp sauce)

¼   *pound raw shrimp, plus shells from the shrimp used in making quenelles*
2½   *tablespoons butter*
1   *tablespoon finely chopped shallots*
1   *tablespoon finely minced onion*
2½   *tablespoons flour*
1   *cup dry white wine*
1   *cup fish broth or bottled clam juice*
1½   *tablespoons tomato paste*
½   *cup crushed, skinned, fresh or canned ripe tomatoes*
½   *tablespoon finely chopped fresh tarragon or ½ teaspoon dried*
    Pinch of cayenne pepper
    Salt and freshly ground pepper to taste
1   *cup heavy cream*
1   *tablespoon cognac*

1. Shell and devein the shrimp. Cut them into small pieces and set aside. Combine the shells with the shells reserved from making the quenelles. Set aside.

2. Heat 1 tablespoon of butter in a saucepan and add the shallots and onion. Add the reserved shrimp shells.

3. Sprinkle with flour and stir to blend. Add the wine and broth, stirring rapidly with a whisk. Continue stirring until blended. Bring to the boil and add the tomato paste, tomatoes, tarragon, cayenne, salt and pepper. Simmer 30 minutes.

4. Pour and spoon the mixture, including the shells, into the container of a food processor (see note). This will probably have to be done in 2 steps. Blend until the shrimp shells are coarsely blended. Strain the sauce, pressing with the back of a wooden spoon to extract as much juice as possible from the solids.

5. Return the mixture to a saucepan and add the cream. Cook, stirring, 10 to 15 minutes.

6. Heat ½ tablespoon of butter in a skillet and add the shrimp pieces.

Cook just until the shrimp change color, about 1 minute. Add the cognac and ignite it. Add the shrimp to the sauce. Add the remaining one tablespoon of butter and swirl it in. Serve hot.

Yield: About 2 cups of sauce.

Note: Take care not to overwork the motor of the food processor. The shells should not be finely pulverized.

It Started with an Onion Sandwich

There are many foods in this world indelibly inscribed in our memory, and the gamut goes, almost without saying, from the ridiculous to the sublime.

One of the dishes we remember best is a fantasy we sampled with cocktails many years ago in the home of James Beard, and it took the form of a sandwich, a captivating bit of whimsy made with thin rounds of white bread stuffed with thin onion slices, the sides smeared with mayonnaise and rolled in finely chopped parsley. We found them irresistible trifles, and Jim explained that they were the invention of a former business partner and friend, Irma Rhode.

Somehow we never had the fortune to meet Miss Rhode in all those years until we recently received a copy of her newly published book, *Cool Entertaining* (Atheneum, $8.95), and in it she expounds on the genesis of that devilishly good recipe.

Although the recipe has appeared as "Irma's Onion Sandwiches," she writes, "I cannot claim credit. The true story of the evolution . . . is as follows: In the twenties, in a Parisian establishment described by Polly Alder as 'a house that's not a home,' two slices of leftover breakfast brioche, spread with mayonnaise and filled with a slice of onion, were served with the aperitifs to my brother Bill."

In the 1930s Miss Rhode, James Beard and her brother opened a catering establishment called Hors d'Oeuvres Inc. Bill "remembered the combination, and we started testing. How thick the brioche slices, how thin the onion? What size cooky cutter? Two bites or a bite and a half?

"When the three of us had finally decided on these questions, there arose another one. How to dress them up? There always was a big bowl of chopped parsley around and, of course, mayonnaise. I can still see Jim rolling the edges in mayonnaise and then in chopped parsley, and the new onion rings were born. But it all goes back to the thrifty madam of that establishment in Paris."

We telephoned Miss Rhode to ask if we might visit her to discuss her involvement in the world of food. When we arrived at her apartment in Manhattan, she was in the midst of preparing the ingredients for a fascinating and unusual sweet, a devastatingly rich pumpernickel, chocolate, rum and cream dessert. It was, she explained, a creation remembered from her European childhood in a time when thrifty housewives dried their leftover black bread and put it to numerous uses.

"I was born in 1900 in Berlin," she recalled, "and in the tradition of those days, before I entered the university I had to learn how to run a household. Young women lived under the thumb of their families, and I was obliged to attend the household school of the Grand Duchess of Baden.

Irma Rhode satisfied her friends by collecting her recipes in a book

"Before I came to America in 1928, I had taken a chemistry degree from the University of Kiel, and my specialty was mineralogy and geology. In this country I became involved in the field of clay and ceramics.

"I did a lot of close work with microscopes, and as a result my eyes were weakened. I was advised by a doctor to stay away from microscopes."

It was then that she, James Beard and her late brother opened their hors d'oeuvre shop at 66th Street off Lexington Avenue, across from the Cosmopolitan Club.

"Our business prospered from the beginning, but then the war came along and there was nothing to do. How can you use twenty pounds of butter a day, which we needed, when there were restrictions everywhere?

"We gave up the enterprise, and I joined a marine hardware shop on Staten Island and stayed there working mostly on marine lamp assemblies.

"After the war, Bill had a contract to write an encyclopedia of food, and I helped him with that, but he died before it was completed. It was hard to find a job in those days, and I went to Philadelphia and worked as cafeteria manager for a large department store, then back to New York," where she has been ever since.

Her present book, a fine compendium of recipes to make entertaining look effortless, actually came about because of the demands of her friends for her recipes.

"It seems I was forever getting one recipe or another mimeographed to distribute to people who seemed invariably to ask for recipes when they came to my home for dinner, and this book solves the problem."

Miss Rhode has many interesting thoughts on food, among them that fillet of beef is far simpler to cook than steak. It is also easier to serve and not one bit more expensive in that it is frequently on sale in supermarkets. Her book has a compelling recipe for a sweet potato salad found in a small giveaway cookbook published more than a hundred years ago by a Manhattan baking powder company.

Here is a sampling of recipes from *Cool Entertaining*.

Onion Rings

6   slices firm white bread, on the
    sweet side, or 12 slices challah
    (Jewish bread used for
    Sabbath)
½   cup mayonnaise,
    approximately
    Salt to taste
12   very thin slices onion
¾   cup very finely chopped
    parsley, approximately

1. With a 1½-inch cooky cutter, cut 4 rounds from each slice of bread or 2 rounds from the challah slices. Arrange them in 12 pairs. Spread each round with mayonnaise.

2. Using either a slicer or a potato peeler, cut the slices of onions and put 1 on a bread round. Salt lightly, then top with the second round, sandwich fashion. When all 12 are assembled, spread some mayonnaise on a piece of wax paper and have the chopped parsley ready in a bowl.

3. Take a sandwich between thumb and forefinger and roll the edges first in the thinly spread mayonnaise, then in the chopped parsley. Make sure there are no bare spots; if so, dab a bit of mayonnaise on the spot and dip again in parsley. Place on wax paper on a flat tray or cooky sheet and cover with wax paper. Chill well.

Yield: 12 pieces.

Note: If it is too hard to get very thin slices of onions perfectly round, part slices will do, too; use 2 or more parts. The thinness is important.

Roast Fillet of Beef

1   6-to-7-pound untrimmed beef
    fillet (tenderloin)
4   strips bacon
    Cumberland sauce (see recipe)

1. Preheat the oven to 375 to 400 degrees.

2. If you are courageous, buy the beef tenderloin "as is" with all the fat on. Just start peeling off the layers of fat, trim off the fat on the sides and remove the tendons that run along the sides of the fillet. (Save that strip of meat; it is good ground and also as a goulash.) Dig in at the "head," the thickest part, and don't be discouraged by the mountain of fat that is removed. A 6-to-7-pound fillet "as is" trims down to about 3½ to 4 pounds, but that is enough for 8 to 10 people.

3. The classical way to prepare the fillet for roasting is to lard it with "smoked bacon"; a simpler way is to

put the 4 strips of bacon over the length of the fillet. Roast for 40 minutes for rare. Remove bacon strips after 30 minutes roasting time. Take pan with meat from the oven and let cool, then chill. Slice rather thin when cold. Serve with Cumberland sauce.

Yield: 8 to 10 servings.

Cumberland sauce

1   *orange peel*
2   *tablespoons dry mustard*
4   *tablespoons red wine*
1   *10-ounce jar currant jelly*

1. With a potato peeler remove skin from orange. Do not press hard; just the yellow part is needed, not the white skin underneath. With a pair of scissors snip this peel very fine.

2. Mix the mustard and red wine to a paste. With a fork beat the currant jelly, add the orange peel snippings and mustard paste and blend. Chill before serving.

Yield: 8 to 10 servings.

Sweet Potato Salad

1½   *pounds sweet potatoes (about*
     3 large)
     Juice of 4 limes
2   *large apples*
1   *cup thinly sliced and then*
     chopped celery
6   *ounces coarsely chopped*
     cashews or pecans
1   *cup mayonnaise,*
     approximately

1. Cook the sweet potatoes until soft; drain and cool enough to peel. Quarter lengthwise, then cut into cubes. Place in a mixing bowl and sprinkle with lime juice. Chill.

2. Peel, core and dice the apples. Add to potatoes together with celery and nuts. Add enough mayonnaise to coat well. Chill before serving.

Yield: 1 quart.

Pumpernickel Dessert

8   *ounces pumpernickel bread*
     (usually 1 package)
1   *to 1¼ cups rum*
8   *ounces semisweet chocolate*
1½   *pints heavy cream*
1   *cup sugar*
1   *teaspoon vanilla extract*
1   *cup seedless raspberry jam*

1. Preheat oven 250 to 300 degrees.

2. Crumble the pumpernickel on a baking sheet and dry in a slow oven. Put in a blender and blend fine. Put in a bowl and pour rum over it. The drier the bread the more rum it will soak up.

3. Grate the chocolate in a nut grater or Mouli cheese grater.

4. Whip the cream, gradually adding sugar and ending with vanilla extract.

5. In a deep, 8-cup glass serving bowl, spread a layer of the whipped cream, sprinkle with pumpernickel crumbs and grated chocolate and dot with the jam. Cover with a layer of whipped cream, repeat the layer of pumpernickel, grated chocolate and jam. Cover again with whipped cream and repeat once more. Cover with whipped cream. Dot with dabs of jam and if there is any leftover chocolate, use this for decoration, too. Cover lightly and chill overnight.

Yield: 8 to 10 servings.

A Grande Bouffe

Young wild boar can be cooked exactly like fresh pork. "But one difference between a wild boar ranging the woods and a domesticated pig," Carlo Amato was saying as the plane circled Yarmouth Harbor in Nova Scotia, "a wild boar climbs higher and will step over obstacles in his path. A domesticated pig walks around them."

Mr. Amato owns a 700-acre farm called Shangri-La on this small island about twenty miles from Yarmouth town and raises wild boar experimentally and commercially as well as to keep his ample table supplied not only with wild boar roasts and ragouts but with such Italian delicacies as home-smoked prosciutto, capocollo and sausages.

Over a recent weekend, he and his wife, Lorraine, invited a trio of America's best chefs—Jean Vergnes, chef-owner of Le Cirque Restaurant in Manhattan; Luigi Nanni, chef-owner of both Nanni's Restaurant and Il Valetto in Manhattan; and Pierre Franey, former chef of Le Pavillon and now a vice president of Howard Johnson's—to visit his forest domain. The chefs and their families plus other guests arrived by plane, laden with crates and cartons and tote bags filled with cheeses and spices and plastic bags puffed with fresh basil and parsley and other good things essential to fine cuisine and a prolonged grande bouffe in the country.

Two large vans were needed to accommodate the party that numbered twenty. When Mr. Amato announced that Yarmouth was a splendid source for both fresh and dried fish, both vans stopped—almost automatically—alongside a local fish market. A short while later the owners of the market were considerably enriched and the vans a bit more burdened with the likes of two dozen freshly trapped and highly agitated lobsters; half a bushel of fresh clams, some to be stuffed, some to be turned into soup; seven and a half pounds fresh codfish heads, also to be ordained in a soup kettle; fresh cod tongues and cheeks, which would become a sublime creation with fresh tomatoes, dry white wine and heavy cream; dried cod to be transformed into baccala Livernese; and a pound or so of Digby chicks, the Nova Scotia name for smoked herring fillets. The latter wound up as a celestial appetizer, marinated (after soaking in cold milk) in olive oil with onion rings, carrots and a bit of garlic. One member of the party had discovered a fine source for fresh fiddleheads from New Brunswick, and those, too, were brought along to be cooked and served with hollandaise.

It was shortly after noon when the party arrived at the kitchen of the main house, and Sirio Maccioni, also owner of Le Cirque (and former maître d'hôtel of the old Colony Restaurant), decided with his infinite grace and Italian wisdom that even Shangri-La could be improved with a medicato for all hands. A medicato, we learned, is made of about half a cup of dry white wine (preferably Italian, Mr. Maccioni advises), a teaspoon of Campari, a twist of orange peel, ice and a splash of soda, all served in a tall glass. It offers a distinct improvement to midday vision.

Two of the chefs, Jean Vergnes and Pierre Franey, descended to a butchering room to make ready a couple of forty-five-pound wild boar that had been slaughtered for the three days of feasting to follow. A good occasion for menu linguistics. We learned that a wild boar, approximately one year old, is known as a marcassin in French, a cinghialetto in Italian. Beyond that age it is known as sanglier in French, cinghiale in Italian.

Over our medicato, Mr. Amato told us that he is 38 years old and was born in Rome (actually, he is a baron; his grandfather was senator from Sicily a few decades ago to the Italian kingdom). He first came to America in 1959 and became a Canadian citizen in 1970. He stated that his interest in cultivating wild boar was natural, that his family had raised wild boar as long as he could remember. He added that he is a biology assistant to Georgia State University, that his breeding stock originally came from the Black Forest in Germany and that he does a minor business in selling boar meat to restaurants—he provisions two restaurants in Montreal and Nanni's in New York. The meat appears on Nanni's menu during the winter months. He has studied boar culture all over the world—in Austria, Russia, Africa and South America—and is writing a book that will be illustrated by photographs taken by his friend of many years, Gina Lollobrigida. It is to be published next year.

Someone had brought up from the storeroom below an enormous smoked ham, a prosciutto that the host stated he had been curing for six months. Salamis and a slab of capocollo also appeared and were properly carved and served as finger food, marvelously matched to the medicati.

Vergnes and Franey returned to the kitchen bearing a platter of expertly trimmed, pink-fleshed wild boar chops, and a large basin of cubed boar meat plus the animal's heart, kidneys, liver and other unmentionables, some of which would be marinated and all of which would go into a gruotte of wild boar, the word gruotte being a regional Burgundy name for a game ragout.

Lunch, to include the steamed lobsters with salade russe and a fish soup with pasta, was almost ready and the salt cod was put on to soak.

Mr. Amato lamented his inability to produce Nova Scotia salmon for the occasion. Paradoxically, he pointed out, "most of the lobster eaten in America is from Nova Scotia and only 2 percent of the smoked salmon comes from Nova Scotia. Oddly, most of what is often called Portuguese salt cod also comes from this area."

Here is a sampling of wild boar recipes from that outing, including the most theatrical roast wild boar on a spit. Note that in all cases where wild boar is called for, equivalent cuts of domesticated pork could be substituted.

In New York, wild boar can be purchased at certain times of the year at Regent Food Shop, 1174 Lexington Avenue, between 80th and 81st Streets.

Marcassin à la Broche

(Wild boar on a spit)

1   *45-pound wild boar, cleaned, dressed and ready for the spit but head removed*
Salt and freshly ground pepper to taste
20 *cloves garlic, peeled and cut into slivers*
⅓   *cup dried rosemary*

1. Prepare the base of charcoal more or less to the rear of the pit or grill where the boar will turn. That is to say the fire should be placed in such a fashion that the heat will be thrust at the animal from an angle. Place a pan directly under the animal and in front of the charcoal fire to catch the drippings.

2. Place the boar on the spit.

3. Rub the boar all over with salt and pepper.

4. Make gashes in the fat of the animal and insert slivers of garlic. Sprinkle inside and out with about half the rosemary.

5. Start the spit turning and roast about 15 minutes. Lower the spit cover to partly enclose the boar and continue roasting, basting as necessary. As the boar roasts use your own judgment in adding more salt, pepper and rosemary. Roast about 6½ hours or until thoroughly cooked.

Yield: 36 or more servings.

Pierre Franey's Gruotte de Marcassin

(A ragout of wild boar Burgundy-style)

9   *pounds wild boar or fresh pork, cut into 2-inch cubes*
1½ *bottles (about 4½ cups) dry red Burgundy*
½   *cup coarsely chopped celery*
1   *cup carrot rounds*
½   *cup coarsely chopped onion*
2   *small cloves garlic, coarsely chopped*
Salt to taste
10 *parsley sprigs, tied in a bundle*
½   *tablespoon peppercorns*
½   *tablespoon dried rosemary*
5   *juniper berries, crushed*
2   *bay leaves*
¼   *teaspoon dried thyme*
2   *teaspoons dried basil*
¼   *cup red wine vinegar*
½   *cup corn or olive oil*
Freshly ground pepper to taste
¼   *to ½ cup flour*
½   *pound fresh mushrooms, quartered*
1   *tablespoon butter*
¾   *cup fresh wild boar blood (traditional but optional)*
2   *tablespoons cognac*

1. This dish should be prepared 1 or 2 days in advance and left to marinate before cooking. Cut the lean part of the boar into cubes. Refrigerate the heart, liver, kidney and testicles for later use or discard them as desired. Traditionally all those parts are used in making this dish.

2. Place the cubed meat in a large bowl and add the wine, celery, carrot rounds, onion, garlic, salt and parsley sprigs.

3. Prepare a cheesecloth bag to

enclose the peppercorns, rosemary, juniper berries, bay leaves, thyme and basil. Tie the bag with string and place it in a saucepan. Add the wine vinegar and bring to the boil. Add this to the cubed boar. Cover closely with foil and refrigerate for 24 hours or longer.

4. Drain but reserve the marinade. Separate but reserve in 2 bowls the cubed meat and the vegetables.

5. If the reserved heart and so on are to be used, cut them into 2-inch cubes and set aside. If the testicles are to be used, the transparent membrane surrounding them must be pulled away.

6. Add the oil to a heavy skillet and brown the cubed meat without crowding the pieces. As the cubes become golden transfer them to a large kettle. Brown the pieces of heart and other parts and add them.

7. If the boar blood is to be used, sprinkle the meat with ¼ cup of flour. If the blood is not to be used, sprinkle with ½ cup of flour. Stir to coat the meat well. Add the reserved marinade and vegetables, stirring. Bring to the boil. Cook 3 hours, skimming the surface as necessary to remove the fat that rises. When done, the meat should be quite tender.

8. Remove the meat to another casserole. Strain the sauce and bring it to the boil.

9. Meanwhile, toss the mushrooms in the butter and sprinkle with salt and pepper. Add to the meat.

10. If the blood is to be used, add a little of the hot sauce to the blood, stirring. Add this mixture to the meat, stirring. Bring just to the boil and add the cognac. Pour the hot sauce over the meat and reheat briefly.

Yield: 12 or more servings.

Jean Vergnes' Cotes de Marcassin Sauce Robert
(Wild boar chops with mustard sauce)

8   *to 10 wild boar or pork chops, each about ½ inch thick*
    Salt and freshly ground pepper to taste
    Flour for dredging
5   *tablespoons butter*
½   *tablespoon finely chopped shallots*
½   *tablespoon finely chopped onion*
½   *cup dry white wine*
2   *tablespoons red wine vinegar*
1   *tablespoon imported mustard, Dijon-style*
3   *tablespoons thinly sliced cornichons (imported small French sour pickles) or small sour pickles*
2   *tablespoons finely chopped parsley*

1. Sprinkle the chops on all sides with salt and pepper. Coat lightly on all sides with flour and shake off excess.

2. Heat 3 tablespoons of butter in a large heavy skillet. Add the chops and brown on one side. Turn and brown on the other side, turning often, 15 to 20 minutes. Transfer the chops to a heated platter and keep warm.

3. Add the shallots and onion to the skillet and, when wilted and starting to brown, add the wine, stirring. Add the red wine vinegar and reduce briefly. Stir in the mustard. Add the cornichons. Heat briefly and add the remaining 2 tablespoons of butter, bit by bit, swirling it in. Pour this over the chops and sprinkle with chopped parsley.

Yield: 4 or 5 servings.

Nanni's Sella di Cinghiale Shangri-La

(Roast saddle of wild boar with mushroom sauce)

1   5½ pound saddle of wild boar
    or 1 4-to-5-pound rolled pork
    roast
¾   cup dried, sliced, imported
    mushrooms, preferably Italian
3   sprigs fresh dill
1   tablespoon chopped garlic
2   tablespoons finely chopped
    shallots
2   tablespoons finely chopped
    parsley
2   tablespoons dried rosemary
1   cup chopped scallions
    Salt and freshly ground black
    pepper to taste
    Wild boar bones or pork bones
6   tablespoons butter
4   cups thinly sliced fresh
    mushrooms
2   cups peeled, cored, crushed
    fresh red, ripe tomatoes or use
    imported canned Italian
    tomatoes
¼   cup chopped fresh basil or 1
    tablespoon dried basil
¼   teaspoon Tabasco sauce
½   teaspoon Worcestershire
    sauce
¾   cup dry white wine

1. Preheat the oven to 300 degrees.

2. If the saddle of boar is to be used, it must be boned, but the 2 loin pieces must remain together. Trim off all the fat from the meat inside and out. In addition to the saddle there will be 2 small fillets. Set them aside. If the boned pork roast is used, untie it and open it up to receive a filling.

3. Meanwhile, add the dried mushrooms to a mixing bowl and add hot water to cover. Soak about 20 minutes. Drain and squeeze dry. Set aside.

4. Stuff the opened up saddle of boar or roast pork with dill, a third of the drained dried mushrooms, the garlic, half of the shallots, the parsley, rosemary and scallions. Sprinkle with salt and pepper. If the saddle is used, add the 2 small fillets side by side, matching the large end with the small end of each. Roll the saddle or roast pork to enclose the filling. Tie neatly with string. Sprinkle with salt and pepper.

5. Place the rolled roast in a small roasting pan and surround with the bones. Bake 1 hour and 15 minutes. After the roast has given up some of its fat, start basting the roast. Turn the roast occasionally as it cooks.

6. As the roast cooks, pour off about 3 tablespoons of fat into a saucepan and add 2 tablespoons of butter. Add the remaining shallots and the sliced fresh mushrooms. Cook briefly until the mushrooms give up their liquid. Continue cooking until this liquid evaporates. Add the tomatoes, about half a teaspoon or more of freshly ground black pepper, the basil, Tabasco and Worcestershire sauce. Add the remaining dried mushrooms and continue cooking about 30 minutes. Swirl in the remaining butter.

7. When the roast is done, remove it. Discard the bones. Pour off all the fat from the pan and add the wine, stirring to dissolve the brown particles that cling to the bottom and sides of the roasting pan. Add the mushroom sauce and stir to blend. Untie the roast, slice it and serve with the sauce.

Yield: 8 to 12 servings.

Vinaigrette Dishes

WITH PIERRE FRANEY

In a strictly technical or classic sense, the word vinaigrette is one of the most abused in the entire gastronomic lexicon. What is commonly referred to in this country as a vinaigrette sauce—a combination of three parts oil to one part vinegar plus salt and pepper to taste—is quite simply known in France as a sauce salade. A classic vinaigrette (also called ravigote) consists of oil and vinegar plus capers, chopped herbs such as parsley, tarragon, chives and chervil, a touch of onion, salt and pepper. On this page, we ask Auguste Escoffier to forgive us our sins, for we employ the word vinaigrette loosely and as a matter of convenience. In any event, here are a few personal favorites and some of the recipes even call for lemon juice in lieu of vinegar. We considered coining a name like lemonette or citronette, but obviously we'd rather not.

Belgian Endive and Fennel Vinaigrette

6   heads Belgian endive, approximately
1   fresh fennel bulb
2   tablespoons fresh lemon juice
1   tablespoon imported mustard, preferably Dijon or Düsseldorf
6   tablespoons olive oil
    Salt and freshly ground pepper

1. Trim off the bottoms of the endive. Cut the endive into 1-inch lengths or cut it lengthwise into thin shreds. Drop the pieces into cold water. This will keep them from turning dark. Drain and spin dry or pat dry. Put in a plastic bag and chill.

2. Trim the fennel and slice it thinly. Cut the slices into fine pieces. Rinse, drain and spin or pat dry. Chill.

3. Combine the fennel and endive in a chilled mixing bowl. Blend the remaining ingredients and pour over all. Add more lemon juice or oil to taste. Toss and serve on chilled salad plates.

Yield: 4 to 6 servings.

Salade de Lentilles Vinaigrette

(Lentil salad)

1   1-pound package lentils
1   onion stuck with 2 cloves
2   sprigs fresh thyme or ½ teaspoon dried
1   whole clove garlic, peeled and lightly crushed
1   bay leaf
    Salt and freshly ground pepper
6   cups water

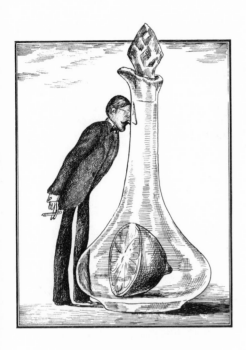

Vegetable Salad Italian-Style

12 *shrimp, cooked, shelled and deveined*
1   *small cauliflower*
1   *or 2 ribs celery*
¼   *pound green beans, as green, young and tender as possible*
12 *pitted or stuffed green or black imported olives*
12 *anchovy fillets, split in half widthwise*
6   *thin onion slices, preferably red onion*
    Salt and freshly ground black pepper
    Sauce vinaigrette (see recipe)

1. Prepare the shrimp and set aside.

2. Cut off the "flowers" from about ¼ of the cauliflower. The weight should be about ¼ pound. Cut the flowers into bite-size "flowerettes." There should be about 2 cups. Set aside.

3. Cut the celery ribs widthwise into ½-inch, bite-size pieces. Set aside.

4. Neatly trim the green beans and cut them into 1-inch lengths. Set aside.

5. Preferably the vegetables should be steamed in a vegetable steamer. However cooked, they must not be overcooked. They must remain crisp-tender. Steam the cauliflower pieces about 4 or 5 minutes. Drain quickly under cold water to chill. Steam the celery about 3 to 4 minutes. Drain and chill. Steam the green beans about 5 to 8 minutes. Drain and chill. Drain all the vegetables well.

2   *cloves garlic, finely minced*
5   *tablespoons finely chopped parsley*
½   *cup finely chopped onion*
1   *tablespoon red wine vinegar or more to taste*
6   *tablespoons peanut, vegetable or corn oil*

1. Empty the lentils into a saucepan and add the onion, thyme, whole clove of garlic, bay leaf, salt and pepper to taste and water. Bring to the boil and simmer about 20 minutes or until lentils are tender without being mushy. Drain well into a mixing bowl and let stand at room temperature. There should be about 7 cups.

2. Add the remaining ingredients and toss well. Add salt and pepper to taste.

Yield: 8 or more servings.

6. Place the vegetables in a salad bowl and add the olives, anchovies, shrimp, onion rings and sprinkle with salt and pepper to taste. Pour the vinaigrette sauce over all and toss. Serve with buttered toast.

Yield: 6 servings.

Vinaigrette sauce

2   *tablespoons lemon juice*
6   *tablespoons olive oil*
1   *tablespoon imported mustard, preferably Dijon or Düsseldorf*
    Salt and freshly ground pepper
1   *clove garlic, finely minced*

Combine all the ingredients in a small jar and seal with a lid. Shake well and chill. Shake before using.

Yield: About ½ cup.

Salade de Moules

(Mussels vinaigrette)

5   *pounds clean, well-scrubbed mussels, the smaller the better*
½   *cup white vinegar*
2   *sprigs fresh thyme or ½ teaspoon dried*
1   *bay leaf*
1½   *cups chopped red onion*
⅓   *cup chopped parsley*
¾   *cup peanut, vegetable or corn oil*

1. Place the mussels in a kettle and add ¼ cup vinegar, thyme and bay leaf. Cover and steam until they open, 5 to 10 minutes. Drain.

2. Empty the warm mussels into a large serving dish or mixing bowl. Toss with remaining ingredients including the remaining ¼ cup vinegar.

Yield: 12 or more servings.

Heart of Palm with Capers Vinaigrette

1   *teaspoon imported mustard, preferably Dijon or Düsseldorf*
    Salt and freshly ground pepper
2   *tablespoons red wine vinegar*
6   *to 7 tablespoons olive oil*
1   *teaspoon finely chopped garlic*
1   *tablespoon drained capers*
1   *14-ounce can heart of palm, chilled*
8   *flat anchovy fillets*

1. Combine the mustard, salt and pepper to taste and vinegar in a mixing bowl. Using a wire whisk, gradually add the oil, beating vigorously. Add the garlic and capers.

2. Drain the heart of palm and cut each heart lengthwise in half. Arrange the heart of palm neatly on 4 chilled plates. Garnish each serving with 2 flat anchovy fillets. Stir the sauce and ladle it over.

Yield: 4 servings.

Jefferson the Epicure

Is connoisseurship in the world of fine food intuitive, or is it learned? Or both? How does it come about that two men, each endowed with uncommon sensibilities, can be exposed for an extended period to the great dining salons of France and return to native soil, one to be immortalized as perhaps America's greatest gastronome, the other far better remembered for going out and flying a kite?

The palates in question are, of course, those of Thomas Jefferson and Benjamin Franklin. Franklin, although gout-ridden late in life, was an advocate of vegetarianism (he also, according to the Encyclopedia Britannica, eleventh edition, took "a cold air bath regularly in the morning, when he sat naked in his bedroom beguiling himself with a book. . . .").

When it came to the pleasures of the table, Jefferson possessed extraordinary, undisputed taste. Oddly, however, this aspect of his nature is mentioned only tangentially by his biographers, if at all. (Pedagogues, we have noted over the years, seem, by and large, to care very little for their stomachs.) They do go on at some length about the ingenious and sometimes highly amusing devices that he invented or created for his dining room, kitchen and cellar, and many of these are remarkable.

To one man's mind, however, the most fascinating aspect of Jefferson, epicure, is the handwritten recipes or "receipts" for dishes he had tasted in France. Some of them are written in a compelling mixture of English and French. His recipe for making meringues, for example, calls for "12 blancs d'oeuf, les fouettes bien fermes, 12 cueillères de sucre en poudre, put them by little and little into the whites of eggs, fouetter le tout ensemble, dresser les sur un papier avec un cueiller de bouche, metter les dans un four bien doux, that is to say, an oven after the bread is drawn out. You may leave them there for as long as you please."

When Jefferson arrived in France in 1784 as Minister Plenipotentiary to the court of Louis XVI (succeeding Benjamin Franklin), the haute cuisine of that nation was long out of its cradle. Cafés and restaurants were flourishing in Paris. Interestingly enough to food historians, he arrived in Paris to serve the year that Antonin Carême, the supreme chef of the eighteenth century and known as the Moses of classic French cooking, was born. Jefferson doubtlessly supped on hundreds of the dishes that Carême was later to record for posterity.

The most comprehensive work yet compiled on Jefferson's gastronomic adventures is Marie Kimball's *Thomas Jefferson's Cook Book* (first published in 1949 and to be reissued in late July or early August by the University of Virginia press). The volume makes note of hundreds of dishes, recipes for which Jefferson

Jefferson's kitchen at Monticello

had culled from his own servants, chefs and the mistresses of various stately homes in the French capital. The dishes include grilled pork cutlets with a piquant sauce Robert; civet de lapin or rabbit in a red wine sauce with bacon and small onions; vol au vents or puff pastry shells filled with any of many creamed or otherwise sauced dishes; and one of the most elegant dishes of all, a galantine of turkey, the skin of the bird stuffed with various meats, pistachios and truffles before poaching, cooling and serving with an aspic coating.

At rural Monticello, there was much game to be had for his home table, and there are numerous French recipes for venison including one for venison, marinated and roasted and served with a sauce piquante, sometimes called a sauce poivrade.

In addition to meringues, his detailed connoisseurship extended to blanc manges, ladyfingers and macaroons. One guest at a dinner given by Jefferson at the White House noted that "the ice cream was brought to the table in the form of small balls, enclosed in cases of warm pastry, a feat." It is reasonable to surmise that this dish was that marvelous and easily made confection, profiteroles—cream puffs—filled with ice cream and served with a hot chocolate sauce.

It is more than conjecture to say that until his sojourn in France the basis of the great man's diet had been soul food, that distinct form of cookery evolved from the hearts and minds of slaves. Without question throughout his lifetime, his table was supplied with such southern staples as fried chicken, country ham, numerous kinds of foods based on corn including corn bread made in a black skillet, grits and whole hominy. The staple greens on the Jefferson table were undoubtedly mustard, turnips and collards plus a variety of peas and beans including cow peas, crowder peas and snap beans. Plus watermelon, hot biscuits, pecan and sweet potato pies.

Mr. Jefferson was once denounced—spitefully and vengefully, no doubt—by Patrick Henry as a man who "abjured his native victuals." The speech was politically motivated.

Whatever his association with the southern table, the Jefferson garden grew an exceptional number of vegetables of great sophistication: broccoli, asparagus, cauliflower, artichokes and endive. Mushrooms were also cultivated at Monticello.

Jefferson is credited with being the first to import many foreign gadgets and delicacies for his kitchen at Monticello, among them a waffle iron from Holland and a pasta-making machine from Italy. He also imported packaged spaghetti from Europe. Jefferson owned an ice cream freezer, a contrivance also owned by George Washington, who spent, according to the recipe, one pound, 13 shillings and four pence for "a cream machine for ice."

Again to quote Mrs. Kimball, Martha Washington left numerous recipes for posterity but none for ice cream. Jefferson discovered his recipe for the dish and wrote it down. "Thus it happens that our first American recipe for ice cream, then no vulgar commonplace, is in the writing of a President of the United States."

Jefferson in Europe developed a lusty appetite for the likes of Parmesan cheese, almonds, fine mustards, tarragon vinegar, oil and anchovies, and these he had shipped to Virginia throughout his lifetime. We have before us the receipt of Mr. Jefferson's hotel in Amsterdam dated 10 to 28 March 1788. It details many of his room service requests and shows that he was long in the tooth for oysters. Fortunately, these he could find in abundance in the waters of Virginia.

Jefferson traveled extensively through the vineyards of France and Germany, making a painstaking study of grape-growing and wine-making, and he had an enthusiastic respect for the wines of both countries. Records show that he imported hundreds of cases of European wines for his home cellar. He seems to have had a special regard for the wines of Bordeaux as well as Sauternes. He seems not to have held the sparkling wines of Champagne in high esteem, preferring the still wines of that region. "The mousseux or sparkling champagne is never brought to a good table in France. The still, or non-mousseux, is alone drunk by connoisseurs," he is said to have written.

Mr. Jefferson went to considerable lengths to obviate the need for servants in the dining room. He was not so much concerned that these "mute but not inattentive listeners" would repeat what they had heard but rather that they would repeat it incorrectly.

Thus, he devised an ingenious silent butler, a one-panel door that turned on a central vertical swivel. One side of the door was a series of shelves where food might be placed. When the door was turned to the dining room, a single waiter or perhaps two would take the food from the shelves and take it to the various tables where guests were seated. There were tiered stands at each table and, presumably, the food was placed on these so that the guests would serve themselves.

Jefferson, when he entertained, also preferred to have several small tables spaced in the dining room rather than one large one. This, he felt, provided a greater intimacy and made conversation more personal.

Jefferson's wine cellar was and is situated directly below a mantelpiece in the dining room. On either side of the mantel two more "dumbwaiters" were installed. The person in charge of the cellar would position the bottles from below as they were required above and hoist them up by an "endless" conveyor belt. Open the door and, voila! Le vin. It was thought for many years that this was a Jefferson original, but it now appears that he visited, on occasion, a place called the Café Mécanique in Paris and this same conveyor belt system was used there.

In Paris, Jefferson's first staff consisted of a cuisinière. Later he acquired a valet de chambre named Adrien Petit and there was James Hastings, a black slave who had followed him from Monticello. Hastings received extensive training in the art of French cookery and Jefferson signed a document on 15 September 1793, witnessed by Petit, in which he offered Hastings freedom if he agreed to return to Monticello and teach "such person as I shall place under him to be a good cook . . ."

During his tenure as President, the White House staff consisted of Joseph Rapin, a French maître d'hôtel who was succeeded by Etienne Lemaire (at $20 a month). There was a French chef named Julien and an assistant to the chef named Noel. Jefferson brought two slaves from Monticello, known simply as Edy and Fanny, to be trained under Julien and it was they who staffed Jefferson's kitchen when he retired to Monticello. Jefferson's wife had died early on in their marriage and his household on retirement was presided over by his daughter, Martha Jefferson Randolph.

It would be interesting to know the genesis of one dish for which Mr. Jefferson had a particular fondness and which he frequently requested for breakfast. It is for chicken hash, known in French as capillotade. It was often served at Monticello. Throughout his lifetime, Mr. Jefferson was unstinting in his hospitality, and he died on the 4th of July, 1826, impoverished.

There follows a series of recipes for dishes that Mr. Jefferson might very well—and probably did—dine on in Paris or Monticello or both.

Profiteroles au Chocolat

(Cream puffs with vanilla ice cream
and chocolate sauce)

36 cream puffs (see recipe)
36 small scoops vanilla ice cream
    (see recipe)
    Chocolate sauce (see recipe)

1. Split the cream puffs in half for stuffing.

2. Scoop a small portion of ice cream onto the bottom of each cream puff and cover with the cream puff tops. Spoon the chocolate sauce over and serve immediately.

Yield: 12 or more servings.

Profiteroles
(Cream puffs)

8 tablespooons butter plus
   additional butter for greasing
   a pan
1 cup flour plus additional flour
   for flouring a pan
1 cup water
   Salt to taste
½ teaspoon sugar
4 whole, large eggs

1. Preheat the oven to 425 degrees.

2. Lightly but thoroughly butter a jelly roll pan. Sprinkle the pan with flour and shake it around until well coated. Shake and tap out excess flour.

3. Add the water to a saucepan and add the 8 tablespoons of butter, salt to taste and sugar. Bring to the boil and add the flour, all at once, stir-

ring vigorously and thoroughly in a circular fashion until a ball is formed and the mixture cleans the sides of the saucepan.

4. Add the eggs, one at a time, beating thoroughly and rapidly with the spoon until the egg is well blended with the mixture. Add another egg, beat and so on. When all the eggs are added, fit a pastry bag with a round-tipped, number 6 pastry tube. Spoon the mixture into the bag. Holding the pastry bag straight up with the tip close to the floured surface of the pan, squeeze the bag to make mounds of pastry at intervals all over the pan. There should be about 36 mounds.

5. The mounds may have pointed tips on top. To flatten these, wet a clean tea towel and squeeze it well. Open it up, fold it over in thirds. Hold it stretched directly over the mounds, quickly patting down just enough to rid the mounds of the pointed tips. Do not squash the mounds.

6. Place the pan in the oven and bake 30 minutes or until the cream puffs are golden brown and cooked through. Remove and let cool.

Yield: About 36 cream puffs.

Glace à la vanille
(Vanilla ice cream)

4   cups milk
1   cup heavy cream
1½   cups sugar
10   egg yolks
1   teaspoon pure vanilla extract
     or 1 split, 3-inch length of
     vanilla bean

1. Combine the milk and cream

in a saucepan and bring just to the boil.

2. Place the sugar and yolks in a mixing bowl and beat with a whisk to the ribbon stage; i.e., until thick and pale yellow in color and, when the beater is lifted, the mixture falls back on itself ribbonlike.

3. Pour a cup or so of the hot milk and cream mixture into the egg mixture, beating rapidly with the whisk. Return this mixture to the hot milk mixture in a saucepan. Rinse out the bowl with the hot mixture. Add the vanilla bean if used.

4. Using a wooden spoon, cook the sauce over low heat, stirring this way and that all over the bottom of the saucepan, taking care that the sauce does not stick. Also, be cautious that the sauce does not curdle. Cook only until the mixture coats the bottom of the spoon like very thick cream. Do not at any point boil the sauce, or it will curdle. If the vanilla bean is not used, add the vanilla extract at this time.

5. Immediately strain the sauce into a mixing bowl. Let stand until cool. Chill thoroughly in the refrigerator or freezer without freezing.

6. Pour the custard into the canister of a hand-cranked or electric ice cream machine and freeze according to the manufacturer's instruction.

Yield: About 1½ to 2 quarts ice cream.

Sauce au chocolat
(Chocolate sauce)

1   *pound dark, sweet chocolate*
⅔   *cup water*
3   *tablespoons sugar*

1   *cup heavy cream*
4   *tablespoons butter*

1. Break up the chocolate and add it to a saucepan. Add the water and sugar and cook, stirring as necessary, until chocolate melts.

2. Off heat add the cream and butter. Keep warm without boiling.

Yield: About 3½ cups.

Capillotade
(A French chicken hash)

1   *3-pound chicken, simmered in chicken broth until done*
½   *pound fresh mushrooms*
4   *tablespoons butter*
¼   *cup finely chopped onion*
    Salt and freshly ground pepper to taste
½   *cup dry white wine*
¼   *cup flour*
1   *cup heavy cream*
⅛   *teaspoon freshly grated nutmeg*
    Pinch of cayenne pepper
1   *egg yolk*
3   *tablespoons grated Gruyère or Swiss cheese*

1. Preheat the oven to 425 degrees.

2. Remove the flesh from the chicken bones. Pull off the skin. Add both skin and bones to the broth in which the chicken cooked and continue cooking 30 minutes or longer.

3. Cut the chicken into bite-size pieces. There should be about 2 cups.

4. Finely chop the mushrooms. There should be about 2 cups.

5. Heat 1 tablespoon of butter in a skillet and add the onion. Cook until wilted. Add the mushrooms, salt and pepper to taste. Cook about 2 minutes and add the wine. Cook over high heat until reduced by half. Add the chicken and stir to blend. Cook about 4 minutes and set aside.

6. Add remaining 3 tablespoons butter to a 1-quart saucepan. Add the flour and stir to blend with a wire whisk. Add 2 cups of the simmering stock, stirring rapidly with the whisk. Strain and reserve remaining stock for another use. Add the cream, nutmeg and cayenne. Add about ⅔ of this to the chicken mixture. Simmer about 5 minutes and set aside.

7. To the remaining sauce add the egg yolk and stir. Bring just to the boil, stirring rapidly, but do not cook further. Set aside.

8. Pour the chicken mixture into an oval baking dish and spoon the remaining sauce over all. Sprinkle with cheese and bake until browned in the oven, about 10 minutes.

Yield: 8 to 10 servings.

Canard aux Olives

(Duck with olives)

2   *4-to-5-pound ducks, with
      giblets
      Salt and freshly ground
      pepper to taste*
1   *cup finely chopped onion*
1   *clove garlic, crushed*
¼   *cup finely chopped celery*
⅓   *cup finely chopped carrots*
1   *sprig fresh parsley*
1   *bay leaf*
2   *sprigs fresh thyme or ½
      teaspoon dried*
1   *tablespoon tomato paste*

1   *cup Madeira wine*
2   *cups chicken broth*
6   *peppercorns, crushed*
1   *cup pitted green olives*
3   *tablespoons butter*

1. Preheat the oven to 400 degrees.

2. Cut off and reserve the wing tips and the second wing joints of the ducks. Leave the main wing bone attached. Sprinkle the ducks inside and out with salt and pepper to taste and truss them with string.

3. Place the ducks on their sides in a roasting pan and bake 30 minutes, basting as necessary.

4. While the ducks are baking, cut the necks into 1-inch lengths and add them to a heavy saucepan. Cut the wing tips and joints into small pieces and add them. Add the hearts and gizzards and sprinkle with salt and pepper. Do not add fat, but cook the duck pieces, stirring often, until nicely browned. Pour off the fat that has accumulated and add the onion, garlic, celery, carrots, parsley, bay leaf and thyme. Add the tomato paste and stir. Add the wine, chicken broth and peppercorns. Bring to the boil and simmer 1½ hours, skimming the fat from the surface as it accumulates.

5. When the ducks have roasted 30 minutes, reduce the oven heat to 350 degrees. Pour off the fat from the pan. Turn the ducks to the other side and continue roasting 30 minutes. Pour off the fat once more and turn the ducks, breast side up. Continue roasting from 1 to 1½ hours longer, pouring off the fat as it accumulates in the pan. The total cooking time is from 2 to 2½ hours. The ducks are done when they are lifted and the liquid from the cavity runs clear.

6. When the ducks are almost done, taste the olives. Soak them briefly in water if they are salty or, if you wish, blanch them for about 10 seconds in boiling water. Drain.

7. When the ducks are done, remove them from the pan. Drain the pan of all fat and place the pan on the stove. Add the Madeira sauce, stirring and scraping to dislodge any brown particles that cling to the bottom and sides of the roasting pan. Strain the sauce through a fine sieve, pushing with the back of a heavy spoon to extract as much liquid from the solids as possible. Bring the sauce to the boil and add the olives. Swirl in the butter. Serve the duck carved with the sauce.

Yield: 8 or more servings.

Meringue Shells

Butter for greasing pans
Flour for flouring pans
6   egg whites, preferably from
     extra large eggs
1½   cups sugar

1. Preheat the oven to 200 or 250 degrees. The lower heat is preferable.

2. Rub one or two pastry sheets or jelly roll pans with butter. Sprinkle with flour, shaking the pan until bottom is coated. Shake and tap out the excess flour.

3. Add the egg whites to the container of an electric mixer and start beating on low speed. When soft peaks form, gradually add the sugar, beating on high speed until very stiff peaks form.

4. Use a pastry bag fitted with a round-tipped number 8 pastry tube. Spoon the meringue into the bag and squeeze ovals of meringue measuring about 3 to 3½ inches long and 1½ to 2 inches wide onto the prepared pans. Space them in neat rows and slightly apart. Place the pans in the oven and bake at the lower heat for 2½ hours or at the higher temperature for 2 hours.

5. Remove the pans from the oven and let cool. Serve 2 meringue shells per person with a scoop of ice cream sandwiched between the shells. Serve preferably on chilled plates.

Yield: 24 or more meringue shells, depending on size.

July 1976

I N BROWSING through the food columns that appeared in *The New York Times* during the month of July last year, I discovered an article on clams freshly harvested from the waters near our home in East Hampton. I have a confession to make.

I had never really been conversant with clams in my childhood. The first time I ever sampled a clam was in my young adulthood in Chicago. Come to think of it, I had never given much thought to the age, sweetness, tenderness, size or anything else when it came to clams, be they littleneck, cherrystone or quahog, a name that fascinated me because of its unusual, melodic North American Indian ring. Shortly after I joined the *Times*—young, eager and infinitely self-assured where some facts of reporting were concerned—I interviewed a neighbor of mine, a Frenchman, a dear friend in his late 70s who, in his retirement, spent hours each day clamming in the waters of Accabonac Bay. I took it upon myself to interview him during one of his low-tide excursions to explore the ins and outs of what's what in clamdom. His name was Auguste and, after an hour or so, his clam bucket buoyed up with a small tire, he must have gathered something like six dozen clams, or whatever the limit was in that year. "Auguste," I asked, "what's the difference between littleneck and cherrystone clams?" He was a bit distracted, I suppose, and told me littlenecks were the larger of the two. When I wrote the article, I stated thusly with sublime self-assurance: "Littlenecks, of course, are larger than cherrystones." The night the article was to appear, I bought a copy of the early edition of the newspaper on my way home. I hastily opened it to my column, only to find treason in the editing: "Cherrystones," the copy read, "are, of course, larger than littlenecks." With considerable anger, I telephoned the copy desk and yelled that my copy must stand as written. They revised it. The next morning, at dawn perhaps, I started wondering: Could it be that Auguste, my friend, had not been accurate? That he had been inattentive? Or that I perhaps had misheard? I called him and said: "Tell me, Auguste, didn't you say that littlenecks were larger than cherrystones?" "Of course not," he answered. When I went to the paper that morning, I learned that the original correction had been made by Theodore M. Bernstein, one of the great clam fanciers of all time and the gentleman who was in charge of language at the newspaper. I went to see him, taking with me a solitary broken littleneck clam by way of apology.

A Chinese Buffet

May Wong Trent was born in Hong Kong, the daughter of a well-to-do eye surgeon who, at 85, still teaches. As a child, she noted, she—with youthful defiance—spent most of her time in the kitchen.

"Like many families in Hong Kong those days," she stated, "we had two kitchens. One American, one Chinese. This was the one area of the house that was absolutely forbidden to children. But my sisters were older than I and largely they ignored me. The cooks were my favorite playmates and I would take my chances of getting a spanking.

"My husband and I had known each other closely for more than three years," Mrs. Trent said recently, "before he knew I could even make tea. Whenever we were together in Hong Kong or New York, we spent endless hours talking and going to restaurants, but he never asked if I could cook and I never volunteered to tell him.

"We met on a blind date in Hong Kong about eleven years ago when he came there on business. Peter is an investment banker and when we entertained his friends or business acquaintances, it was always in public. One afternoon he telephoned to say he would be stopping by that evening with a friend. So I cooked. It took me weeks to persuade him the food hadn't been catered or something I'd picked up in a fast-food shop."

The reed-slender Mrs. Trent tends her own immaculately weeded garden, which is currently flourishing with such Sino-American vegetables and herbs as basil, tomatoes, corn, green beans, leaf lettuce, bok choy or Chinese cabbage, Chinese mustard greens, Chinese squash, long Chinese beans, green peppers and three kinds of parsley—Italian flat leaf, Chinese (fresh coriander) and curly.

The Trent table is international and follows a vague pattern.

"Whenever we entertain it is generally Chinese, and we always have a noodle lunch for the family on Sundays. Peter has a passion for southern food— he spends a good deal of time in the South on business—and I generally serve him grits with grated cheddar and melted butter on Sunday mornings. And grillades, a spicy Louisiana dish. Otherwise, we dine on simply grilled meats and salads and gazpacho. I make a large batch of gazpacho once a week and keep it in the refrigerator when tomatoes are ripe."

Mrs. Trent states that she and her husband entertain on the average of once a week, generally for eight or ten guests in the belief that ten is the maximum number suitable for their dining table, which, incidentally, is a handsome piece in the Chinese chippendale-style that they had custom-made on Long Island.

It is her concept (an idea we explored in another context some weeks ago) that a Chinese meal for eight or ten isn't all that difficult when properly planned. Quite often such a dinner in her home takes the form of a buffet.

May Wong Trent entertains eight or ten guests each week with buffets

"Today," she said, as she relaxed over a glass of very dry, very good California white wine, "the meal will begin with cold rice noodles with a bean sprout salad on top." This served to get the guests properly seated. Afterward, the guests helped themselves to two more room-temperature dishes—spiced seafood Chinese-style and sesame chicken with asparagus ring. Mrs. Trent had used her crockpot to prepare slow-cooked Chinese spareribs with a black bean sauce. The single hot dish was put on to simmer shortly after the guests began the buffet. It was steamed beef balls with two kinds of mushrooms. The meal ended with cold fruits, pineapple and lychee nuts with candied ginger. There was rice, of course, and tea.

Mrs. Trent feels that the elements of a Chinese meal should be like painting. There should be harmonies in flavor, textures, temperatures and colors.

In the meal that she served on this occasion, one dish had a "chivey" taste, another tasted of celery, another of sesame, and so on.

Mrs. Trent, incidentally, has given Chinese cooking classes both in Short Hills and in their cottage on Fire Island.

Here is the outline of dishes recently served as a Chinese buffet in Mrs. Trent's home. Prior to the meal she served an assortment of vegetables and quail eggs with a satay dip.

Cold Spiced Seafood Chinese-Style

3 quarts water
1 pound sea scallops
1 pound shrimp, shelled and deveined
3 ribs celery
10 to 12 scallions
3 tablespoons white vinegar
1 clove garlic, finely chopped
2½ tablespoons fish sauce, available in Chinese grocery stores
2 teaspoons sugar
¼ teaspoon ground white pepper
¼ cup chopped fresh, hot green chilies

1. Bring the water to the boil.

2. Cut the scallops against the grain into ¼-inch rounds. Add the rounds to the boiling water for about 1½ minutes or until the scallops lose their translucent look. Take care not to overcook. Drain. Let cool.

3. Add the shrimp to the boiling water for about 40 seconds. Drain immediately. Let cool.

4. Trim off and discard the ends of the celery. Use a swivel-bladed paring knife and scrape the celery. Cut the ribs into 2-inch lengths and cut the lengths into thin shreds. There should be about 2 cups.

5. Trim off the ends of the scallions. Slice off the white part and discard the green tops or put them to another use. Shred the white parts lengthwise.

6. In a mixing bowl, combine the scallops, shrimp, celery and scallions. Blend the remaining ingredients and pour over the salad. Toss well. Serve at room temperature.

Yield: 8 to 12 servings.

Sesame Chicken with Asparagus Ring

3 to 4 whole chicken breasts (enough to make 5 cups of shredded meat when cooked)
3 tablespoons sesame paste, available in Chinese and other oriental and Middle-Eastern markets
2 tablespoons thin (light) soy sauce
¼ teaspoon hot oil (see note)
¼ cup plus ⅓ cup corn oil
¼ cup water
¼ cup Szechwan peppercorns (see note)
Salt to taste
1 pound asparagus
4 thin slices fresh ginger
Freshly ground pepper to taste

½   tablespoon shao hsing or dry
    sherry
¼   teaspoon sugar
¾   cup loosely packed leaves of
    Chinese parsley (also called
    cilantro and fresh coriander)

1. Place the chicken breasts in a kettle and add water to cover. Bring to the boil and simmer 10 to 15 minutes, depending on size. Turn off the heat and let stand until cool.

2. Drain the chicken and pull the skin and meat from the bones. Shred the skin and meat. There should be about 5 cups.

3. Combine the sesame paste, soy sauce, hot oil, ¼ cup corn oil and water.

4. Place the peppercorns in a small skillet and cook briefly, shaking the skillet until the peppercorns give off a pleasant roasted aroma. Pour out onto a flat surface and crush lightly. Hold a sieve over the sauce and add the peppercorns to the sieve. Sift the fine, loose particles into the sauce. Reserve the coarse peppercorns for another use.

5. Scrape the asparagus with a swivel-bladed vegetable knife. Cut the stalks and tips on the bias into 2-inch lengths.

6. Heat the remaining ⅓ cup of corn oil in a wok or skillet and add the ginger. When it is quite hot but not smoking add the asparagus pieces and immediately add the pepper, wine and sugar. Cook, stirring constantly, about 30 seconds. Cover with the wok cover about 15 seconds. Uncover and cook, stirring, about 15 seconds longer. Take care not to overcook.

7. Scoop out the asparagus.

8. When ready to serve, make a border of asparagus around an oval or round serving dish.

9. Add the leaves of Chinese parsley to the sesame sauce and stir. Pour this over the chicken and toss to blend. Spoon the chicken into the center of the asparagus. Garnish with sprigs of fresh Chinese parsley. Serve at room temperature.

Yield: 8 to 12 servings.

Note: All the ingredients listed above are available in Chinese markets in Chinatown.

Steamed Beef Balls with Two Kinds of Mushrooms

40   small or 20 large dried black
     mushrooms
¾   pound ground, not too lean,
     beef
½   tablespoon finely chopped
     fresh ginger
3   tablespoons light soy sauce
½   tablespoon shao hsing or dry
     sherry
½   tablespoon cornstarch
½   teaspoon sugar
⅛   teaspoon ground white pepper
     Salt to taste
1½   teaspoons sesame oil
24   fresh or frozen shelled green
     peas
1   tablespoon corn oil
1   14-ounce can straw
     mushrooms, available in
     Chinese markets

1. Place the mushrooms in a mixing bowl and add very hot water to cover. Let stand 20 minutes or longer.

2. Combine the beef, ginger, 1 tablespoon soy sauce, wine, cornstarch, half the sugar, pepper, salt and 1 teaspoon sesame oil in a mixing bowl. Blend well. Using the fingers, shape the mixture into 24 small meatballs. Press 1 pea halfway into each ball as a garnish. As the meat is shaped, arrange the balls in pairs, pea-side up, down the center of a round baking dish.

3. Squeeze the black mushrooms to extract most of the liquid. Cut off and discard the stems.

4. Combine the remaining soy sauce with the remaining sesame oil, corn oil and remaining sugar.

5. Add the black mushroom caps and bring to the boil, stirring. Remove from the heat and spoon the mushrooms to one side of the row of meatballs.

6. Drain the straw mushrooms and squeeze them to extract most of the moisture. Add these to the small amount of sauce in the saucepan. Stir around and pour these to the other side of the meatballs.

7. Arrange the baking dish on a rack over but not touching boiling water. A steamer may be used. A pair of chopsticks placed separate but parallel in a wok partly filled with water is also convenient. Cover and steam about 10 minutes.

Yield: 6 to 12 servings.

Crockpot Chinese Spareribs with Black Bean Sauce

3   *pounds baby spareribs, preferably of the kind to be found in Chinese meat markets*
¼   *cup flour*
½   *cup coarsely chopped fermented black beans, available in Chinese markets*
1   *10-ounce can mock abalone (chai powyu), available dry packed in Chinese markets*
¼   *cup dark soy sauce*
1½ *cups water*
1   *teaspoon sugar*

1. Prepare this dish a day in advance.

2. Have the butcher crack the spareribs across the bones into 3 lengthwise slabs. Cut these slabs into fairly large bite-size pieces.

3. Roll the spareribs in flour and add them to a dry crockpot. Do not add fat. Sprinkle the top evenly with black beans and the mock abalone. Sprinkle with the remaining ingredients. Cover and cook on low heat for 7½ to 8 hours without removing the cover. The next day reheat for 30 minutes and serve.

Yield: 8 to 12 servings.

Cold Noodles with Bean Sprout Salad

2   *ounces rice vermicelli (rice noodles, see note)*
2   *small eggs*
5   *cups fresh bean sprouts, about 1 pound*
4   *canned sweet white cucumbers (see note)*
¾   *cup loosely packed chives, preferably Chinese chives, cut into 2-inch lengths (see note)*
1   *cup shredded Chinese roast pork (see note) or home cooked*
⅓   *cup light soy sauce*
10   *to 20 tiny hot green chilies in vinegar (see note)*
2   *teaspoons sesame oil*
1½   *teaspoons sugar*
⅔   *cup black Chinese vinegar (see note), or red wine vinegar*
1½   *tablespoons loosely packed, chopped fresh ginger*
    Salt to taste

1. Drop the rice vermicelli into boiling water to cover and turn off the heat. Let stand 10 minutes. Drain and rinse under cold water until thoroughly chilled. Drain.

2. Beat the eggs thoroughly and pour them into a lightly oiled skillet with a nonstick surface. Tilt the skillet this way and that so the eggs cover the surface. Cook just until the eggs set and turn the "omelet" out onto a flat surface. Let cool. Cut the omelet into 2-inch shreds and add it to a mixing bowl.

3. Place the bean sprouts in a sieve or colander and pour about 4 quarts of vigorously boiling water over them. Drain well and let cool to room temperature.

4. Shred the cucumbers and add them to the mixing bowl. Add the bean sprouts, chives and roast pork.

5. Combine the soy sauce, hot green chilies, sesame oil and sugar in a small saucepan and bring to the boil, stirring. Remove from the heat and let cool.

6. Combine the black vinegar and ginger and set aside.

7. Add ¼ cup of the vinegar mixture and 2 tablespoons of the soy sauce mixture to the bean sprout salad. Toss with salt to taste.

8. To serve, arrange equal portions of the noodles on individual small plates. Arrange a small amount of the bean sprout salad on top. Serve the remaining 2 sauces in small bowls on the side.

Yield: 8 to 12 servings.

Note: All the ingredients listed above are available in Chinese markets in Chinatown. The sweet cucumber pickles used by Mrs. Trent are the Tung Chun brand packed in 1-pound cans. Two excellent sources for rice noodles are the Central Asian Food Market, 212 Canal St., and Shin Kwong Co, 232 Canal St. Three preferred brands of rice vermicelli (rice noodles) are Kweilin, Kongmoon and Sailing Boat. Bottled Tabasco peppers, widely available, may be substituted for hot green chilies.

Satay Peanut Dip

1   *teaspoon red pepper flakes, more or less to taste*
2   *tablespoons finely chopped onion*
1   *clove garlic, finely minced*

1   tablespoon corn oil
3   tablespoons peanut butter
½   teaspoon turmeric
½   teaspoon brown sugar
¾   cup water
½   tablespoon lime juice
½   tablespoon dark soy sauce
¼   teaspoon grated fresh ginger

1. Using a spice grinder or the container of an electric blender, blend the pepper flakes to a powder.

2. Combine the pepper powder with the remaining ingredients in the container of an electric blender and blend until thoroughly mixed. Spoon into a sauce dish and serve.

Yield: About 1 cup.

Assorted foods with satay peanut dip

Arrange plucked-over snow peas, drained Chinese baby corn and drained quail eggs (both available in tins in Chinese markets), pieces of fresh tender broccoli and other fresh vegetables cut into bite-size pieces in small bowls. Serve them with satay peanut dip.

Sweet Basil

WITH PIERRE FRANEY

It is indisputably true that a single dish can cause an upsurge of interest in one herb or spice that may border on the phenomenal. That is certainly the case with oregano, which was little known in this country until the pizza craze arrived after World War II. It is also true of basil, which has gained a vast following in America during the last decade, due largely, in our books at least, to pesto genovese, that seductive sauce made with fresh basil, garlic, grated Parmesan or pecorino cheese and nuts, generally pine nuts. Basil is, of course, one of the most delectable of all sweet herbs. We offer several recipes here for basil that is now flourishing in thousands of gardens in this country. We also offer a new twist on pesto genovese—this one made with pistachio rather than pine nuts. Pine nuts or walnuts may be substituted, however.

Pesto Genovese

1   cup loosely packed basil
⅓   cup pistachio nuts
2   cloves garlic, peeled
¾   cup freshly grated Parmesan
      cheese
½   cup olive oil
1   pound spaghetti, cooked
      according to package
      directions
3   tablespoons butter

1. Place the basil in the container of an electric blender and add the pistachio nuts and garlic. Blend, stirring down carefully with a rubber spatula if necessary. When well blended, add the cheese.

2. Gradually add the olive oil while blending on a low speed.

3. When the spaghetti is cooked, drain it quickly and pour it into a hot serving dish. Toss with the butter. Add pesto sauce to taste and toss well.

Yield: 4 servings.

Gigot d'Agneau au Pistou

(Braised lamb with basil and garlic stuffing)

1   5-pound leg of lamb, boned
¼   pound bacon or salt pork
6   cloves garlic, finely minced
3   sprigs fresh parsley
10   fresh basil leaves
      Salt and freshly ground
      pepper
1   cup coarsely chopped onions
½   cup coarsely chopped carrot
¾   cup dry white wine

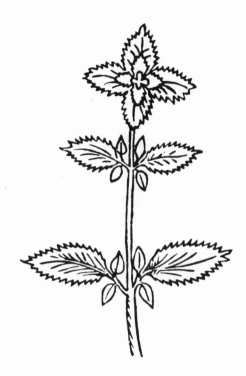

4. Place the lamb fat-side down in a heavy casserole and arrange the bones around it. The lamb and bones should fit snugly inside the casserole. Brown the lamb on all sides and sprinkle onions and carrots around it. Cover and cook about 5 minutes.

5. Carefully pour off and discard all fat that has accumulated. Add the wine, tomatoes, salt and pepper to taste. Cover and bring to the boil. Cook over moderate heat about 2 hours.

6. Remove the lamb and strain the sauce into a saucepan. Bring to the boil and skim the surface as necessary to remove as much fat as possible. Cook the sauce down until it is properly concentrated and saucelike. Slice the meat and spoon a little of the sauce over each serving.

Yield: 8 to 12 servings.

2   *cups chopped, peeled tomatoes (if canned tomatoes are used, use the imported Italian peeled tomatoes)*

1. When the lamb is boned, ask the butcher to reserve the bones and crack them.

2. Combine the bacon, garlic, parsley and basil in a food processor or use an electric blender. Blend the ingredients to a fine puree with salt and pepper to taste.

3. Sprinkle the lamb inside with salt and pepper to taste. Spread the bacon mixture inside the lamb to fill it. If some of the stuffing oozes out, no matter. Sew up the lamb, tucking in torn pieces of lamb as necessary. Sprinkle the lamb all over with salt and pepper. Rub the lamb with any excess bacon and herb mixture.

Soupe au Pistou

(Bean soup with basil sauce)

The soup

¾   *cup dried pea beans*
3   *quarts water*
2   *potatoes, about 1¼ pounds*
½   *pound green beans*
1½ *pounds lima beans in the shell or 1 10-ounce package frozen Salt and freshly ground pepper*
2   *red, ripe tomatoes, about 1¼ pounds, or 2 cups chopped canned imported tomatoes*
3   *or 4 small zucchini, about 1 pound*
¼   *cup broken small pasta, preferably capellini or vermicelli or use spaghettini or spaghetti*

The pistou

10   *or 12 leaves fresh basil*
2   *to 4 cloves fresh garlic, peeled*
3   *tablespoons olive oil*

1. Place the beans in a kettle and add the water. Bring to the boil and simmer 30 minutes.

2. Peel the potatoes and cut them into ½-inch cubes. There should be about 3½ cups. Add them to the kettle.

3. Trim the green beans and cut them into ½-inch lengths. There should be about 2 cups. Add them to the kettle.

4. Shell the fresh lima beans if used. There should be about 1 cup of beans. Add them to the kettle. If frozen lima beans are used, do not add them at this point.

5. Add salt and pepper to taste. Cover and simmer 50 minutes.

6. Peel and core the tomatoes and cut them into ½-inch cubes. Add them to the kettle.

7. Trim and discard the ends of the zucchini and cut them into ½-inch cubes. Add them to the kettle. If frozen lima beans are used, add them. Cover and cook 30 minutes longer.

8. Meanwhile, blend to a paste the basil and garlic. Stir in the oil gradually. This is the pistou.

9. When ready to serve, add the pasta to the soup and simmer about 1 minute. Stir in the pistou and serve piping hot in hot bowls.

Yield: 8 or more servings.

Zucchini with Basil

¾   *pound small zucchini*
1   *tablespoon flour*
      Salt and freshly ground
      pepper
2   *tablespoons olive oil*
1   *clove garlic, finely minced*
3   *tablespoons chopped fresh*
      basil
3   *tablespoons freshly grated*
      Parmesan cheese

1. Preheat oven to 400 degrees.

2. Trim off and discard the ends of the unpeeled zucchini. Cut the zucchini into ¼-inch slices. Toss the slices in the flour mixed with salt and pepper to taste.

3. Heat the oil and add the zucchini, tossing occasionally and taking care not to break up the slices. When golden brown, slide the zucchini onto an 8-inch pie plate. Sprinkle with garlic, basil and cheese and bake 5 minutes.

Yield: 4 small servings.

Clams, American-Style

One of the most bizarre questions to greet our ears—and it is asked on an astonishing number of occasions—is whether there is such a thing as traditional American cooking. The answer is, of course, a resounding yes. For the most part, and in its pure state, it is both regional and intraregional in character.

American cooking at its best can be superb, with such mouth-watering recollections as crab cakes in Baltimore; she-crab soup in Charleston; cioppino soup in California; the groaning board with the seven sweets and sours of the Pennsylvania Dutch; the fried chicken, Brunswick stews and gumbos of the south and, intraregionally, the Creole cooking of Louisiana, to name but a few morsels of American inventiveness where food is concerned.

A short while ago we set upon the mission of finding the recipes of a lady who years ago made those "scrumptious" baked clams at a small, family-style rooming and boarding house on Main Street in East Hampton. The name of the house shall go nameless in that it is at present under new management.

We sought out the former owner of that establishment and learned in short order that the place had been famous not only for its baked clams but for its clam chowder and clam fritters, three dishes that we reckon to be Americana, pure and simple.

We learned that the lady who produced these dishes when they enjoyed such esteem is Eleanor Hutflas, who agreed to demonstrate her techniques in cooking.

Mrs. Hutflas is what is known affectionately in these parts as a Bonacker. That is to say she was born within a stone's throw of a small body of water here called Accabonac Bay. She was actually born in the town of Amagansett, a few miles distant. Christened Eleanor Scott, she is a descendant of a family that has lived in these parts for four generations.

"My recipe for clam chowder," she noted, "was taught me by my grandmother when I was a child. It is basically the same as you'll find in this neighborhood, although I do use bay leaf and thyme for seasonings. My grandmother would never use spices. Some people may use green pepper and carrots and celery and things like that," and "that," she implied, was not quite traditional.

She concedes that she can't recall the genesis of her stuffed clams and that this dish, too, is the result of a few personal touches she has added over the years—chopped basil to give them delicacy of flavor and a bit of Parmesan to liven up the flavor.

Mrs. Hutflas makes the most delicious clam fritters we've ever had the good fortune to sample and serves them with a sauce that may or may not be a traditional accompaniment on the eastern end of Long Island.

Eleanor Hutflas prepares one of her specialties, stuffed clams Amagansett style

    Mrs. Hutflas told us that a few years ago, when her daughter was a student at Arizona State University, she oftentimes would dispatch these dishes in a frozen state to the Southwest. We offer three of these as a sampling of Americana.

East End Clam Chowder

2   *cups shucked clams plus 3 cups clam liquid*
¼   *pound not-so-lean salt pork*
7   *cups water*
½   *pound onions, peeled*

1   *pound potatoes, peeled*
1   *bay leaf*
1   *teaspoon dried thyme (more or less to taste)*
    Freshly ground pepper to taste
1   *pound fresh, red, ripe tomatoes or use 1 14-ounce can imported peeled plum tomatoes with tomato paste, crushed*
    Salt to taste (optional)

1. Open the clams or have them opened, reserving both clams and liquid.

2. Put the salt pork through a food grinder, using the medium blade. A food processor may be used for this and other ingredients in this recipe, although there is a tendency to chop the ingredients a bit too finely when the food processor is used.

3. Add the salt pork to a kettle and cook, stirring, until rendered of all fat and starting to brown. Add the water and clam juice.

4. Quarter the onions and put them through the same food grinder. Add them to the kettle. Quarter the potatoes and put them through the food grinder. Add them to the kettle. Add the bay leaf, thyme and pepper. Cook about 20 minutes and add the crushed tomatoes. Simmer 25 minutes. Wash the meat grinder and put the clams through it. Add the clams to the kettle. Simmer gently just until clams are piping hot. Do not boil or clams will toughen.

5. Taste the chowder and, if you desire, add a touch of salt.

Yield: About 9 cups.

Stuffed Clams Amagansett-Style

2 *cups shucked clams*
2 *tablespoons melted butter*
2 *tablespoons finely grated onion*
1 *small egg, beaten*
1½ *teaspoons chopped fresh basil or half the amount dried*

2 *tablespoons finely chopped parsley*
   Freshly ground pepper to taste
1 *tablespoon lemon juice*
6 *tablespoons clam juice*
2¼ *cups fine bread crumbs*
2 *tablespoons grated Parmesan cheese*
8 *to 10 squares of bacon Lemon quarters*

1. Preheat the oven to 400 degrees.

2. Grind or chop the clams and place them in a sieve to drain.

3. Add the clams to a mixing bowl and add the butter, onion, egg, basil, parsley, pepper, lemon juice, clam juice, 2 cups of bread crumbs and 1 tablespoon of cheese. Blend well.

4. Use the mixture to fill 8 or 10 well-cleaned cherrystone clam shells

(larger or smaller shells may also be used, if desired).

5. Blend the remaining bread crumbs and cheese and sprinkle liberally on the clams. Top each clam with a square of bacon. Arrange on a baking dish and bake 20 to 25 minutes or until the clams are piping hot throughout and the bacon is crisp. Serve with quartered lemons.

Yield: 4 or 5 servings.

Clam Fritters Bonacker-Style

1   cup chopped clams
1   egg, lightly beaten
1   teaspoon lemon juice
1   tablespoon finely chopped
     parsley
1   teaspoon baking soda
1   cup flour
¼   cup clam juice
¼   cup milk
4   teaspoons melted butter
     Pinch of cayenne pepper
     Freshly ground pepper to taste
     Oil for shallow frying
     Shrimp sauce (see recipe)

1. To prepare the clams, chop them on a flat surface or put them through a food grinder, using the medium blade. Add the clams to a mixing bowl.

2. Add the egg, lemon juice, parsley, baking soda and flour and stir.

3. Blend the clam juice and milk and add this gradually to the clam mixture, stirring constantly. Add only enough of the clam juice and milk to make a batter that is not too runny. Add the butter, cayenne and pepper.

4. Heat an eighth of an inch of oil in a skillet and drop the batter, about 2 tablespoons, into the oil. Continue

adding batches of batter without letting the sides touch. Turn the fritters as they brown on one side and continue cooking until cooked through. Continue cooking until all the batter is used. Serve hot with shrimp sauce.

Yield: 4 servings. The number of fritters will depend on the quantities added to the skillet.

Shrimp sauce

½   pound shrimp in the shell
2   tablespoons butter
2   tablespoons flour
¾   cup clam juice
¾   cup cream or evaporated milk
1   tablespoon dry sherry
1   bay leaf
⅛   teaspoon ground nutmeg
½   teaspoon or more packaged
     seafood seasoning, if
     available, or blend equal
     amounts—about ⅛ teaspoon
     each—celery salt, mace,
     ground cloves, mustard
     powder, paprika, ground
     ginger and ground cardamom
     and add to taste
     Salt and freshly ground
     pepper to taste

1. Cook the shrimp in the shell about 5 minutes in water to cover. Drain and let cool. Shell and devein the shrimp and cut them into small, bite-size pieces.

2. Melt the butter in a saucepan and add the flour, stirring with a wire whisk. Blend the clam juice and cream and add it to the saucepan, stirring rapidly with the whisk. When thickened and smooth, add the sherry, bay leaf, nutmeg and seafood seasoning. Add the salt and pepper to taste. Let simmer about 5 minutes. Serve hot.

Yield: About 1½ cups.

Viva the Zesty Mexican Way

Before she emplaned for Mexico a short while ago, Diana Kennedy, the English-born authority on Mexican cooking, scribbled a hasty postcard.

"Thought you might like to know that a couple of excellent cooks are coming to the Hamptons to cater Mexican dinners this summer. They are Kathleen Haven and Marie Zazzi."

Aficionados of Mexican cooking to the core, we telephoned the young women who told us they were in the middle of preparing several native foods and would we like to join them. We said we certainly would and a brief time later turned our car into the driveway to the side of a small, bright yellow-painted house on Montauk Highway. Out of the kitchen came a highly appetite-whetting assortment of smells, including that of corn tortillas on a griddle, the delicately mingled odors of onion, green peppers and garlic, simmering oil and freshly chopped coriander.

"Someone passed by and dropped off a striped bass they had just hauled out of the water, so we decided to add pescado zeracruzana to the menu," Miss Haven told us. The fish, bright in the eyes, as all fresh fish should be, and newly cleaned, lay on an aluminum baking dish. Miss Zazzi was in the business of pricking it with a fork, rubbing it with lime juice and stuffing the lime shells in the cavity.

"We let it marinate like that a few hours before baking," she explained.

Miss Haven was turning her attention to four or five dried ancho chilies heating up on a separate griddle. She turned them occasionally, giving them a feel now and then, a sort of massage to make sure they were becoming soft to the touch and did not burn. The chilies gave off a splendid aroma that smelled vaguely both of light tobacco leaf and sweet chocolate and Miss Haven described the odor as "exquisite."

"In addition to the fish," she explained as she transferred the chilies to a bowl and poured boiling water over them, "we're having puerco adobado, or boned loin of pork with ancho chilie sauce. The chilies will be seeded and blended to make the sauce." Both the young women, we learned, have been disciples of Diana Kennedy over the years. Miss Zazzi, in fact, has been the cookbook author's assistant during her years as a cooking instructor on Riverside Drive. Miss Haven, who has been collaborating on a Mexican cookbook, lived in Mexico City for several years and studied for several months with Mrs. Kennedy. We inquired into the logistics of "cooking Mexican" in East Hampton, and they told us it wasn't difficult after the first week.

When they first came they loaded the back seat and trunk with a few hundred pounds of staples, including black beans, dried chilies, canned chilies, canned Mexican tomatoes and masa harina, that ground corn mixture essential to tor-

Marie Zazzi buys kitchen utensils in many of the countries she visits

Kathleen Haven prepares Mexican dinners in her East Hampton home

tillas. They also brought along two tortilla presses—one Mexican, one Guatemalan—and, one of Miss Zazzi's prize possessions, a heavy deep alabaster mortar and pestle.

Miss Zazzi, who describes herself as a "gypsy" ("I can spend the rest of my life traveling around the world," she says) bought the tortilla press in Guatemala; the mortar and pestle were purchased from an old pharmacy at Second Avenue and 27th Street in Manhattan shortly before it went out of business.

"I paid $3 for it. I should have bought a dozen."

The couple have an interesting sauce for that other staple of Mexican cooking, fresh coriander leaves, known in Spanish as culantro or cilantro.

"Some husbands may come out here and bring their wives roses," Miss Haven stated. "My husband arrives on weekends with his arms full of cilantro. He is a never-ending supply."

Miss Haven, who has been professionally involved in graphic design for many years—for a time with the Museum of Modern Art—is married to Douglas Newton, the present director of the Museum of Primitive Art in Manhattan and soon to move with the collection to the new wing of the Metropolitan Museum.

Miss Zazzi, by the way, has had extensive professional training in various kitchens. She was for six months in the kitchen of the Waldorf Astoria and later a principal cook at the Pier 77 Restaurant on 77th Street and Amsterdam Avenue. Her late father was owner of Chez Cardinale, a well-known Italian restaurant in New York until it closed some years ago.

Pescado Veracruzano

(Fish Veracruz-style)

1   *4-pound fish such as striped
    bass, red snapper or weakfish
    with head left on but gills
    removed*
2   *limes*
    *Salt and freshly ground
    pepper to taste*
3   *tablespoons olive oil*
2   *cups thinly sliced onions*
3   *tablespoons finely chopped
    garlic*
4   *cups diced, peeled tomatoes*
3   *tablespoons drained capers*
20 *to 24 stuffed green olives*
2   *or more jalapeno peppers,
    drained, seeded and coarsely
    chopped*
1   *teaspoon chopped fresh
    oregano or half the amount
    dried*
1   *bay leaf
    Lime wedges for garnish
    Fresh coriander (cilantro)
    sprigs for garnish, optional*

1. Place the fish on a dish and prick the skin all over with a fork. Sprinkle all over with the juice of the limes. Stuff the cavity of the fish with the lime shells. Let stand 3 hours. Remove the lime shells.

2. Preheat the oven to 375 degrees.

3. Sprinkle the fish all over with salt and pepper and place it on a large baking dish. It may be necessary to cut off the head to make the fish fit the pan.

4. Heat the oil in a saucepan and add the onions and garlic. Cook until onions are wilted. Add the tomatoes, capers, olives, jalapeno peppers, oregano, bay leaf, salt and pepper to taste. Simmer about 10 minutes.

5. Pour the sauce over the fish and place in the oven. Bake, uncovered, about 30 minutes. Turn the fish carefully and continue baking 30 to 40 minutes longer or until the flesh flakes easily when tested with a fork. Serve garnished with lime wedges and coriander sprigs.

Yield: 8 or more servings.

Boned Loin of Pork en Adobo

1   *4-pound boned, tied loin of
    pork
    Salt and freshly ground
    pepper to taste*
4   *large, dried ancho chilies (see
    note)*
½   *teaspoon cumin seeds*
½   *teaspoon dried thyme*
1   *teaspoon coarsely chopped
    fresh oregano or half the
    amount dried*
10 *whole peppercorns*
2   *cloves garlic*

2   *tablespoons orange juice*
2   *tablespoons white vinegar,*
    preferably rice vinegar

1. Sprinkle the pork with salt and pepper and set aside.

2. Meanwhile, place the ancho chilies on a griddle and let roast, turning often, until the chilies start to expand. Take care that they are cooked evenly and do not burn. The chilies will give off a nice odor and soften when they are ready.

3. Place the chilies in a mixing bowl and add boiling water to cover. Let soak at least 20 minutes. Drain but save both the chilies and the soaking liquid.

4. Preheat the oven to 350 degrees.

5. Remove and discard the stems from the chilies. Split the chilies open and remove and discard the seeds. Add the chilies to the container of an electric blender.

6. Using a spice mill or small coffee grinder, grind together the cumin, thyme, dried oregano, if used, and peppercorns. Grind to a powder and add to the blender. If fresh oregano is used, add it to the blender. Add the garlic, orange juice, vinegar and salt. Blend, taking care not to overblend. The sauce should be a trifle pulpy and not too fine.

7. Spread out a length of heavy-duty aluminum foil large enough to enclose the pork. Add the pork loin and bring up the sides of the foil. Spoon the chili sauce over the top of the pork. Seal the foil and place in the oven. Bake about 1½ hours.

8. Open up the foil so that the pork will brown as it cooks. Continue cooking about 30 minutes or until a

meat thermometer inserted in the roast registers 180 degrees. Serve sliced.

Yield: 8 or more servings.

Note: Sources for ancho chilies are Casa Moneo, 210 West 14th Street, and Trinacria Importing Company, 415 Third Avenue (at 29th Street).

Tortillas with Pork en Adobo, Sour Cream and Salsa Verde

For each tortilla, spoon a little black beans into the center. Add a small slice of pork en adobo, a little salsa verde and sour cream. Fold up and eat.

Salsa Verde

(Mexican green sauce)

3   *tablespoons finely chopped onion*
2   *tablespoons fresh coriander (cilantro), available in Chinese and Spanish markets that specialize in fresh greens*
1   *or more serrano chilies, split and seeded*
    Salt to taste
1   *15-ounce can tomatoes verdes, available in grocery stores that specialize in Mexican foods*

1. Using a mortar and pestle or electric blender, grind together the onion, coriander, chilies and salt to taste.

2. Add the drained tomatoes verdes and blend to a sauce consistency.

Yield: About 2 cups.

Albondigas

(Meatballs)

1   pound ground beef or pork
¼   cup finely chopped onion
2   tablespoons chopped fresh
      coriander (cilantro), available
      in Chinese and Spanish
      markets that specialize in fresh
      greens
¼   cup finely diced, well-drained
      tomato
¼   cup finely crumbled English
      muffin
      Salt and freshly ground
      pepper to taste
1   small raw egg or half a large
      egg, beaten
      Oil for frying or soup for
      poaching the meatballs

1. Combine the meat, onion, coriander, tomato, English muffin, salt, pepper and egg in a mixing bowl. Blend well with the hands.

2. Shape the mixture into about 24 meatballs of approximately the same size.

3. Cook the meatballs in a skillet with a little oil until they are golden brown all over and cooked through, or cook them—raw—as indicated in the Mexican soup with albondigas and zucchini. If the meatballs are fried, serve with a tomato sauce or green sauce (see recipe).

Yield: 2 dozen meatballs.

Mexican Soup with Albondigas and Zucchini

3   tablespoons corn oil or solid
      white vegetable shortening
½   onion, finely chopped, about
      ½ cup
2   cloves garlic, finely minced
2   cups cubed, peeled, fresh
      tomatoes
3   sprigs fresh coriander
      (cilantro), available in Chinese
      and Spanish markets that
      specialize in fresh greens
      Salt and freshly ground
      pepper to taste
8   cups rich chicken broth
2   small zucchini
24   uncooked meatballs (see
      recipe), optional
1   small serrano chili, left whole
      (available in tins in Spanish
      and Mexican stores and many
      supermarkets)

1. Heat the oil in a kettle and add the onion and garlic. Cook until the onion is wilted. Add the tomatoes, coriander, salt and pepper. Cook, stirring, about 5 minutes.

2. Add the broth and continue to simmer about 10 minutes.

3. Meanwhile, trim off and discard the ends of the zucchini. Cut the zucchini into 1½-inch lengths. Cut the lengths into quarters or eighths, depending on size. Drop the pieces into the soup and simmer about 10 minutes. Add the meatballs, if they are to be used, and continue cooking 10 to 15 minutes or until the meat is cooked through. Add the chili and serve piping hot.

Yield: 8 or more servings.

Picacillo

(Spiced ground meat)

2 tablespoons lard, solid
   vegetable shortening or oil
1½ pounds ground beef or pork
¾ cup finely chopped green
   onion
¾ cup finely chopped green
   pepper
3 tablespoons raisins
3 tablespoons capers
24 stuffed green olives, sliced
4 cups cubed, cored, peeled,
   red, ripe tomatoes or an equal
   amount drained canned
   tomatoes
4 whole cloves
15 peppercorns
1 1-inch piece stick cinnamon,
   broken, or use ½ teaspoon
   dried cinnamon
¼ teaspoon ground allspice
4 cloves garlic, finely minced
1 tablespoon white vinegar,
   preferably rice vinegar

1. Heat half the shortening in a skillet and add the ground meat. Cook, stirring to break up any lumps that may form, until meat loses its red color.

2. Separately, heat the remaining shortening and add the chopped onion, green pepper and cook, stirring, until wilted. Add the raisins, capers and olives and cook briefly. Add this to the ground meat. Add the tomatoes and continue cooking about 10 minutes.

3. Meanwhile, combine the cloves, peppercorns and cinnamon stick in the container of a spice mill or small coffee grinder and blend to a powder. Or combine the ingredients in a mortar. Add the allspice, garlic and vinegar and pound to a paste with a pestle. Or blend all these ingredients. Scrape the mixture into the ground meat mixture and stir. Cook 10 minutes. Serve as a filling for tortillas or simply as a meat course with rice. It has many uses in Mexican cooking including as a stuffing for baked cheese.

Yield: 6 or more servings.

Frijoles de Olla

(Black beans in a pot)

1 pound black turtle beans,
   available in stores that
   specialize in Mexican, Spanish
   and Cuban foods
⅛ pound lean salt pork, cut into
   1-inch cubes
½ onion, coarsely chopped
10 cups water
   Salt to taste

1. Wash the beans and drain them. Put them in a kettle with the pork, onion and water. Do not add salt. Bring to the boil and simmer 1 hour.

2. Add salt to taste and continue cooking about 2 hours longer.

Yield: About 8 servings.

Note: These beans are best if they are allowed to simmer a while the second day.

August 1976

I T WOULD BE possible, of course, to examine the writing of any critic and, after a certain period of time, to discover trends and tastes, or, to put it another way, predilections. I know full well that such an examination would come up with at least one predilection of mine in this month of August. This is for what is to me the most refreshing dessert ever created—the granités one finds in Europe. I specify Europe because they are so rarely found on menus in America. Granités are pure fruit ices and the trouble is, I suspect, these are confused with sherbets in the public mind. A sherbet is made with two pure additives—eggwhites in the form of meringue or gelatin—which give them a smoother quality. While I am by no means opposed to sherbets, and enjoy them on numerous occasions, they seem to lack that astringent ice cold purity of the granité. If I had to name my ultimate dessert in this category, it would most assuredly be a granité of pamplemousse, otherwise known as grapefruit ice.

Seafood Italiano

WITH PIERRE FRANEY

There is rarely an Italian restaurant in Manhattan, or throughout the country for that matter, that does not list stuffed clams as a specialty among appetizers. Most of them are outrageously banal, chewy and clumsily seasoned, the predominant flavor being that of oregano. The best stuffed clams, Italian-style, we've ever dined on anywhere are those of Luigi Nanni, friend and chef-owner of Nanni's Restaurant at 146 East 46th Street and Il Valetto at 133 East 61st Street in Manhattan. We recently spent some time cooking with Nanni in a kitchen in a private home in Nova Scotia. He made those clams and several other fish and seafood related specialties, which we dutifully recorded.

Nanni's Stuffed Clams

36 *to 48 littleneck clams*
6 *shallots, peeled*
4 *cloves garlic, finely minced*
½ *cup loosely packed fresh basil*
½ *cup loosely packed fresh parsley leaves*
1 *small tomato, about ⅓ pound, cored and quartered*
4 *fresh mushrooms sliced*
¾ *cup freshly grated Parmesan cheese*
½ *cup fresh bread crumbs*
2 *slices lean bacon, cut into pieces*
 Salt and freshly ground pepper
½ *teaspoon red pepper flakes, more or less to taste, optional*
1 *tablespoon finely chopped chives, optional*
¼ *cup olive oil*
½ *cup dry white wine*

1. Preheat oven to 400 degrees.

2. Open the clams or have them opened, discarding the top shell and loosening the clam on the bottom half shell.

3. Combine the shallots, garlic, basil, parsley, tomato, mushrooms, half a cup of grated cheese, bread crumbs, bacon, salt and pepper to taste. Do not add much salt because the clams are salty. Grind the ingredients or blend them coarsely in a food processor. Grind or blend to a medium fine puree. Fold in the red pepper flakes, if used, and chives.

4. Spoon the mixture over the clams and smooth it over. Arrange the clams on a baking dish and sprinkle with the remaining cheese. Sprinkle with the oil and wine. Bake 20 minutes or until golden brown and piping hot. Run briefly under the broiler for a deeper glaze.

Yield: 36 to 48 clams.

Fish Soup with Pasta

7½ pounds fish heads, gills
    removed
6   quarts water
¾   cup olive oil
6   cloves garlic, finely chopped
1½ cups coarsely chopped onion
1½ cups chopped celery
¾   cup chopped carrots
2   bay leaves
1   cup potatoes, peeled and cut
    into ½-inch cubes
¾   cup chopped parsley
4   cups shredded Swiss chard or
    lettuce
3½ cups imported Italian canned
    tomatoes or an equal amount
    of red, ripe fresh tomatoes
¾   pound broken perciatelli,
    linguine or lingue di passeri
1   cup grated Parmesan cheese

1. Wash the fish heads well under cold running water. Place in a kettle and add the water. Bring to the boil and simmer 45 minutes. Strain and press the solids with the back of a heavy spoon to extract as much juice as possible. Discard the solids.

2. Heat the oil in a skillet and add the garlic and onion and brown lightly. Add the celery, carrots and bay leaves. Cook 10 minutes. Add this mixture to the fish broth and bring to the boil.

3. Add the potatoes, parsley, Swiss chard and tomatoes and simmer 45 minutes to 1 hour.

4. Add the broken up pasta and simmer just until the pasta is tender, about 10 minutes. Stir in the cheese and serve.

Yield: 16 to 20 servings.

Clam Soup

4   quarts soft shell clams
    Salt
½   cup olive oil
6   shallots, peeled and thinly
    sliced
4   cloves garlic, thinly sliced
3   dried hot red peppers, crushed
10 sprigs fresh basil
1   cup dry white wine
2¼ cups crushed canned imported
    Italian tomatoes
1   cup water
½   cup coarsely chopped parsley
1   teaspoon dried oregano
    Freshly ground pepper

1. Soak the soft shell clams for several hours in several changes of cold, salted water. Wash thoroughly.

2. Heat the oil in a kettle and add the shallots and garlic. Cook about 30 seconds, stirring, and add the clams and crushed red peppers. Add the basil, wine and cover. Cook 5 minutes and add the tomatoes, water, parsley and oregano. Stir. Add salt and pepper to taste and cook 20 minutes.

Yield: 8 servings.

Calamari alla Nanni

(Squid in wine sauce)

⅔ cup olive oil
6 cloves garlic, finely chopped
⅓ cup finely chopped scallions
4 bay leaves
1 2-ounce can flat anchovies
6½ pounds fresh squid,
thoroughly cleaned and cut
into 1-inch rounds
½ cup chopped fresh parsley
½ cup chopped fresh basil
¾ cup dry white wine
½ teaspoon oregano
1 pound peeled, cored, crushed
fresh tomatoes, about 1½
cups, or use canned imported
tomatoes
Salt and freshly ground
pepper
1 tablespoon Pernod or other
anise-flavored liqueur,
optional

1. Heat the oil in a large kettle and add the garlic, scallions and bay leaves. Add the anchovies along with the oil in which they are packed. Simmer about 5 minutes and add the remaining ingredients except the liqueur. Cover and let simmer 1 hour.

2. Stir in the Pernod, if used, and serve hot with rice.

Yield: 12 or more servings.

Anguilla Scarpione

(Fried eels with oil and vinegar)

12 fresh, skinned eels, each
weighing about ¾ pound
Salt and freshly ground
pepper
Flour for dredging
1 cup olive oil
4 cups thinly sliced onion
6 bay leaves
⅓ cup white wine vinegar
⅔ cup dry white wine

1. Cut off and discard the heads and small tail ends of the eels. Cut the eels into 2-inch pieces. Sprinkle the pieces with salt and pepper to taste and dredge lightly in flour. Shake off excess.

2. Heat the oil in a skillet and brown the eels on all sides, a few pieces at a time. Drain the pieces as they cook. Transfer them to a platter.

3. Pour off the oil but do not wipe out the skillet. Add the onions and cook, stirring, until wilted. Add the bay leaves, salt and pepper to taste, vinegar and wine. Cook 5 minutes and pour this over the eels.

Yield: 12 servings.

Getting on the Grits Bandwagon

Grits, the cereal that has crept—swept is more like it—into the public consciousness within recent weeks, are no joke, despite that unfortunate name, which lends itself to humor. The name, incidentally, is not the lackluster invention of a dimwitted backwoodsman. It stems, rather, according to scholarly sources, from a Middle English word gryt meaning bran and from the Old English grytt. Ditto groats.

Although grits are thought of mostly as a deep-South breakfast specialty, they are sold in supermarkets nationwide: even in chic outposts like the Hamptons where it costs 61 cents for the two-and-one-half-pound box. Heaven knows, one box of grits goes a long way. The cooking directions on the box sitting just aft of this typewriter state that one serving can be made by cooking three tablespoons of the fine white grain in one cup of water.

A liking for any food may be highly subjective. We know people who can't abide caviar. We like both caviar and grits and can speculate that the two together would be quite compatible in the same way that fresh caviar and a hot buttered baked potato is a marriage made in heaven.

Grits are, after all, like snails, noodles and potatoes, a somewhat neutral food whose character depends on what you serve with them or on them. A pat of butter is the most elementary and universal addition to hot grits. One of the glories of this world—to a southern palate that is—is a slice of fried, country-cured ham served with grits and red-eye gravy. Red-eye gravy, for the enlightenment of those unaccustomed to the nobler things in life, is what results when you fry that slice of country ham and remove it from the skillet. To the skillet you add a touch of black coffee and swirl and scrape it around to incorporate and make liquid all the brown particles that cling to the bottom and sides of the pan. Water will do, but coffee gives more character.

Other foods notably suited to grits are sautéed chicken livers or calves liver; braised wild birds and other game; and a Louisiana specialty known as grillades, a savory, braised meat dish.

One of the most championed of all grits dishes in the deep South is one that became a regional rage two or three decades ago. This is freshly cooked grits combined with a commercially made six-ounce roll of garlic cheese, a soft, yellow processed cheese with garlic flavor. We discovered yesterday it is not sold in chic outposts like the Hamptons but grated cheddar plus a touch of garlic is an admirable substitute. Cheese and grits, incidentally, have a remarkable affinity for one another.

Last evening we had a dear friend for dinner, a lady from Memphis, Tennessee, who has excellent taste in most things but with a lapse in one area. She announced over cocktails she didn't like grits. Fine thing. We were on the verge of serving a grits-and-cheese soufflé conjured up by our French-born colleague, Pierre Franey. Also at table was a lady of unfaltering palate from Paris, who had never heard of, much less eaten, "greets." Well, to put it in a word, when the soufflé was served, the lady from Memphis flipped. The lady from Paris fleeped.

Grits are, to put it as briefly and mercifully as possible, made from white or yellow corn kernels. Dried corn with 14 percent moisture, for some reason or other, brings the best price. We know, because a producer of an excellent product, Honey Suckle Quick Cooking Grits from Memphis, told us when we contacted him by telephone. He told us that the dried kernels are shelled in the field and sent to a milling company. The kernels are put through a cleaning process and are ground through mill rolls six times. The heart of the corn is taken out and the hull of the kernels are removed. What's left is ground into corn meal or grits. Grains of grits are larger than grains of corn meal.

The largest producer of grits in this country and the brand most commonly found in America is Quaker Oats. That's the brand we grew up on as a child. The person we spoke to at Quaker told us that 140,000,000 pounds of grits are sold each year in America. That's a silo-full.

Here is an assortment of grits recipes culled—with the execption of Pierre Franey's grits and cheese soufflé—from various southern cookbooks. The recipe for baked grits is taken from the *Jackson Cookbook*, compiled by the Symphony League of Jackson, Mississippi. We make special reference to this work because it contains one recipe title we treasure most. The book has a foreword by the much-admired Mississippi author, Eudora Welty. In tribute to her, the first recipe in the book is for Squash Eudora. All we can say is, don't you dare!

Pierre Franey's Grits and Cheese Soufflé

1   cup quick-cooking or regular
    grits
2   cups milk
2   cups water
    Salt and freshly ground
    pepper to taste
¼   teaspoon grated nutmeg
½   teaspoon Tabasco sauce or
    according to taste
⅓   pound grated sharp cheddar
    cheese, about 1¾ cups
6   large eggs, separated

1. Generously butter a 2-quart soufflé dish and place it in the freezer until ready to use.

2. Cook the grits in the milk and water according to package directions. Add salt to taste.

3. As the grits cook preheat the oven to 425 degrees.

4. When the grits are cooked, scrape them into a mixing bowl. Add pepper, nutmeg and Tabasco. Stir in all but ½ cup of grated cheese.

5. Let cool slightly and add the egg yolks, stirring until well blended. Beat the whites until stiff. Add half of them to the grits mixture and beat them in. Add the remaining whites and fold them in, using a rubber spatula.

6. Spoon the mixture into the prepared soufflé dish and smooth over the top. Sprinkle the top with the remaining cheese. Place in the oven and bake 25 minutes or to the desired degree of doneness.

Yield: 6 servings.

Baked Garlic Cheese Grits

(Adapted from *Cane River Cuisine,* published by the Service League of Natchitoches, Louisiana)

1   cup raw quick-cooking grits
1   6-ounce roll garlic cheese (see
    note)
8   tablespoons (1 stick) butter
½   cup chopped green onions,
    green part and all, optional
2   eggs, lightly beaten
¾   cup milk

1. Cook the grits according to package directions. Stir in the cheese, butter and green onions. Pour the mixture into a buttered 2-quart casserole. Let cool.

2. Preheat the oven to 375 degrees.

3. Blend the eggs and milk and pour over the grits. Bake about 1 hour.

Yield: 4 to 6 servings.

Note: If garlic cheese is not available, use 1½ cups grated cheddar cheese and 1 teaspoon finely chopped garlic.

Fried Grits

(Adapted from the *Christ Church Cook Book,* published by the women of the Christ Episcopal Church of Savannah, Georgia)

2   cups water
2   cups plus 2 tablespoons milk
    Salt to taste
1   cup regular or quick-cooking
    grits

3   *eggs*
1   *cup fine, fresh bread crumbs*
2   *tablespoons or more butter*

1. Combine the water and two cups of milk with salt in a saucepan and gradually add the grits, stirring often. Cook until done according to package directions for the grits.

2. Remove from the heat and beat in 2 eggs, lightly beaten. Pour the mixture into an 8-inch square pan. Chill until firm.

3. Cut the mixture into 1½-inch squares.

4. Beat the remaining egg and dip each square into the egg. Coat with the bread crumbs.

5. Heat the butter in a skillet and cook the grits squares until golden brown on both sides, turning once.

Yield: 8 servings.

Baked Grits

(Adapted from the *Jackson Cookbook,* compiled by the Symphony League of Jackson, Mississippi)

1   *cup regular grits*
½   *pound grated sharp cheese*
8   *tablespoons butter*
3   *eggs, well beaten*
⅓   *cup plus 1 tablespoon milk*

1. Preheat the oven to 350 degrees.

2. Cook the grits according to package directions.

3. Stir in the cheese, butter, eggs and milk and pour into a buttered baking dish. Bake 40 minutes or longer or until set.

Yield: 6 to 8 servings.

Cheddar Cheese Grits

(Adapted from *Cane River Cuisine,* published by the Service League of Natchitoches, Louisiana)

1   *cup uncooked regular grits*
5   *cups boiling water*
     Salt to taste
1½   *cups grated sharp cheddar cheese*
8   *tablespoons butter*
4   *eggs, lightly beaten*
     Freshly ground pepper to taste
1   *teaspoon Worcestershire sauce*

1. Add the grits gradually to the boiling water with salt to taste. Cook, stirring often, about 25 to 30 minutes.

2. Meanwhile, preheat the oven to 350 degrees.

3. When cooked, remove the grits from the heat and add the cheese and butter. Add the eggs and blend well. Add salt and pepper to taste and the Worcestershire sauce. Pour this mixture into a 2-quart baking dish and bake 1 hour.

Yield: 6 to 8 servings.

As a child of the South (and one who has not infrequently been described as having corn-meal mush in his mouth) we felt notably secure in stating that grits, that celebrated Southern cereal, constituted a plural noun. We staunchly defend this opinion, but we do feel moved to give the opposition a moment of self-defense. We heard from a fellow-Mississippian, who shall go nameless, as follows:

"I wonder whether you have quietly fallen victim of a Yankee malaise, one which causes even editors of dictionaries, alas, to refer to grits as a plural noun. Never mind what these Yankee dictionaries say, come back home where grits is IT, not them. Do Yankees refer to those oatmeal? Does one eat one grit or many? Isn't it supposed, at least by tradition, to be a singularly singular noun? Please say it's so.

"I remember, growing up on the Mississippi Gulf Coast, laughing with smirking pleasure over Yankee references to grits as 'them' and 'those.' I do not recall whether any of them referred to the finer-ground cousin of grits, corn meal, as 'them' or 'those' corn meal, but maybe I was not listening.

"Until I hear better, I am going to assume that you remain well, and the dictionary usage for grits was insinuated (or were insinuated) into your otherwise impeccable article by some scurrilous (Yankee) copy editor.

"P.S.: Now, repeat after me: 'I like grits. It is good. I eat it (not them) whenever possible.' "

Fruit Ices and Ice Creams

WITH PIERRE FRANEY

One of our earliest associations of food and rhyme consists of four lines of nonsense, "I scream, you scream, we all scream for ice cream." Where ice cream is concerned, we find such a tribute richly deserved. But if we go wild for ice cream, we go absolutely bananas for any pure fruit ice, the kind known in French as a granité and in Italian as a granita. Our tribute to these frozen desserts for summer is a sampling of same.

Granité de Fraises

(Strawberry ice)

2   cups water
2½   cups sugar
4   pints strawberries
¼   cup lemon juice

1. Combine the water and sugar in a saucepan and bring to the boil. Simmer 5 minutes. Remove from the heat. Pour the syrup into a bowl and let cool. Chill.

2. Meanwhile, pick over the strawberries. Remove and discard the stems. Put the strawberries into the container of a food processor or electric blender and puree. There should be about 6 cups. Add the syrup and lemon juice.

3. Pour the mixture into the canister of a hand-cranked or electric ice cream machine and freeze according to the manufacturer's instructions.

Yield: About 2 quarts.

Granita di Caffe con Panna

(Coffee ice with whipped cream)

3½   cups very strong espresso
     coffee (see note)
2   tablespoons freeze-dried or
     instant espresso
2½   cups sugar
2   cups water
1   cup heavy cream
     Kahlua and/or sweetened
     whipped cream, optional

1. Prepare the coffee and stir in the freeze-dried or instant coffee.

2. Combine the sugar and water in a saucepan and bring to the boil. Cook 5 minutes. Cool and add to the coffee mixture. Chill.

3. Add the cup of cream. Pour the mixture into the container of a hand-cranked or electric ice cream machine and freeze according to the manufacturer's instructions. Serve in individual portions with a little Kahlua and/or whipped cream on top.

Yield: 12 or more servings.

Note: To make relatively strong espresso coffee, brew 1 cup of ground espresso or dark roast coffee with 4 cups of water. Or increase the coffee to 1½ cups for very strong coffee.

Granité de Pamplemousse

(Grapefruit ice)

2 *cups water*
2 *cups sugar*
4 *cups fresh grapefruit juice*
   Grated rind of 1 grapefruit
½ *cup lemon juice*

1. Combine the water and sugar in a saucepan and bring to the boil. Simmer 5 minutes. Remove from the heat. Pour the syrup into a bowl and let cool. Chill.

2. Add the grapefruit juice and rind and stir to blend. Add the lemon juice.

3. Pour the mixture into the canister of a hand-cranked or electric ice cream machine and freeze according to the manufacturer's instructions.

Yield: About 7 cups.

Uta Hagen's Love for Cooking

Murmurs of approval at the end of a meal or the sound of clapping hands across footlights, it all adds up to the same thing: "the sound that says love," to borrow a phrase from a Broadway musical of a few years back.

"Applause," Uta Hagen, the actress, was saying, "that's why I cook. If there's no one there to say, 'thank you very much, that was delicious,' I stand up and eat from the refrigerator."

For years, we have known of Uta Hagen's reputation as an excellent and enthusiastic cook. Thus, when we learned that she was a neighbor and had completed the manuscript for a highly personal cookbook, we telephoned for an interview. We were received around noon on the terrace of the actress's ocean-view home here, the sun sweeping brilliantly across the far horizon. She offered us a preprandial drink, a small and insidiously good glass of pale yellow, homemade lemon vodka poured from a frosty bottle taken directly from the freezer.

"A lot of the recipes in my book," she told us, "are those I've made up myself or borrowed from friends. This is indexed as Jennifer's vodka supreme. I got the formula from Jennifer Scanlon, a member of the Jose Limon dance company.

"Some of my recipes are from my childhood in Germany. My mother was a professional singer—she sang lieder and opera—and a marvelous cook. Unfortunately I didn't cook as a child, and I've simply had to recreate the dishes I liked best from memory."

For this particular occasion Miss Hagen had prepared a midsummer luncheon composed of three irresistible cocktail appetizers—cheese puffs, olive puffs and smoked beef roulades—a cold chicken in aspic dish, new peas and new potatoes harvested that morning from her garden.

A catalogue of the various items in that garden, which she tends herself, is enough to send a lizardlike nongardener into a state of terminal exhaustion. There over the railing in immaculately tended beds is a summer-full of trailing cucumbers, red tomatoes, yellow and green zucchini, green beans, carrots, lettuce and Brussels sprouts. The indefatigable, endlessly resourceful lady also boasts herbal plots of basil, rosemary, tarragon, thyme, arugula, dill and assorted mints. Not to mention proliferating stands of gladioli, roses, daisies, dahlias and "anything that will grow by the sea." When she has nothing else to do, she mows the lawn and does needlepoint.

The dessert for that lunch, incidentally, would be a splendid fruit tart, a crisp

For Uta Hagen, cooking makes her feel like a star

crust filled with rings of fresh blueberries and fresh blackberries and topped with toasted almonds.

"I got up and picked those blackberries," she told us, "at six this morning while the dew was on the vines." We looked around for an almond tree and, seeing none, decided they must have come out of a can.

We have always been curious as to how actors and actresses can eat on stage and deliver their lines with their mouths full. We asked Uta Hagen how she managed such a feat, and she recalled two plays in particular in which food was a vital part of the action.

"One of them was *Farewell Supper* by Arthur Schnitzler, adapted from *The Affairs of Anatole*. The heroine was about to leave her lover who had considerable wealth and in saying goodbye she consoled herself by gorging on a whipped cream torte. We faked it by using yogurt for the cream, but eating it was no small feat, particularly on matinee days when one performance followed another.

"The second was a play called *In Any Language*. I played a Betty Grable type on an art junket to Italy. To assuage her anxieties I had to eat an *entire* loaf of bread, dunked morsel by morsel in red wine, and half a provolone cheese, and there was no way to fake either one. The worst of this, of course, was matinee day, and to this day I can't swallow provolone."

Miss Hagen created the role of Martha in *Who's Afraid of Virginia Woolf?* and this involved a very minor alimentary matter. The character spends the evening drinking, and in this case she resorted to water.

We mentioned the pleasure we had found in watching her performance in *Saint Joan* by George Bernard Shaw and stated that we couldn't recall if she had eaten food in that play or not.

"No, but my daughter, who was very young at the time, thought carefully when someone told her I had agreed to the role."

"Ummmm," she said with a serious look on her face and with a tone that smacked of relish, "Mummy's gonna burn good." Her daughter is a child by Miss Hagen's first marriage to José Ferrer.

Miss Hagen is now married to Herbert Berghof, the Broadway director, and together they direct the H. B. acting studios on West Bank Street in the Village. The studio has an enrollment of approximately 1,800 students, and Miss Hagen teaches acting three days a week.

"Some years ago I went on a pasta-making binge—someone had just given me a new machine for making it, and I cooked up a batch for one of my classes at the studio. I baked the dish in the oven and when it was piping hot I started to remove it. Somehow I got a nasty burn on my fingers, so I threw the hot casserole up in the air with the strands of spaghetti falling on my head. A moment before I had opened the oven door I had said to the students, 'Get a load of this,' and to this day some of them think it was an exaggerated and ludicrous exercise in dramatics."

Miss Hagen has appeared in scores of theatricals to critical acclaim since her debut in 1936 and has written a book on the profession titled *Respect for Acting*. The title is in a sense related to her new book, which is titled *Uta Hagen's Love for Cooking*. It will be published by Macmillan in mid-October.

We feasted well on Miss Hagen's terrace and as we said our goodbyes she handed us a small paper tote bag. In it was a lavish assortment of relishes and chutneys made with green tomatoes, zucchini, pickle pears and regular pears. Just a few little things she'd put up for the love of it when she had nothing else to do.

Here is an assortment of recipes from that summer afternoon.

Olive Puffs

⅔ cup sifted flour
¼ cup butter at room
    temperature
1 cup grated sharp cheddar
    cheese
Salt to taste
1 teaspoon paprika
¼ teaspoon dry mustard
30 or more stuffed Spanish olives

1. Combine all the ingredients except the olives in a mixing bowl. Knead briefly until well blended and smooth.

2. Pinch off pieces of the dough and flatten with the hand to make small circles, each large enough to wrap around an olive. Place one olive in a circle of dough, bring up the edges and roll between the palms of the hands to form balls with the olives inside. Arrange the balls on a baking sheet and place in the freezer. Transfer the balls to plastic bags and freeze until ready to use.

3. To cook preheat the oven to 400 degrees and bake on an ungreased baking sheet about 15 minutes or until golden brown.

Yield: About 30 olive puffs.

Cheese Puffs

1	*1-pound loaf of unsliced bread*
8	*tablespoons butter*
¼	*cup finely diced mozzarella cheese*
¼	*cup grated sharp cheddar cheese*
¼	*cup grated Swiss cheese*
1	*3-ounce package cream cheese*
½	*teaspoon dry mustard*
⅛	*teaspoon cayenne pepper Salt to taste*
2	*egg whites*

1. Trim off and discard the crusts from the top, bottom and sides of the loaf. Cut the bread into 1-inch cubes and set aside.

2. In a saucepan, combine the butter, all the cheeses and stir over moderate heat until blended. Add the mustard, cayenne and salt.

3. Beat the egg whites until stiff and fold them into the cheese mixture. Using a two-tined fork or fondue fork, spear the bread cubes one at a time and dip them into the mixture until well coated. Arrange the cubes side by side but not touching on a baking sheet. Freeze immediately until firm. Remove the cubes from the baking sheet and store in plastic bags in the freezer until ready to use.

4. To cook, preheat the oven to 400 degrees and bake on an ungreased baking sheet for about 10 minutes or until nicely browned. Serve 4 to 6 for each guest.

Yield: About 12 servings.

Smoked Beef Roulades

1	*3-ounce package thinly sliced smoked beef, available in supermarkets*
4½	*ounces cream cheese (the contents of 1½ packages)*
¼	*teaspoon lemon juice*
5	*small sweet pickles (gherkins)*

1. Use 12 slices of the smoked beef and reserve the other slices for another use. Prepare 3 rows of smoked beef, using 4 slices to each row. Arrange the slices with the ends slightly overlapping.

2. Combine the cream cheese and lemon juice in a bowl and place the bowl in a warm place or in an oven preheated to 200 degrees. Let stand about 10 minutes until the cheese softens and can be spread easily.

3. Spread the cheese over the beef.

4. Cut the pickles into ⅛-inch, lengthwise strips. Arrange the strips horizontally and evenly at intervals, starting from the top to the bottom of the cheese. Roll the meat into a sausage-shape about 1 inch thick. Roll the sausage in foil and refrigerate at least 2 hours. To serve, cut the rolls into 1½-inch lengths.

Yield: 10 to 12 pieces.

Note: These rolls freeze well and should be defrosted before cutting into pieces.

Midsummer Tart with Fruits and Berries

1   baked 9-inch pastry crust
1   quart fresh berries such as strawberries, blueberries, blackberries, raspberries and so on, including a combination of berries, if desired
1   cup fruit jelly such as crab apple, currant, beach plum or apple
2   tablespoons liqueur such as Grand Marnier, kirsch or framboise
¼   cup toasted almonds
    Whipped cream

1. Place the tart on a serving dish and fill with the berries. Place the largest and best berries in the center with the other berries piled around.

2. Heat the jelly over low heat and stir in the liqueur. Let cool slightly and spoon this over the fruit. Garnish with toasted almonds, sprinkling them in a ring around the berries. Chill at least 1 hour before serving. Serve with whipped cream on the side.

Yield: 6 to 10 servings.

Jennifer Scanlon's Lemon Vodka

1   bottle imported Russian, Finnish or Polish vodka
3   lemons
1   to 2 teaspoons sugar
¼   teaspoon salt
5   drops glycerine, available at drug stores

1. Pour out and reserve for another occasion ¼ cup of the vodka.

2. With a paring knife or swivel-bladed vegetable peeler, remove large pieces of yellow rind from the lemons. Stuff the pieces into the bottle. Add the remaining ingredients. Seal and refrigerate 1 week. Before serving place the bottle in the freezer for at least 3 hours. Serve in chilled liqueur glasses.

Yield: 1 bottle of lemon vodka.

The Time of the Lobster

WITH PIERRE FRANEY

In 1885, the *Lewiston* (Maine) *Journal* noted that fishermen were getting splendid prices for their lobster—ten cents a lobster—the public was paying ten to twelve cents a pound, and people were still complaining about high prices. Right now, lobsters are as plentiful and as inexpensive ($4 a pound) as they are likely to be for the rest of this year. Hence a pair of lobster dishes—lobster in cognac and cream sauce and lobster with tomatoes and tarragon.

Homard Chavontaise

(Lobster in cognac and cream sauce)

4   *live lobsters, about 1¼ pounds each*
¼   *cup olive oil*
3   *tablespoons finely chopped shallots or green onions*
3   *tablespoons finely chopped onion*
1   *teaspoon finely minced garlic*
2   *tablespoons cognac*
1½ *cups chopped fresh or canned tomatoes*
½   *teaspoon dried thyme*
1   *cup dry white wine*
1   *tablespoon chopped parsley Salt and freshly ground pepper*
1   *cup heavy cream*

1. Plunge a knife into each lobster where the body and tail section meet to sever the spinal cord. This will kill the lobster instantly. Break off the tail and set aside in a large bowl. Break off the large claws and add to the large bowl. Cut off the small feeler claws and add to the bowl. Pull out and discard the interior of the chest portion of the lobster.

2. Heat the oil in a deep, heavy skillet large enough to accommodate the lobsters. When the oil starts to smoke, add the lobster pieces. Cook, stirring, about 5 minutes and add the shallots, onion and garlic. Sprinkle with cognac. Add the tomatoes, thyme, wine, parsley, salt and pepper to taste and cook, stirring, over high heat about 1 minute. Cover and cook 15 minutes.

3. Remove the tail and claws from the skillet and let them cool briefly.

4. Continue cooking the remainder of the ingredients and add the cream. Cook, uncovered, over high heat about 10 minutes to reduce the sauce.

5. Meanwhile, when the tail and claws are cool enough to handle, break or crack the tail and claws and remove the meat. Add the meat to the sauce along with any accumulated juices. Serve the lobster in sauce, carcass and all, with fluffy rice or buttered noodles.

Yield: 6 to 8 servings.

Lobster with Tomatoes and Tarragon

(For spaghetti)

3   *live lobsters, about 1¼ pounds
     each*
4   *tablespoons butter
     Salt and freshly ground
     pepper*
¼   *cup olive oil*
⅓   *cup finely diced onion*
3   *tablespoons finely minced
     shallots*
½   *teaspoon chopped garlic*
⅓   *cup finely diced celery*
¼   *cup finely diced carrots*
1   *tablespoon finely chopped
     fresh tarragon or 2 teaspoons
     dried*
2   *tablespoons tomato paste*
¼   *cup cognac*
1⅓ *cups finely diced or chopped
     fresh or canned tomatoes*
1   *cup dry white wine*

1. Plunge a knife into each lobster where the body and tail section meet to sever the spinal cord. This will kill the lobster instantly. Save all juices that flow from the bodies. Break off the tails and cut each tail crosswise into 3 pieces. Crack the claws. Discard the tough sac near the eyes. Split the carcass in half widthwise. Remove the lobster liver and coral and place in a bowl. Add 2 tablespoons butter and set aside.

2. Sprinkle the lobster with salt and pepper to taste.

3. Heat the oil in a large, heavy skillet or casserole and add the lobster. Cook, stirring, about 2 minutes or until shell starts to turn red. Add the onion, shallots, garlic, celery, carrots, half the tarragon and tomato paste. Stir to blend and cover. Cook about 3 minutes. Flame with the cognac.

4. Add the tomatoes, any liquid from the lobster and wine. Add salt and pepper to taste. Cover and cook about 5 minutes. Total cooking time should be about 10 minutes.

5. Remove the lobster pieces from the skillet. When cool enough to handle, remove the lobster meat from the tail and claws. Discard the shells. Cut the carcass pieces in half and set aside with the meat.

6. Blend the coral and liver with the butter and stir it into the sauce. Bring to the boil over high heat. Put the sauce through a food mill, pressing to extract as much liquid as possible from the solids. Discard the solids. Return the sauce to the skillet and add the lobster pieces. Sprinkle with the remaining tarragon and swirl in the remaining butter. Serve with hot spaghetti.

Yield: 4 to 6 servings.

September 1976

THE PRIMARY REASONS for a yacht, one supposes, would include: getting from one place to another; lying on deck absorbing the sun; relaxing; and the sheer romance of the thing. I was invited on a yacht in this month and I accepted with alacrity because of none of those things. I happened to know this skipper (it also happened that his yacht was berthed in a boatyard not far from my home) and I knew him to be not only a marvelously amusing man but a highly inventive and ingenious chef. His name is Paul Steindler and he tempted me to come along with the likes of fish chowder and sweetbread omelets and veal scaloppine with avocado and mushroom risotto. It was, indeed, a lure beyond resisting. We boarded the yacht along with other friends and the skipper's beautiful wife, Aja, an Olympic skating champion before fleeing Czechoslovakia some years ago. The trip was unforgettable, starting on the upper deck with trays of sliced imported sausages and cheeses and breads and, following a nap, a dinner that began with large grains of caviar and a touch of iced vodka. It was a blissful orgy of fine wines and, to tell you the truth, I remember not one single detail of the water and the navigation, and I had to refer to my notes to remember precisely where we had rested at anchor that night.

Taking It Easy

There is no more obvious method of eliminating labor from a feast on Labor Day than assembling an assortment of good things in advance. It has long been our contention that some of the best dishes in the world are those that bear the unseemly and unpalatable label "leftovers." Two of the merest cases in point are roast turkey and roast beef (or even roast pork, a recipe for which is below). We like them piping hot from the oven, but how much more delectable we find them the day after, thinly carved and tucked between slices of a decent loaf of bread, the slices smeared with freshly made mayonnaise. That and a pickle. Omar, the tentmaker, probably never knew his "paradise enow."

With a single exception—a splendid corn and cheese pudding that can be assembled in advance and baked at the last hour—all of these dishes may be made to advantage a day in advance. But make no mistake, they would be excellent if prepared and served with dispatch.

Chicken and Mushroom Mayonnaise

1   *7-pound chicken, simmered until tender (see recipe) and cooled*
½   *pound fresh mushrooms, preferably button mushrooms Chicken broth to cover*
1   *tablespoon drained green peppercorns out of a bottle or can (see note)*
4   *tablespoons drained capers*
1   *cup homemade mayonnaise (see recipe) Juice of one lemon Finely chopped parsley for garnish*

1. When the chicken is cool, remove it from the kettle. Take the meat from the bones. Remove the skin from the meat. Return the bones and skin to the kettle and continue cooking to reduce the broth to any desired strength.

2. Cut the chicken into bite-size pieces and add it to a bowl.

3. If the mushrooms are small, leave them whole; otherwise quarter them or cut them into eighths. Drop them into a saucepan with chicken broth to cover. Simmer 5 minutes and drain well. Cool and add them to the chicken.

4. Add the peppercorns, capers, mayonnaise and lemon juice. Toss well to blend. The dish is now ready to serve. Before serving, sprinkle with chopped parsley.

Yield: 8 or more servings.

Note: Green peppercorns are available in food shops that deal in imported delicacies.

Poached chicken

1   7-pound chicken, trussed or
    not, plus gizzard, heart and
    neck
20 peppercorns, crushed
3   large ribs celery, trimmed and
    cut into 2-inch lengths
2   large carrots, trimmed and cut
    into 2-inch lengths
1   clove garlic, crushed
6   sprigs fresh parsley
    Salt to taste
    Water to cover

1. Combine all the ingredients in
a kettle and bring to the boil.

2. Partly cover and simmer 45
minutes or until the chicken is
thoroughly tender. Let the chicken
cool in the broth.

Yield: One 7-pound chicken or
about 3½ pounds of chicken meat
when cut into bite-size pieces.

Mayonnaise

1   egg yolk
1   teaspoon prepared mustard,
    preferably Dijon or Düsseldorf
    Salt and freshly ground
    pepper to taste
    Pinch of cayenne pepper
1½ teaspoons white vinegar
1   cup peanut oil
    Lemon juice to taste

1. Place the egg yolk in a mixing
bowl. Add the mustard, salt and pepper to taste, the cayenne and vinegar.

2. Start beating with a whisk, ro-
tary beater or electric beater, gradually adding the peanut oil. Continue
beating and adding the oil until all of
it is used. Beat in the lemon juice to
taste. Taste for seasoning and beat in
more salt, cayenne or lemon juice, if
desired.

Yield: About 1½ cups.

Roast Pork with Fennel

1   3½-to-4 pound center cut pork
    loin roast
3   to 5 cloves garlic
    Salt and freshly ground
    pepper to taste
1   tablespoon crushed fennel
    seeds
2   small white onions, peeled
½   cup chicken broth

1. The roast will be easier to carve if the chine bone (the continuous flat bone at the top of the ribs) is cut away by the butcher. This is not essential, however. If the chine bone is cut away, save the bone.

2. Preheat the oven to 400 degrees.

3. Cut the garlic into slivers. Make gashes at various points in the fat of the roast as well as between the meat and the rib bones. Stud the holes with garlic slivers. Sprinkle the roast with salt and pepper. Rub the fennel seeds on top of the roast.

4. Arrange the roast meaty side down in a shallow baking pan. Chop the bone into pieces and scatter them around the roast. Add the onions. It is not necessary to add any liquid at this time.

5. Place the roast in the oven and bake. Baste the roast at frequent intervals as the fat accumulates. When the roast has baked 30 minutes, turn it bone side down. Continue basting and roasting 30 minutes.

6. When the roast has cooked a total of 1 hour, pour off all the fat from the pan. Add the chicken broth and cover the roast lightly with foil. Bake 30 to 45 minutes longer. Serve hot or cold.

Yield: 6 to 10 servings.

Corn Pudding with Cheese

6   or more ears of freshly
    shucked corn
1   tablespoon butter
1   cup finely chopped onion
1   cup finely diced green peppers
3   cups milk
3   eggs, lightly beaten
    Salt and freshly ground
    pepper to taste
3   cups grated sharp cheddar
    cheese (about ½ pound grated)

1. Drop the corn into a large quantity of boiling water. Cover. When the water returns to the boil, remove pan from the heat and let stand 5 to 10 minutes. Drain the corn.

2. Meanwhile, preheat the oven to 325 degrees.

3. Cut and scrape the corn kernels from the ears. There should be exactly 3 cups for this recipe. Add the corn to a mixing bowl.

4. Heat the butter in a small skillet and cook the onion and green peppers until wilted. Add this to the corn. Add the milk and stir to blend. Add the eggs, salt and pepper to taste. Add all but ½ cup of the cheese. Blend well.

5. Pour the mixture into a 2½-to-3-quart casserole. Sprinkle with the remaining ½ cup of cheese. Bake 1 hour or until the pudding is set. Serve piping hot.

Yield: 8 to 12 servings.

Ed Giobbi's Cold Pasta and Broccoli with Pesto

4   to 6 tablespoons fresh pesto
    genovese (see recipe)
1   bunch of broccoli
    Salt
1   pound rigatoni or any tubular
    pasta, preferably imported
3   tablespoons olive oil
1   clove garlic, finely chopped
½   teaspoon or more hot red
    pepper flakes, optional
1   firm red, ripe tomato

1. Prepare the pesto and have it ready.

2. Cut the broccoli into small flowerettes. Trim the stalks and stems of the broccoli and cut the stems and stalks into bite-size lengths. Steam the broccoli pieces over boiling water or cook in boiling salted water until crisp tender. Do not overcook. Set aside.

3. Cook the rigatoni in boiling salted water more or less according to package directions, but take care not to overcook. The pasta must be tender and in no sense mushy. Drain but reserve a little of the boiling pasta water to dilute the pesto.

4. Heat the oil in a saucepan and add the garlic and blanched broccoli. Sprinkle with pepper flakes. Cook, stirring gently, just to heat it through. Remove it from the heat.

5. Meanwhile, core the tomato and cut the tomato into small bite-size wedges.

6. When ready to serve, put the rigatoni in a bowl. Add 1 or 2 tablespoons of the hot pasta water to the pesto and stir until slightly thinned. Do not make it soupy. Pour this over the rigatoni. Add salt to taste. Add the broccoli and tomato and toss to blend. Serve at room temperature.

Yield: 8 to 10 servings.

Pesto genovese

½   cup loosely packed basil
2½ tablespoons hulled pumpkin
    seeds (available in health food
    stores) or pine nuts
1   clove garlic, peeled
6   tablespoons freshly grated
    Parmesan cheese
¼   cup olive oil

1. Place the basil in the container of an electric blender and add the pumpkin seeds and garlic. Blend, stirring down carefully with a rubber spatula if necessary. When well blended, add the cheese.

2. Gradually add the olive oil while blending on low speed.

Yield: About ½ cup.

Beets in Sour Cream and Mustard Sauce

1¼ to 1½ pounds fresh beets
    Salt to taste
2   small red onions
1   tablespoon imported mustard
    such as Dijon or Düsseldorf
2   teaspoons white vinegar
½   cup sour cream
    Freshly ground pepper to taste

1. Cut off the leaves of the beets, but leave an inch or so of the beet top intact. Do not cut off the root ends of the beets. Wash the beets well and place in a kettle. Add cold water to cover and salt to taste. Bring to the boil and simmer until beets are tender. This may take anywhere from 20 minutes to an hour depending on the size and age of the beets.

2. Drain the beets and let cool. When cool, trim off and discard the ends of the beets. Peel the beets and cut them into ¼-inch thick or slightly smaller slices. Place the slices in a mixing bowl. Peel and slice the onions and add them to the bowl. Combine the remaining ingredients and blend well. Pour this mixture over the beets and toss well.

Yield: 6 to 10 servings.

Zucchini with Coriander Vinaigrette

1½ to 2 pounds green or yellow zucchini
2 or 3 large, sweet, seedless oranges
1 large red onion, peeled and cut into rings
3 tablespoons white vinegar
¼ cup olive oil
  Salt and freshly ground pepper to taste
¼ teaspoon sugar
¾ teaspoon ground coriander

1. Trim off and discard the ends of the zucchini. Cut the zucchini into ½-inch lengths and place in the top of a vegetable steamer. Steam, covered, over boiling water about 5 minutes or less. Take care not to overcook. The vegetable must retain a bit of its crisp texture. Transfer the vegetable to a bowl and let cool.

2. Peel the oranges and cut them into wedges or slices. There should be about 1½ cups. Add this to the bowl. Add the onions and chill thoroughly.

3. Combine the remaining ingredients and shake or blend thoroughly. Pour this over the ingredients in the bowl and toss well.

Yield: 8 or more servings.

Lustrous Aspics

WITH PIERRE FRANEY

One of the nicer and more elegant conceits of the French kitchen is just a trifle tricky to handle but, to use a favorite old-fashioned phrase, the game is worth the candle. The conceit in question is aspic dishes, which, properly prepared, add a certain glitter to any occasion, the simple reason being that aspics are basically lustrous. Aspics are used to "dress up" foods. We recently devised an assortment of seafood appetizers, all with aspic coatings. The basic foods are crab meat, mussels and clams. The inspiration for the aspic-coated clams on the half shell is, incidentally, from the new and much-heralded Windows on the World restaurant atop the World Trade Center. It is included among the restaurant's appetizers.

How to Make a Clear Aspic

For every cup of aspic to be used, in a saucepan combine 1 cup of well-seasoned stock or broth with 1 envelope of unflavored gelatin, 1 egg white, beaten until frothy, and 1 crushed egg shell. Beat with a whisk and place over low heat. Let simmer, without stirring, about 30 seconds.

Ideally, the stock or broth to be used in coating a dish should derive from the same or a related source as the food to be coated. For instance, chicken broth should be used to coat a chicken dish; fish stock for a fish dish; clam broth for a clam dish and so on.

On the other hand, fish stock could be used for any fish or seafood dish and it will produce a clearer aspic than, for example, clam or mussel broth. Chicken aspic is a fairly neutral broth and could be used on most meat dishes and, failing all else, would be acceptable for fish and seafood dishes.

Remove the aspic from the heat and strain it through a fine sieve, preferably lined with a clean linen napkin wrung out in cold water. Let cool to room temperature and use as indicated in the following instructions for garnishing foods.

How to Use an Aspic for Garnishing Foods

Once the aspic is made, let it cool to room temperature. This process may be hastened by placing the aspic in the refrigerator for a brief period. The foods to be coated with aspic should be well chilled in the refrigerator or briefly in the freezer. The aspic when applied must be cool but still liquid.

Spoon or brush a little of the aspic onto the surface to be coated and refrigerate. When that layer sets, apply another coating and so on until the foods are well coated. Should the aspic set at any point, it may be reheated by placing the utensil that holds it in a basin of warm or even hot water just until the aspic becomes liquid again.

Leftover aspic may be held for several days in the refrigerator and made liquid before using it.

Raw Clams on the Half Shell with Aspic

12 raw littleneck clams
½ to 1 cup aspic made with fish broth, fresh or bottled clam juice or chicken broth
Salt
Tabasco sauce
Juice of half a lemon
Freshly ground pepper
¼ cup finely chopped scallion

1. Open the clams or have them opened. Loosen the clams totally and return each clam to the bottom shell. Discard the top shells. Refrigerate.

2. Meanwhile, prepare an aspic, adding salt, Tabasco sauce to taste and the juice of half a lemon to the broth before making the aspic.

3. Sprinkle each clam with pepper and about 1 teaspoon of finely chopped scallion on each clam. Coat the clams with aspic following the instructions for garnishing foods. Chilled leftover aspic may be chopped and added as a further garnish around the stuffed clams.

Yield: 12 stuffed clams.

Stuffed Mussels with Aspic

2 pounds (1 quart) well-scrubbed mussels
¼ cup thinly sliced onion
4 sprigs fresh parsley
½ cup dry white wine
Freshly ground pepper
1 cup aspic made with mussel liquid
3 stems fresh tarragon, coarsely chopped, optional
⅓ cup freshly chopped tarragon leaves, optional

1. Place the mussels in a kettle and add the onion, parsley, wine and pepper. Cover. Bring to the boil and steam about 5 minutes or longer, until the mussels open.

2. Strain but reserve both the mussels and liquid. When mussels are cool enough to handle, take the meat from the shell. Arrange 1 mussel in each bottom shell. Discard the top shells. Cover the mussels on the half shell with plastic wrap and refrigerate.

3. Prepare an aspic with the mussel liquid, adding enough water to make a cup of liquid. If a tarragon flavor is desired, add the chopped stems to the saucepan while making the aspic. Strain.

4. Sprinkle each mussel with about half a teaspoon of tarragon. Coat the stuffed mussels with aspic.

Yield: 40 or more mussels.

Crab-Stuffed Clam Shells with Aspic

12   or more small or medium clean
      clam shells, purchased or
      cleaned at home
½   pound crab meat
½   cup mayonnaise, preferably
      homemade
1   teaspoon lemon juice
½   cup finely chopped heart of
      celery
1   tablespoon chopped chives
2   teaspoons well-drained capers
      Tabasco sauce
      Salt and freshly ground
      pepper
½   to 1 cup aspic made with fish
      broth, fresh, or bottled clam
      broth or chicken broth

1. If the clam shells are to be cleaned at home, cover with water and bring to the boil. Simmer 10 minutes and drain. When cool, use a knife and scrape them clean. Rinse and dry.

2. Combine the crab meat, mayonnaise, lemon juice, celery, chives, capers, Tabasco sauce to taste, salt and pepper to taste. Blend. Stuff the clam shells with the mixture.

3. Coat the crab meat filling with aspic. Chilled leftover aspic may be chopped and added as a further garnish around the stuffed shells.

Yield: 12 or more crab-stuffed shells.

Stuffed Soft-Shell Clams with Aspic

1   quart soft-shell clams, about
      13

3   tablespoons salt
2   tablespoons vegetable oil
½   cup dry white wine
⅓   cup mayonnaise, preferably
      homemade
2   tablespoons prepared
      mustard, preferably imported
      such as Dijon
1   tablespoon finely chopped
      scallion
½   to 1 cup aspic made from the
      clam broth

1. Wash the clams thoroughly in several changes of cold water. Place them in a mixing bowl and add the salt and lukewarm water (not too hot) to cover. Add the oil. Cover with a clean kitchen towel and let stand several hours.

2. Drain the clams and wash them well under cold running water. Place them in a kettle and add the wine. Cover closely and cook 3 to 5 minutes or until they open.

3. Drain the clams and reserve both the clams and the broth. There should be about 1½ cups of broth. Use the broth to prepare an aspic, and set aside half the clam shells for stuffing.

4. When the clams are cool, remove them from the shells. Pull off and discard the rubbery black "shield" attached to each clam neck. Add the tender clam bellies to a mixing bowl and chop the necks. Add them to the bowl. Add the mayonnaise, mustard and scallion. Blend well. Use the mixture to fill 14 to 16 clean clam shells. Chill well on a rack. Coat with several layers of aspic.

Yield: 14 to 16 stuffed clams.

The Best Captain's Table Around

It isn't the largest galley afloat and it certainly isn't the smallest. It measures about nine by twelve feet, about the size of a decent apartment kitchen in Manhattan. Whatever its size, out of it come some of the best meals in the Atlantic and surrounding waters.

We've known for decades that when a good chef works, it is frequently for a twelve-hour day with demonic devotion. We also know that when a good chef plays, it is generally with equal dedication and fervor. Paul Steindler and his wife, Aja, were on a two-day spree that would carry them and a party of six from the Shagwong Marina on Three Mile Harbor in East Hampton to the waters of Block Island, where the boat would be anchored overnight. It was, Paul explained, only his second holiday after a long hot summer of gutting and rebuilding the interior of a restaurant scheduled to open in late October. That plus his frequent daily and nightly presence at The Duck Joint, a popular Manhattan eatery owned jointly by him and his wife.

The anchor was hoisted, the boat moved away from the pier and Paul, at the wheel, was playing. The bits and pieces of his game that weekend would include a case or two of Dom Pérignon champagne, some in a cabin below, a constant supply being iced on deck; a pound of fresh Iranian caviar, the grains the size of buckshot; three kinds of pâtés; a quintet of fire-engine red lobsters recently cooked ashore and now being iced; an impressive pinkish-white hunk of veal for scaloppine; avocados; tomatoes fresh from the garden; a splendid jar of highly concentrated fish stock to be turned into chowder; a pair of sweetbreads braised in port wine (these would become the filling for a Sunday omelet). In the hold there were other wines with labels like Puligny-Montrachet, Bâtard-Montrachet and Chateau Talbot.

Paul set the automatic pilot and settled down, offered his guests wine while his wife passed the assorted pâtés—a country pâté, a delicate sweetbread pâté and a fish pâté.

Paul sampled the country pâté and shook his head. "It's not as robust as it should be. It should have a touch more cognac and a bit more garlic. It's a bit dry." The guests thought it was delicious.

Paul, who is 55 years old, explained that he was born in a small town close to Prague, that he fled his native Czechoslovakia at the time of the Communist takeover in 1948. He was at one time an Olympic wrestler, which is quite interesting because his wife, Aja, a handsome woman with dark hair and a graceful,

A holiday aboard the Caraja means hard work for Paul Steindler

athletic walk, was four times the Olympic ice-skating champion. She was born in Prague and defected in 1950.

"Aja," Paul said, "was a star of the Ice Capades for sixteen years. She spends most of her time in the restaurant, but she is still a talent scout for Ice Capades."

Aja is Paul's second wife and the name of his boat is *Caraja*, named for Aja and his daughter, Carol, by his previous marriage.

Cooking on the boat has never been a problem because of his organization. The kitchen is also remarkably well equipped, which helps. There is a small electric stove with three top burners and an oven with a broiler above. When he uses the broiler, he generally gets down on his knees to tend whatever is being cooked. Next to the stove is a cutting and chopping area equipped with a small, rectangular cutting board.

He also has the smallest professional version of the French food processor that has recently become so popular in this country. His processor is one size larger than the Cuisinart machine and is called a Robot Coupe. (It is available at the Bridge Kitchenware Corp., 212 East 52d Street, and is primarily designed for small restaurants.) He also has an electric skillet that he admires for its versatility and maneuverability. With it he has made sukiyaki for twenty guests on the fantail of his boat during a tour around Manhattan.

As the day progressed and after the boat had been safely anchored, more champagne was poured and eggs were cooked "mollet-style," which is to say less than hard-cooked so that they could be unmolded but with a soft center. He cracked the tops of the eggs, scooped out the insides, which he mashed. The egg shells were refilled with mashed egg and scallion. A touch of sour cream was piped into each and a large spoonful of the fresh caviar was placed on top. More champagne. As the chef proceeded to the main course of the evening, a veal scaloppine with cubed avocados and tomatoes, we learned a good number of things about boat cookery. Mr. Steindler, for instance, prepares ashore a fairly sizable assortment of foods with keeping qualities and brings them aboard.

He prepares an assortment of "bases" such as concentrated fish broth to be turned into soup; an assortment of herb and vegetable butters, some made with shallots, some with garlic, onion, celery, carrots and so on, which are kept in plastic containers. This, of course, eliminates a good deal of chopping while underway or at anchor.

The Steindlers prefer to entertain with six to eight at table, because, they explain, "anything beyond that is camping out."

The couple also told us that they like to come to Block Island because each Sunday morning a boatman comes alongside singing "O Sole Mio" and selling freshly baked bread and meat pies. He also carts away any garbage that may have accumulated overnight.

Breakfast of sweetbread omelets was followed by a superior fish chowder for lunch and an excellent lobster salad.

During the course of the weekend, we learned that Mr. Steindler had recently purchased a landmark-designated building, the old Humane Society edifice at 313 East 58th Street. He has completely gutted the building and excavated a basement. When it is transformed into a restaurant, tentatively named Paul's Landmark, it will have an inner dining room with a seating capacity of eighty-five, plus a patio and a kitchen area of 2,500 square feet. That's no broom closet.

Veal Scaloppine with Avocado and Tomato

6   medium slices of veal cut as
     for scaloppine (about 6 ounces
     each)
     Salt and freshly ground
     pepper to taste
2   firm but ripe avocados, about
     1 pound each
     Juice of 1 lemon
2   firm but ripe tomatoes,
     about ¾ pound each
7   tablespoons butter
¼   cup chopped onion
2   cloves garlic, finely chopped
2   teaspoons curry powder
5   tablespoons flour, preferably
     Wondra flour
½   chicken bouillon cube (see
     note)
1   cup milk
¼   cup heavy cream
¼   cup olive oil
¼   cup scotch whiskey
6   thin slices Muenster cheese

1. Place the scaloppine on a flat surface and pound with a mallet. Sprinkle with salt and pepper.

2. Peel the avocados and discard the skin and seeds. Cut the avocados into ½-inch cubes or slightly larger and place in a mixing bowl. There should be about 4 cups. Add the lemon juice and toss to coat.

3. Core, peel and seed the tomatoes. Cut into ½-inch cubes. There should be about 2 cups. Add this to the avocados.

4. Heat 4 tablespoons of butter and add the onion. Cook briefly to wilt and add the garlic. Cook briefly and remove from the heat. Add the avocado mixture, sprinkle with half the curry powder and add salt to taste. Stir and cook briefly just to heat thoroughly. Set aside.

5. In a saucepan, heat the remaining 3 tablespoons of butter and add half the flour, stirring with a wire whisk. Sprinkle with remaining curry powder, stirring. Add the bouillon cube, milk and cream, stirring with the whisk. Cook about 10 minutes, stirring often.

6. Dust the scaloppine lightly on both sides with the remaining flour.

7. Heat the oil in an electric or other skillet and when it is quite hot, add the meat. Cook about 45 seconds and turn. Cook for 5 seconds and transfer to a baking dish. This may have to be done in two stages.

8. Add the scotch to the pan, stirring. Reduce quickly by half and add the avocado mixture. Stir and turn off the heat.

9. Spoon equal amounts of avocado mixture over the veal and spoon half the cream sauce over this. Place 1 slice of Muenster cheese, folded in half, on top. Cover with remaining cream sauce and run briefly under the broiler. This may have to be done in two stages. Serve piping hot with mushroom risotto (see recipe), if desired.

Yield: 6 servings.

Note: Chef Steindler recommends the use of the Knorr Swiss bouillon cubes. He states, however, that they may be eliminated and rich chicken broth substituted for part of the liquid recommended in any given recipe.

Mushroom risotto

4   tablespoons butter
½   cup finely chopped onion
3   cups mushrooms cut into ½-inch cubes, about ½ pound
½   teaspoon saffron
2   cups uncooked rice
1   large chicken bouillon cube (or use 3 cups of rich chicken broth and do not use the water that follows)
3   cups water
2   whole cloves
1   bay leaf
    Salt and freshly ground pepper to taste

1. Heat half the butter in a heavy saucepan or casserole and add the onion. Cook, stirring, to wilt. Add the mushrooms and cook until they give up their liquid. Continue cooking until the liquid evaporates.

2. Add the saffron and stir. Add the rice and bouillon cube and stir. Add the remaining ingredients except butter and stir until the bouillon cube is melted. Cover closely and cook 17 minutes. Stir with a fork and add the remaining butter.

Yield: 6 or more servings.

Fish Chowder à la Caraja

5 tablespoons butter
¾ cup finely chopped onion
1 cup finely chopped celery
1 cup finely diced carrots
¾ cup white part of leek cut into very fine julienne strips
2 cloves garlic, finely minced
4 cups concentrated fish broth (see recipe)
2 tablespoons flour
3½ cups potatoes (about 1½ pounds), peeled and cut into ¼-inch cubes
2 cups white-flesh, non-oily fish such as sea trout (weakfish), sole or striped bass cut into 1-inch cubes.
1½ cups heavy cream or milk
Salt and freshly ground pepper to taste

1. Melt 3 tablespoons of butter in a saucepan and add the onion, celery, carrots, leeks and garlic. Cook, stirring often, about 10 minutes. Add the fish broth and bring to the boil.

2. Blend remaining 2 tablespoons of butter with the flour and add it, bit by bit, to the soup, stirring constantly.

3. Add the potatoes and continue cooking until the potatoes are tender but firm. Do not overcook or the potatoes will become mushy. Add the fish and simmer briefly just until fish is piping hot, about 2 minutes.

4. Add the cream or milk, salt and pepper to taste, and bring to the boil. Do not boil but serve piping hot.

Yield: 6 or more servings.

Fish stock

2½ pounds fish bones (may include head of fish with gills removed)
2 cups coarsely chopped celery
2 cups thinly sliced onions
1 whole clove garlic, unpeeled, sliced in half
2 cups chopped, well-washed green part of leeks
3 sprigs fresh thyme or 1½ teaspoons dried
1 bay leaf
2 quarts water
½ bottle dry white wine
¼ teaspoon peppercorns
¼ teaspoon anise seeds, crushed
Salt to taste

1. Run the bones under cold running water.

2. Place bones in a kettle and add the remaining ingredients. Bring to the boil and simmer about 20 minutes. Strain.

3. Return the strained stock to the kettle and reduce by half.

Yield: 4 to 6 cups.

Note: Leftover stock may be frozen.

Sweetbread Omelet

The filling

1 pair sweetbreads braised in port wine (see recipe)
3 tablespoons butter
1 cup finely chopped onions
2 cups cubed mushrooms, about ½ pound or slightly less
Salt and freshly ground pepper to taste

1 teaspoon *flour*
¼ *chicken bouillon cube (or use*
¼ cup very rich chicken broth
and eliminate the water
indicated below)
¼ *cup water*

The omelet

12 *to 16 eggs*
12 *to 16 tablespoons heavy cream*
Salt and freshly ground
pepper to taste

1. Cut the sweetbreads into 1-inch cubes. There should be about 4 cups.

2. Heat the butter in a skillet or casserole and add the onion. Cook until wilted and add the mushrooms, sweetbreads, salt and pepper to taste and cook, stirring often, about 5 minutes. Sprinkle with flour and add the chicken bouillon cube and water. Cook, stirring often, 10 to 15 minutes or until the liquid has evaporated.

3. Use 2 eggs, 1 tablespoon of cream, salt and pepper to taste for each omelet and prepare according to any standard recipe. Fill with equal amounts of the sweetbread mixture and turn out onto hot plates.

Yield: 6 to 8 omelets.

Sweetbreads braised in port wine

1 *pair of sweetbreads, about 1*
pound
Port wine to cover
2 *sprigs fresh thyme or 1*
teaspoon dried
1 *bay leaf*

1. Soak the sweetbreads overnight in cold water to cover. Drain.

2. Place the sweetbreads in a large saucepan and add port wine to cover. Add the thyme and bay leaf. Bring to the boil and simmer 5 minutes or slightly longer. Drain immediately. Run under cold water and let cool. Trim the sweetbreads by cutting away the connective tissue and cartilage. Chill well.

3. Place the sweetbreads in a dish large enough to hold them and cover with a weight. Weight them down at least 6 hours and refrigerate.

Yield: 1 pair of braised sweetbreads

We were subsequently happy to learn that Mr. Steindler's restaurant was ready to open in June of 1977. It is called Paul's, and is in the landmark-designated building at 313 East 58th Street.

A Robust Neapolitan Feast

It looked for all the world like a cooking marathon but it was in truth just another day in the life of the Migliucci family. The only difference was, on this day they were doing it for pleasure. They were cooking a dinner for twenty, which included themselves, their family and friends.

The Migliuccis—Mario, the father; Clemente, the brother; and Joseph, the son and nephew—are the principals in the kitchen at Mario's Restaurant in the East Tremont section of the Bronx. We had heard on two separate occasions that it has one of the best Neapolitan-style kitchens in the area and that they are famous for, among other things, their spiedini alla romana, a deep-fried batter-coated sandwich made with slices of mozzarella cheese between bread, served hot and crisp with an anchovy sauce. The kind of dish, we reflected, the thought of which can trigger salivation.

We visited the Migliuccis at Mario's on two occasions and what we found was much to our liking. First-rate, unpretentious but adventurous Neapolitan cookery, a trifle more robust than one would find it in northern Italy.

In our presence—and the presence of their family—the chefs prepared an impressive array of dishes, accompanied by an assortment of cheeses, both fresh and aged, plus various salamis and breads purchased on that bustling street of great Italian delicacies, Arthur Avenue in the Bronx. The menu for the day would include a selection, extravagant in number, of things like a lighter-than-air potato gnocci; the spiedini with anchovy sauce; striped bass marechiare with clams and mussels; fillet of beef scaloppine with Marsala and mushroom sauce; stuffed clams; octopus salad; assorted pastas with three tomato sauces; and a ricotta cheese cake.

As Mario Migliucci kneaded the potato gnocci ("You must be careful," he cautioned, "not to add too much flour or the dumplings will be gummy"), Clemente occupied himself with the striped bass fillets for the marechiare dish, and Joe chopped and assembled the ingredients for the octopus salad.

The gnocci finished, Mario moved toward a platter of raw octopus and a kettle of boiling water.

"A Sicilian fisherman taught me how to cook octopus and keep it tender," he told us. "After cleaning it, you drop it into boiling water. When the water comes back to the boil, you take out the octopus and let it cool. You do that three times before the final cooking, which may take from ten to forty-five minutes, depending on the size and age of the octopus." This technique, he added, keeps the "nerve ends" of the creature from toughening.

Mario told us that his family had entered the restaurant field more than sixty years ago, by way of Cairo.

Mario Migliucci

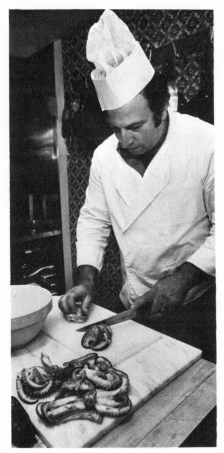

Joseph Migliucci

"My grandparents left Naples with my father in the early 1900s and opened the first Italian restaurant ever to open in Egypt," he said. "It was a success, but my father became restless and decided to come to America. When my grandfather died, my grandmother came too and the three of us opened Mario's on the same site where it stands today. It was much smaller, of course, and I was very little. I remember I had to stand on Coca-Cola boxes in the kitchen to make pizza.

"I suppose you could say we've become famous over the years. The restaurant is mentioned in *The Godfather* and they wanted to shoot some of the film there but we refused, thinking it might be bad publicity. A lot of well-known people have eaten with us—Governor Rockefeller, Anna Moffo, Elizabeth Taylor, Eddie Fisher, back in the days when they were married, the Yankees and the Giants, all of them as far as I know."

Mario, who is 62 years old and more or less in overall charge of the restaurant, explained that his brother, Clemente, 58, is the key man in the kitchen. He believes that the restaurant life can literally run in the family blood and he is prideful of the fact that Joe, 37, is a dedicated cook in the establishment.

"His mother and I tried everything we knew to discourage him from going into the business," Mr. Migliucci said. "When he was in college he would help out on holidays. Then he decided he wanted to work full time. We made him mop the floors, then wash the dishes full time, then the pots and pans. Nothing fazed him. Finally I put him behind the range and thought, 'This will kill him, he's gonna hate it.' Not a bit. And now he's good at everything. Terrific bartender, good host, the works."

Here is a sampling of the Migliucci family specialties.

Octopus Salad

Clemente Migliucci

4   *or 5 baby octopus, about 5 pounds*
5   *cloves garlic*
2   *cups finely chopped celery*
15 *pitted California black olives*
½   *cup olive oil*
8   *to 12 tablespoons lemon juice, according to taste*
    Salt to taste
    Freshly ground pepper to taste
1   *teaspoon red pepper flakes*
⅓   *cup finely chopped parsley*
1   *tablespoon fresh basil leaves, snipped with scissors, or use 1 teaspoon dried*

1. Have a fish dealer prepare the octopus for cooking.

2. Bring a large quantity of water to the boil and add the octopus, 1 or 2 at a time. When the water returns to the boil remove the octopus and cool briefly. Return the octopus to the boiling water, let the water return to the boil and remove. Let cool briefly. Repeat this one more time. Cook all the octopus in the same fashion and let cool.

3. Bring another large quantity of water to the boil and add salt to taste. Add all the octopus and simmer 20 to 40 minutes or until the octopus are tender. Cooking time will depend on the size and age of the octopus. When the octopus are tender, drain them and chill under cold running water.

4. Cut off and discard any non-fleshy parts of the octopus if there are any. If the "beak," a plasticlike small ball, is in an octopus, remove and discard it.

5. Cut the octopus into bite-size pieces. There should be about 5 cups.

6. Place the octopus pieces in a bowl and add the remaining ingredients. Toss to blend and let stand an hour or longer before serving.

Yield: 12 or more servings.

Gnocci di Patate

3   large potatoes, preferably Idaho potatoes, about 1¾ pounds
    Salt to taste
2   eggs yolks
1¾ to 2 cups flour
6   tablespoons melted butter, optional
    Grated Parmesan cheese, optional
2   cups filetti di pomodoro sauce (see recipe)
    Freshly ground black pepper

1. Place the potatoes in a kettle and add cold water to cover. Add salt to taste and bring to the boil. Simmer until the potatoes are tender but not mushy. Drain and let cool.

2. Peel the potatoes. Put them through a ricer, or food mill. Or put

them through a meat grinder using the medium blade. Add egg yolks and blend well.

3. Scoop the flour onto a flat surface. Start kneading the potatoes, adding the flour gradually. Add only enough flour to make a firm, soft and delicate dough. If too much flour is added they become tough when cooked. Knead thoroughly, then shape the dough, rolling with the palms to make a thick sausage shape about 12 inches long. Using a knife or pastry scraper cut the roll into 11 equal slices. Roll each slice into a long cigar shape. Cut each cigar into 18 or 19 pieces. These pieces will resemble miniature pillows. Flour the pieces and set aside until ready to cook.

4. Drop the pieces of dough, half of them at a time, into a large quantity of boiling salted water and let cook until they rise to the surface. Drain quickly and chill under cold running water. Drain well.

5. When ready to serve, drop the pieces once more into a large quantity of boiling salted water. When they float the second time, drain them and return them to the pot. Add the melted butter and cheese, if desired. Add the sauce and sprinkle with pepper. Serve with additional sauce on the side.

Yield: 6 or more servings.

Filetti di pomodoro
(Tomato and onion sauce)

8   cups canned tomatoes, preferably imported from Italy
¼   pound lard
3   cups thinly sliced onions

⅓ pound ham, preferably
prosciutto, cut into very thin
strips, about 1½ cups
Salt and freshly ground
pepper to taste
¼ cup freshly snipped basil
leaves, or 1 tablespoon dried
crushed basil.

1. Using the hands, crush the tomatoes

2. Heat lard and add the onions. Cook, stirring often, until the onions are golden brown, about 20 minutes.

3. Add the ham and cook 5 minutes. Add the tomatoes and cook about 2 hours, stirring often to prevent sticking. Add salt, pepper and basil.

Yield: About 6 cups of sauce.

Striped Bass Marechiare

2 fillets of striped bass with skin
left on, about 4 pounds
Flour for dredging
Oil for deep frying
12 cherrystone clams
12 well-cleaned large mussels
2 cups crushed imported
tomatoes
4 cloves garlic, finely slivered
1 tablespoon finely chopped
parsley
Salt and freshly ground
pepper to taste
2 tablespoons snipped fresh
basil leaves, or 1 teaspoon
dried
½ cup salad oil
¾ cup fresh or bottled clam juice

1. Cut each fillet crosswise into 8 pieces of approximately equal size. Coat the pieces with flour.

2. Heat the oil and, when it is hot but not smoking, add the fish pieces. This may have to be done in 2 steps. Deep fry for 6 or 7 minutes. The pieces should be half cooked. Drain on towels.

3. Arrange the pieces of fish in one layer in a baking dish. Arrange the clams and mussels around the fish. Spoon the crushed tomatoes over the fish and sprinkle with garlic and parsley, salt, pepper and basil. Sprinkle with oil. Cover and simmer on top of the stove about 5 minutes. Sprinkle with clam juice. Continue simmering about 20 minutes or longer, until fish flakes easily when tested with a fork.

Yield: 8 servings.

Beef Scaloppine Casalinga

(Beef fillets with marsala and mushroom sauce)

8 slices fillet of beef, each about
½ inch thick
¾ cup salad oil
½ cup finely chopped onion
½ cup prosciutto or baked ham
cut into very thin strips
⅓ pound fresh mushrooms,
thinly sliced, about 2 cups,
sprinkled with lemon juice
2 tablespoons butter
⅓ cup canned brown beef gravy
1 cup marsala wine
2 tablespoons finely chopped
parsley
Flour for dredging
Oil for shallow frying

8 *rounds of mozzarella cheese, about ⅓ inch thick and 3 inches in diameter*

1. Preheat the oven to 500 degrees.

2. Place the beef slices on a flat surface and pound lightly with a mallet. Set aside.

3. Heat the oil in a skillet and add the onion. Cook, stirring often, to brown lightly, about 10 minutes. Add the prosciutto and mushrooms. Cook slowly, about 10 minutes. Empty the mixture into a sieve and drain well, pressing down with the back of a wooden spoon to extract most of the oil.

4. Heat the butter in another skillet and add the mushroom mixture. Blend well and add the beef gravy and marsala wine. Sprinkle with parsley and simmer about 20 minutes.

5. Dredge the meat lightly in flour. Add oil to a depth of about ½ inch to a skillet and add the meat. Cook quickly, turning once, until golden on both sides, about 2 minutes. Transfer the meat to a colander and let drain.

6. Spoon half the mushroom sauce over a baking dish and arrange the beef slices on top. Spoon remaining sauce over and top each slice with a slice of mozzarella cheese.

7. Bake 10 to 15 minutes or until piping hot and the cheese melted.

Yield: 8 servings.

Spiedini alla Romana

(Skewered, deep fried mozzarella sandwiches)

The sandwiches

14 *slices ordinary, supermarket white bread with crust*
Sliced mozzarella cheese, each slice about ¼-inch thick (see instructions below)
Flour for dredging
5 *eggs, well beaten*
Fat for deep frying

The anchovy sauce

8 *tablespoons butter*
1 *tablespoon finely chopped parsley*
¼ *cup drained capers, optional*
½ *cup brown beef gravy, available in cans*

1. Trim the crusts from the bread to make neat squares (see note). If you can purchase mozzarella cheese in a loaf shape (the loaf size is approximately that of a loaf of bread), cut off 12 slices, matching the shape and sizes of the bread slices as closely as possible. Make 2 stacks of sandwiches with bread slices top and bottom. If regular package of mozzarella is used, proceed differently. Cut the bread slices in half to make 28 rectangles. Cut the mozzarella into 24 slices, matching the shape and sizes of the rectangles of bread as closely as possible. Make 4 stacks of sandwiches with slices of bread top and bottom. Skewer each stack of sandwiches with 2 skewers, to hold the sandwiches together as they cook.

2. Dredge all the skewered sandwiches in flour. Coat thoroughly with the egg and place the sandwiches on a rack until ready to fry. This may be done ½ hour or so in advance.

3. Preheat the oven to 400 degrees.

4. Heat the oil for deep frying and, when it is very hot and almost smoking, add the sandwiches. Cook about 3 minutes turning once, or until golden brown all over. It may be necessary to fry the sandwiches in two steps. Drain on paper toweling.

5. Combine the sauce ingredients in a saucepan and simmer briefly, stirring, until anchovies are "melted" and the sauce smooth.

6. Place the skewered sandwiches on a buttered dish and bake about 5 minutes or until the sandwiches are piping hot throughout. Remove the skewers, cut each sandwich crosswise into 2 or 3 portions. Serve with the anchovy sauce spooned on top.

Yield: 8 to 12 servings.

Note: It is possible, and perhaps much easier, to simplify the preparation of this dish as follows: Use two rectangles of bread and fill with a ½-inch-thick slice of mozzarella cut to fit the size and shape of the rectangle as closely as possible. Skewer the sandwich and dip it first in flour then in beaten egg. Deep fry in hot oil and serve with anchovy sauce.

Zucchini Fritti

3 zucchini, about ½ pound each
   Flour for dredging
3 eggs, beaten
   Oil for deep frying

1. Trim off the ends of the zucchini. Cut the zucchini into 3-inch lengths. Cut each length into ¼-inch slices. Cut the slices into ¼-inch strips. Drop the strips into cold water and let stand briefly.

2. Drain the zucchini well. Place in a bowl, sprinkle with enough flour to coat the pieces, and toss well with the hands.

3. Add the eggs to a large bowl. Add the floured zucchini and mix well with the hands until the pieces are coated.

4. Heat the oil until it is hot and almost smoking. Add a portion of the zucchini, half of it or less at a time, and cook, stirring to separate the pieces, about 6 or 7 minutes or until crisp. Drain on a clean towel. Serve hot sprinkled with salt.

Yield: 6 or more servings.

Salsa Monachina

(An anchovy and tomato sauce)

 6   cups imported Italian plum
     tomatoes
 ⅔   cup vegetable or olive oil
 1   tablespoon thinly sliced garlic
 1¼ cups drained capers, preferably
     salt-cured rather than packed
     in vinegar
15   pitted black California olives,
     sliced
 5   whole anchovies
     Salt and freshly ground
     pepper to taste

1. Empty the tomatoes into a bowl and crush them with the hands.

2. Heat the oil in a kettle or casserole and add the garlic. Cook until brown and add the capers and olives. Add the anchovies and stir until anchovies "melt."

3. Add the tomatoes and cook, stirring occasionally, about 1½ hours. Add salt and pepper to taste.

Yield: About 4½ cups.

Melanzane Ripieni

(Stuffed eggplant)

The eggplant

1½   pounds eggplant
      Flour for dredging
3   large eggs
2   tablespoons finely chopped parsley
      Oil for deep frying

The filling

½   pound mozzarella cheese
½   cup finely shredded ham, preferably prosciutto
1   egg
2   cups ricotta cheese
¼   cup Parmesan cheese
1   tablespoon finely chopped parsley
      Salt and freshly ground pepper to taste
2   to 3 cups marinara sauce (see recipe)

1. Preheat the oven to 500 degrees.

2. Trim off the ends of the eggplant and cut the eggplant lengthwise into 8-inch slices. There should be about 12 center-cut slices. Discard the trimmings.

3. Dredge the slices in flour to coat on all sides. Shake off excess. Beat the eggs with parsley and dip the slices in egg to coat well. Fry the slices, a few at a time in hot oil, about 3 minutes for each batch. Drain well.

4. Cut the mozzarella into ¼-inch slices. Cut the slices into ¼-inch strips. Cut the strips into ¼-inch cubes. Combine the mozzarella with the remaining ingredients for the filling.

5. Place the fried eggplant slices on a flat surface. Add equal amounts of filling toward the base of each slice. Roll to enclose the filling.

6. Spoon about ½ inch of marinara sauce over a baking dish large enough to hold the stuffed slices. Arrange them over the sauce. Cover with more sauce and place in the oven. Bake about 10 minutes.

Yield: 8 to 12 servings.

Marinara sauce

8   cups imported Italian plum tomatoes
¾   cup salad oil
⅓   cup thinly sliced garlic
10   snipped fresh basil leaves, or 1 tablespoon dried
1   tablespoon chopped fresh parsley
      Salt and freshly ground pepper to taste

1. Empty the tomatoes into a bowl and crush them by hand.

2. Heat the oil in a casserole and add the garlic. Add the remaining ingredients and simmer 30 minutes, stirring often.

Yield: About 5 cups.

October 1976

THERE ARE usually good reasons why a much-favored recipe will languish and lie on the brain for years before it ever surfaces in print. Years ago, when I was a student at the Hotel School in Lausanne, Switzerland, I sampled my first "dish," if you could call it that, of raclette, that marvelous melted cheese served with hot potatoes, pickled onions and cornichons. That was a glorious experience, going down into a celler especially designed for the feast, a kind of room that is called in certain parts of Switzerland a carnotzet. The dish was served then under highly specialized and controlled circumstances. The carnotzet was equipped with a neat, vertical brazier that held the hot charcoal. To make a raclette, a whole wheel of bagnes, or raclette, cheese is held against the brazier until the surface melts. This is scraped off onto a dish, the cheese is replaced against the brazier, scraped off, and so on. Originally, this was done before an open fire. The reason why I have never written about a raclette is obvious—the inaccessibility of a vertical grill and the cumbersome nature of an outdoor fire. Later, I discovered an ultraviolet machine for making raclette, but that proved too expensive for the ordinary pocketbook. Then came individual, small raclette cookers, which made it possible to serve the dish in the home. I was fascinated to learn only recently from the chef at the Swiss Embassy in Washington that these small electric cookers are now used at the Embassy when they serve raclette.

In the Mogul Tradition

"In our day-to-day food," Ayesha Singh was saying recently, "there is always the taste of Mogul dining."

As she spoke, Mrs. Singh quickly, deftly and with utmost caution applied small squares of varek—the Indian word for silver foil—to the surface of the rose petal ice cream that she had prepared and offered in a frozen silver bowl. After the foil, of such fragile nature it all but defies the laws of gravity, she added slivered, chilled, blanched almonds and, as a final filling a scattering of fresh rose petals.

The ice cream—known in India as kulfi—is by all accounts one of the most delicate and exotic frozen desserts we've ever known.

Mrs. Singh, a woman of great elegance, sensitivity and style, is the wife of a late brigadier in the Indian Army. She had come to New York to visit her only child, Reeva, and while here acted briefly as a friendly consultant for Raja, an establishment on Second Avenue (near 63rd Street), which specializes in the frozen desserts and other chilled sweets of India.

When we learned that Mrs. Singh, a native of Pakistan who now lives in Delhi, was in town, we telephoned for an interview and to our delight she invited us to sample a grand assortment of Indian specialities miraculously prepared in her daughter's spacious and handsome one-room apartment with a kitchen that seemed tiny even by New York standards. Off the range and out of the oven came shahi biryani, a variously spiced chicken and rice casserole; shahi pasanda, a fork-tender lamb creation flavored with cardamom; and a very special dal made with small black Indian beans.

Desserts included, in addition to the rose petal ice cream, an incredibly subtle and delicious creation made with a rich chilled milk custard spooned over fried pieces of bread with pistachios and almonds.

"All of these dishes," she stated, "are handed down, generation by generation, from the kitchens of the Mogul empire." The Moguls, she informed us, came to the north of India during the sixteenth century from southern Russia, Persia and Turkey, bringing with them the food inspirations of their native lands and these were adapted to the numerous spices to be found in India.

We noted that several of the dishes on that evening bore the name shahi, and she explained that the word means royal.

"The recipe for the rose petal ice cream must be hundreds of years old," she said, "and in the old days when there were lots of servants it was made by stirring raw milk for hours by hand. Today I reduce the milk by cooking it in double boilers. By the way, rose perfume was first distilled by the wife of the third Mogul emperor Noorjehan Jehangir. Noorjehan means light of the world.

Ayesha Singh serves an exotic rose petal ice cream

"Most of the Mogul emperors were great gourmets, including Akbar the great, who consolidated northern and central India as the Mogul empire. The recipe for shahi biryani, the rice with chicken, is said to be that of Shah Jehan who built the Taj Mahal.

"Biryani can be made with almost any kind of meat—with mutton, lamb, fish and so on, but Mogul-style is always with chicken."

Mrs. Singh's kitchen pantry is stocked with a quantity of garam masala, a powdered blend of cardamom, cloves, peppercorns and cinnamon. We were fascinated to learn that turmeric, the spice that is the base of most commercial powder in America, has no place in her kitchen. "I dislike the flavor," she states firmly.

Mrs. Singh, who dresses in resplendent saris, even in the kitchen, stated that she had learned cooking from her grandmother who supervised her family's large kitchen staff. "She spent most of her time in the kitchen, and I was the eldest grandchild. I simply trailed in her footsteps."

"Most people," her daughter, Reeva, told us, "look at her and say, 'I'm sure she doesn't know how to boil an egg.'"

Kulfi Gulab

(Rose petal ice cream)

8 cups raw milk, available in
   some health food stores
2 cups heavy cream
1½ cups heavy rose syrup,
   available in bottles in shops
   where Indian delicacies are
   sold (see note)
6 pods of green cardamom (see
   note)
2 tablespoons rose water
¼ cup slivered, blanched
   almonds
   Varek (silver foil) for garnish
   (see note)
   Rose petals for garnish

1. Place the raw milk in a double
boiler. A double boiler may be impro-
vised by placing a metal bowl inside a
close-fitting and slightly larger container with boiling water beneath the
metal bowl. Cook, uncovered, over
boiling water until reduced almost by
half. Take care that the water beneath
the milk is replenished as it evaporates.

2. Add the heavy cream and rose
syrup. If 2 double boilers are used,
add half the cream and syrup to each.
Continue cooking about 10 minutes
longer.

3. Strain the mixture and let cool.

4. Crush the cardamom and discard the husks. Continue crushing the
seeds. Add the rose water. Stir this
into the rose milk mixture.

5. Pour the mixture into a bowl
and place in the freezer. When the
mixture is almost thoroughly frozen,
stir it with a whisk until creamy. Continue to freeze until it has the consistency of ice cream.

6. Meanwhile, as the ice cream
freezes, drop the almonds in a basin of
ice water and let stand until well
chilled.

7. Garnish the rose ice cream
with silver foil.

8. Drain the almonds well and
scatter them over the foil. Garnish
with a few rose petals and serve.

Yield: 8 or more servings.

Note: The traditional Indian ingredients for these dishes are available
in shops around Manhattan that specialize in Indian delicacies. All the ingredients are available, for example,
at Spice and Sweet Mahal, 135 Lexington Avenue (at 29th Street).

Shahi Pasanda

(Royal fillets of lamb)

3 pounds boneless leg of lamb
½ cup yogurt
1 teaspoon garam masala (see
   recipe)
¾ cup peanut, vegetable or salad
   oil
8 cups chopped onion
3 cloves garlic, finely minced
1 2-inch piece of ginger,
   finely grated
1½ cups water
   Salt to taste
4 large bay leaves
12 green cardamom pods (see
   note)
¾ cup skinless, blanched
   almonds

1. The meat should be well
trimmed of skin and surface fat. Cut
the meat or have it cut into about 25
3-by-2-inch fillets. Add the yogurt and

garam masala and blend the ingredients. Cover and refrigerate overnight or longer.

2. Heat ¼ cup oil in a heavy saucepan or small casserole and add the onion, garlic and ginger. Cook, stirring often, until the mixture is dark caramel colored. This may take 45 minutes or even longer, and care must be taken that the mixture does not stick or burn.

3. Preheat the oven to 350 degrees.

4. Heat the remaining ½ cup oil in a Dutch oven or heavy casserole and add one cup of the onion mixture. Add the water and stir to make a smooth blend. Add salt and bay leaves. Crush the cardamom pods and add them. Add the almonds.

5. Scoop out approximately ¾ of the sauce. Arrange ⅓ of the lamb fillets over the sauce in the casserole. Add ¼ of the sauce and another ⅓ of lamb. Add another quarter of the sauce, the remaining lamb and add a final layer of sauce. Cover, bring to the boil on top of the stove and place in the oven. Bake 1 hour.

6. Uncover and remove the pieces of meat. Skim off as much of the surface fat from the sauce as possible. Return the meat to the sauce.

7. Reduce the oven heat to 200 degrees. Continue baking the lamb about half an hour or until lamb is fork tender.

Yield: 8 to 12 servings.

Note: Cardamom pods are available in shops that specialize in Indian delicacies, including Foods of India, 120 Lexington Avenue (at 28th Street), and Indian Spice Store, 126 Lexington Avenue (between 28th and 29th Streets).

Garam masala

Remove the seeds from 75 pods of brown cardamon, available in Indian stores. Add them to a small coffee grinder or spice mill. Add 50 whole cloves, 50 peppercorns and 4 cinnamon sticks, about 1½ inches each, crushed into small pieces. Blend to a powder. Garam masala is also available commercially in Indian stores.

Shahi Biryani

(A chicken and rice casserole)

2	pounds skinned, boneless chicken breasts
1½	cups peanut, vegetable or corn oil
	Salt to taste
¼	teaspoon red paprika
4	cups thinly sliced onion
3	cups short-grain rice, preferably purchased in Indian markets
¾	cup raisins
1	tablespoon crushed cumin seeds
6	bay leaves
6	whole cloves
½	teaspoon slivered garlic
¼	cup thick yogurt (see recipe)
1	teaspoon crushed cardamom seeds
4¼	cups chicken stock (see recipe)
½	teaspoon kewra (see note), optional

1. The chicken should be cut into flat pieces, each about a 3-inch square. Very thick pieces of chicken should be butterflied before cutting. Set aside.

2. Heat ½ cup of oil in a casserole and cook the chicken pieces sprinkled

with salt and red paprika until chicken pieces lose their raw look. Set aside.

3. Heat the remaining cup of oil in a heavy casserole and cook the onions, stirring, until golden brown, about 20 minutes.

4. Wash the rice well and cover with cold water. Let stand for ½ hour.

5. Cover the raisins with cold water and let stand.

6. Place the casserole with onions on low heat. Add cumin seeds, bay leaves, whole cloves, garlic slivers and drained raisins. Cook, stirring, for 3 minutes. Add the yogurt and salt to taste.

7. Drain the rice and add it to the casserole along with the chicken pieces and any liquid that may have accumulated. Add the crushed cardamom seeds and chicken broth. Sprinkle with kewra. Cover and let it cook for 15 minutes.

8. Meanwhile, preheat the oven to 250 degrees.

9. Do not uncover and do not stir, but pick up the casserole firmly with both hands and toss to redistribute the chicken and the rice. Or, if the casserole is too heavy and seems unwieldy, uncover it and gently stir the rice with a rubber spatula to redistribute it.

10. Place the casserole in the oven and bake 30 minutes.

11. It is preferable to scoop the rice mixture from the casserole to a rice dish with a saucer so that the rice grains do not become sticky.

Yield: 8 to 12 servings.

Note: Kewra is a white spirit that smells vaguely and pleasantly like nasturtiums. It is available in bottles in Indian stores.

Thick yogurt

Line a bowl with cheesecloth. Empty the contents of 1 pint of commercial yogurt into the cheesecloth. Bring up the edges of the cheesecloth and tie with a long string. Suspend the cheesecloth bag with the string over the bowl. Let stand about 2 hours.

Chicken stock Indian-style

> *The bones of a 3-pound chicken*
> *Water to cover*
> *Salt to taste*
> 2 *cinnamon sticks, each about 1½ inches*
> 4 *crushed brown cardamom pods*

Combine all the ingredients in a saucepan. Bring to the boil and cook, uncovered, about 45 minutes. Strain.

Yield: About 5 cups.

Chicken Korma

> 3½ *pounds skinned, boned chicken breasts*
> ⅔ *cup oil*
> 8 *cups chopped onions*
> 3 *cloves garlic, finely minced*
> 1 *2-inch piece ginger, finely grated*
> ¾ *cup water*
> 2 *teaspoons red paprika*
> *Salt to taste*
> ½ *cup tomato paste*
> 1 *teaspoon crushed green cardamom seeds taken out of the pods*

2 *to 4 chopped fresh, hot green chili peppers*
1 *tablespoon chopped fresh coriander leaves, available in Chinese and Spanish as well as Indian markets*

1. Cut the chicken into 2-inch cubes. There should be about 5 cups.

2. Heat ¼ cup of the oil in a heavy saucepan or small casserole and add the onion, garlic and ginger. Cook, stirring often, until the mixture is dark caramel colored. This may take 45 minutes or even longer and care must be taken that the mixture does not stick or burn.

3. Heat the remaining oil in a Dutch oven or heavy casserole and add 1 cup of the onion mixture. Add the water, paprika, salt, tomato paste and crushed coriander seeds. Add the chicken and stir to blend. Add the chopped chili peppers and cover. Cook about 12 to 15 minutes, just long enough so that the chicken pieces are cooked through without drying out. Remove from the heat and let stand until ready to serve. When ready to serve, reheat briefly. Serve sprinkled with fresh coriander.

Yield: 8 to 12 servings.

Sweet and Rich

WITH PIERRE FRANEY

If chocolate truffles are, as we have been told, of Italian origin, then the desserts on this page are, indeed, international in scope. There are Swiss walnut fingers (the recipe for which came to us through the predominately Mexican kitchen of Diana Kennedy, who is English); pears à la vigneronne, the name of which smacks of the vineyards of France; and finally, an outrageously rich pecan pie, the origin of which is the Mississippi Delta. There is only one shameful thing about chocolate truffles: They are like fresh roasted peanuts, insidiously good and, therefore, irresistible.

6   *egg yolks*
6   *tablespoons dark rum*
¾   *cup powdered cocoa*
¾   *cup confectioners' sugar*

1. Preheat oven to 200 degrees or lower.

2. Place the chocolate in a heat-proof bowl and place the bowl in the oven. Watch carefully and remove the bowl just when the chocolate has softened.

3. Immediately beat in the butter, yolks and rum with a wire whisk. Beat with the whisk until the mixture becomes workable. If your kitchen is quite warm, it may be necessary to chill the chocolate mixture briefly until it can be shaped into balls between the palms of the hands. Shape the chocolate into round balls about 1 inch in diameter and roll them in powdered cocoa and/or confectioners' sugar. Arrange the "truffles" on a rack and let stand in a cool place several hours.

Yield: 80 to 90 truffles.

1   *pound semisweet chocolate*
½   *pound butter at room temperature*

6. Bring the liquid in the saucepan to the boil and add the remaining ingredients. Bring to the boil and cook about 10 minutes. Pour the sauce over the pears. Let cool and chill.

Yield: 6 servings.

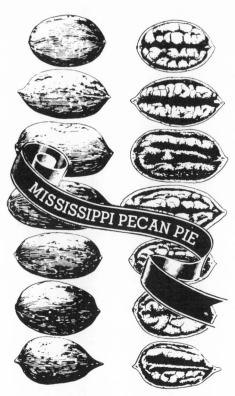

2½   *pounds fresh, ripe, unblemished pears*
2   *cups dry white wine*
½   *cup sugar*
1   *lemon*
1   *2-inch length of cinnamon or ¼ teaspoon ground*
1   *1-inch length vanilla or 1 teaspoon vanilla extract*
¼   *cup orange marmalade*
¼   *cup apricot preserves*

1. Peel and core the pears and cut each of them into eighths.

2. Place the pears in a saucepan and add the wine and sugar.

3. Peel the lemon and cut the peel into very fine, julienne strips. Reserve the lemon for another use. Add the peel to the saucepan.

4. Bring to the boil and simmer 5 to 10 minutes or until pears are tender.

5. Transfer the pears and lemon peel to a serving dish.

Pastry for a 10-inch pie
1¼   *cups dark corn syrup*
1   *cup sugar*
4   *whole eggs*
4   *tablespoons melted butter*
1½   *cups chopped pecan meats*
1   *teaspoon pure vanilla extract*
2   *tablespoons dark rum*

1. Preheat oven to 350 degrees.

2. Roll out the pastry and line a 10-inch pie tin.

3. Combine the corn syrup and sugar in a saucepan and bring to the boil. Cook, stirring, just until the sugar is dissolved.

4. Beat the eggs in a mixing bowl and gradually add the sugar, beating. Add the remaining ingredients and pour the mixture into the pie shell. Bake 50 minutes to 1 hour or until the pie is set.

Yield: 8 servings.

DIANA KENNEDY'S SWISS WALNUT FINGERS

The cookies

1 cup ground walnuts, about ¼ pound
1 cup ground almonds, about ¼ pound
½ cup flour
3 tablespoons superfine sugar
1 teaspoon grated orange rind
¼ teaspoon ground allspice
¼ teaspoon ground mace or nutmeg
¼ teaspoon ground cinnamon
½ cup chopped citron or other fruitcake mixture
1 egg white, stiffly beaten
1 tablespoon honey
1 tablespoon Grand Marnier or cognac

The glaze

2 tablespoons confectioners' sugar
1 tablespoon water
1 tablespoon Grand Marnier or cognac

1. Preheat oven to 325 degrees.

2. Combine the ground nuts, flour, sugar, orange rind, spices, chopped citron and egg white. Heat the honey with the Grand Marnier and add it. Blend well with the hands.

3. Shape the batter into a rectangle about 3 inches by 12 inches. Cut into fingers about ¾ inch thick. Place the fingers on an oiled baking sheet and bake ½ hour.

4. For the glaze, combine the sugar, water and Grand Marnier. Brush the mixture over the fingers and let stand until dry.

Yield: About 16 fingers.

Passion for Pizza

We discovered in Nova Scotia several months back that we had much in common with the children of Sirio Maccioni, the tall, dapper, soft-spoken co-owner of Le Cirque Restaurant in Manhattan, and his wife, Egi. And that is a passion for homemade pizza.

We made this discovery one Sunday morning while most of the rest of the group, including several chefs, were out in the woods somewhere hunting wild boar. We sat in the kitchen and watched Egi as she went about her task of making pizza.

"Pizza on Sunday has been a tradition in our home since I was a child in Montecatini, Italy," she told us as she squeezed a small handful of presoaked imported black mushrooms. "My children—Mario, Marco and Mauro—love it and if I don't prepare pizza on Sunday, it's like losing a day in the week."

Mrs. Maccioni told us that an interest in baking came naturally to her, for her father was and is "the best baker" in her home town, which is, of course, one of the most famous spas in Europe, a place for taking the cure.

As she sliced half a pound of fresh, snow-white mushrooms and grated a hunk of mozzarella cheese for her mushroom pizza, she told us that before her marriage she had been a professional singer and had sung in many places throughout the world including Carnegie Hall. Cooking today for her family has become something of an avocation.

When all the ingredients were assembled and readied—in addition to the mushroom pizza she would cook an anchovy pizza made with capers, oregano and cheese—the pastry she had prepared was divided in half and each half placed on an oiled pizza pan. She pressed it out by hand, covered each round with the savories including the cheese.

As the pizzas were taken from the oven her husband, Sirio, arrived. "She makes the best pizza," he stated as he sampled a hot mouthful, "this side of Naples."

Pizza with Anchovies and Cheese

Pizza dough for 2 13-inch pizzas (see recipe)
8　*tablespoons olive oil*
8　*tinned anchovies, drained and cut in half crosswise (use more anchovies if you prefer a more pronounced flavor)*
¼　*cup drained capers*
1　*cup well-drained canned tomatoes cut into ½-inch pieces*
1　*teaspoon dried oregano*
　　Salt to taste

Egi Maccioni makes "the best pizza this side of Naples" every Sunday

2   *cups grated whole-milk*
    mozzarella cheese
    Freshly ground pepper to taste

1. Prepare the dough and let it rise.

2. Pour 2 tablespoons of olive oil into the center of each of 2 13-inch pizza pans. Spread it around the bottom and inner rim of the pans.

3. Using lightly floured fingers, work the dough into a ball. Divide it in half and, with floured fingers, pat each half into a somewhat thick circle. Add 1 circle of dough to the center of each pizza pan. Using the fingers, pat and press the dough to cover the bottom of the pans, rim to rim. Cover and let stand in a warm place about ½ hour.

4. Meanwhile, preheat the oven to 350 degrees.

5. Scatter equal amounts of anchovies over the 2 pizzas. Sprinkle with capers and cover with tomato pieces. Sprinkle with oregano and just a touch of salt. Sprinkle the grated cheese over all and sprinkle generously with black pepper. Sprinkle with the remaining oil.

6. Place the pizzas in the oven and bake about 15 minutes or until the cheese is bubbling. Place the pans on the floor of the oven and continue baking about 5 minutes or until dough is crisp on the bottom.

Yield: 8 to 12 servings.

Pizza dough
(For 2 pizzas)

2½   cups flour
2   tablespoons olive oil
1½   tablespoons (envelopes) dry
      yeast
1   cup lukewarm water

1. Place the flour in a mixing bowl and stir in the olive oil.

2. Dissolve the yeast in the water. Stir this into the flour mixture, using a wooden spoon and a plastic spatula to scrape around the edges so that all the flour is incorporated. This will be a somewhat sticky dough. Scrape the dough into a compact mass. Cover with a cloth and let stand in a warm place 30 minutes or longer until it rises.

Yield: Enough dough for 2 13-inch pizzas.

Pizza with Mushrooms and Cheese

Pizza dough for 2 13-inch
pizzas (see recipe)
12   or more dried black
      mushrooms, preferably
      imported Italian mushrooms,
      available in grocery stores that
      specialize in Italian delicacies
8   tablespoons olive oil
4   cups thinly sliced fresh
      mushrooms
      Salt to taste

2   cups grated mozzarella cheese
      Freshly ground pepper to taste

1. Prepare the dough and let it rise.

2. Place the dried mushrooms in a bowl and add warm water to cover. Let stand ½ hour or longer, until mushrooms soften.

3. Pour 2 tablespoons of olive oil into the center of each of 2 13-inch pizza pans. Spread it around the bottom and inner rim of the pans.

4. Using lightly floured fingers, work the dough into a ball. Divide it in half and, with floured fingers, pat each half into a somewhat thick circle. Add 1 circle of dough to the center of each pizza pan. Using the fingers, pat and press the dough to cover the bottom of the pans, rim to rim. Cover and let stand in a warm place for about ½ hour.

5. Meanwhile, preheat the oven to 350 degrees.

6. Scatter a layer of fresh mushroom slices all over the dough in both pans. Drain the dried mushrooms and squeeze to extract most of the moisture. Shred them and scatter these over the fresh mushrooms. Sprinkle lightly with salt.

7. Scatter the grated cheese over all and sprinkle generously with pepper. Sprinkle the remaining olive oil over all.

8. Place the pans in the oven and bake about 15 minutes or until the cheese is bubbling. Place the pans on the floor of the oven and continue baking about 5 minutes or until dough is crisp on the bottom.

Yield: 8 to 12 servings.

Raclette

When we recall our first encounters with the good things of the Swiss table—it was at least a couple of decades ago—our mind fairly aches and reeks with nostalgia and pleasure.

We remember our first sampling of deep-fried fresh perch and truite au bleu, the perch and the trout taken from the then crystal-clear waters of Lac Leman (or, as the English would have it, Lake Geneva). There were platters of fine-textured and slightly salted, wind-dried beef from the Grisons and our first taste of a kirsch-perfumed genuine fondue made with a full-bodied, nutty-flavored Gruyère cheese. At the same time we discovered another cheese dish that had, perhaps, an even greater impact on our gastronomic sensibilities and the dish was called raclette.

It was in our student days then and, when cold weather came on, it was our pleasure and persuasion to visit what is called in the French-speaking canton of Valais, a carnotzet, of which there were several. A carnotzet originally was the sampling room of a cellar, situated in front of the wine storage area. Gradually it came to be a place where one sampled both wine and cheese dishes as well. A typical carnotzet has steps leading down into a room, generally quite small with walls sketched with Swiss scenes—mountains, ski-slopes, ski-lifts, chalets, Saint Bernard dogs, wine casks and Swiss cheese in numerous shapes.

There were three sorts of dishes served in the carnotzets we visited: The Grisons beef (called viande sèche in French, Bundnerfleish in German), served as the preface to the others; fondues; and the raclette, which we consider the most interesting and certainly the most festive of cold weather foods.

The name raclette stems from the French word, racler, which means to scrape. The name is applied to the cheese dish because of the traditional technique for serving it. Originally half a wheel of a cheese known as "bagnes" or "raclette" cheese was placed before a blazing wood fire and, as the surface of the cheese melted, it was scraped onto a small plate to be eaten along with small, boiled potatoes in the skin, small, sour pickles known as cornichons, and small pickled cocktail onions. Plus a loaf of crusty bread, a glass of dry white Swiss wine or, perhaps, a glass of kirschwasser. And a pepper mill on the side to give the dish added zest.

This outdoor technique, which still exists in some areas in Switzerland, was modified for the carnotzets. The wood fire was replaced by a perpendicular charcoal brazier with the cheese placed in an upright position close to the heat to melt it. It was served with the traditional accompaniments on small plates. It almost goes without saying that one scraping would scarcely make a meal and thus

Keren Shaw uses an imported electric Swiss oven for her raclette parties

during the course of an hour numerous plates would stack up before the customer. The customer would be charged according to the number of plates.

The possibility of serving raclette in the home has materialized in America within very recent memory. A short while ago, bagnes or raclette cheese was all but unheard of here. We were delighted during the course of a visit in the home of Heidi Hagman (at the time she was called "the barefoot caterer of California"), who is Mary Martin's granddaughter, to be served a genuine raclette party at her hands. Her hands, that is to say, preparing and scraping the cheese for the guests.

Not only was the cheese available to her in half wheels, but she had at her disposal an electric machine for melting the cheese. Both the cheese and that machine are widely available in the New York area. The machine consists of a solid base plus a swinging arm containing an infrared lamp for heating the surface of the cheese. Half a wheel or a quarter of a wheel of raclette cheese is placed between clamps to hold it securely. The heating arm is swung directly over and parallel to the surface of the cheese, which it heats to bubbling. The arm is swung away and the cheese is scraped onto small hot plates. The cost of this unit is about $225 and it may be rented for a few dollars a day.

About a year ago in the Hamptons we were invited to a small raclette party in the home of Keren Shaw, an excellent cook and the wife of Adam Shaw, the writer. She introduced us to a much simplified, much less costly and admirable raclette "oven" imported from Switzerland and widely available here. It consists of a round enameled cover that houses a round electric heating coil. There are four small pans designed to be filled with squares of cheese and situated for heating directly under the hot coil. Four pans will serve for a party of two. It is best (in the interest of uninterrupted dining) to have eight pans for a party of four so that you can eat and heat simultaneously. The cost of this unit with four pans is about $49.98. Four additional pans cost about $7.98.

Have available for each serving small trays of sour pickles, preferably the imported pickles called cornichons and another dish of small pickled cocktail onions. Also vital to a proper raclette, a dish of hot potatoes, preferably boiled in the jacket and unpeeled, although larger potatoes may be boiled, halved or quartered and served. And by all means a pepper mill and a crusty loaf of bread.

In that raclette is a specialty of the Valais region of Switzerland, the best wine to serve with it is a white wine of the same region. That is a Fendant. On the other hand, any very good, light dry white wine would be excellent. If you wish to give a bit of a kick to the party, you might also serve a few small glasses of kirschwasser at room temperature. Beer would also not be amiss. The traditional dessert for the dish is assorted cut fruits and berries tossed with sugar and chilled or, perhaps, a fruit tart.

Sources for purchasing the small raclette "ovens" with four pans include the Ideal Cheese Shop, 1205 Second Avenue (near 63d Street); Cheese of All Nations, 153 Chambers Street; HQZ Cheese Pantry, 1270 Madison Avenue (near 91st Street); The Cheese Shop, 161 East 22d Street; Vermonti Enterprises' The Big Cheese, 35A Jane Street; The Cheese Villa of Massapequa, 219 Sunrise Mall, Massapequa; The Uncommon Market, 26 Hampton Road, Southampton; The Cheese Shop, 134 East Ridgewood Avenue, Ridgewood, N.J.; and The Cheese Shop, 31 Purchase Street, Rye, N.Y.

Large raclette machines with the swing-away arm may also be purchased or rented at several of these shops. The rental cost of the machines ranges from $5 to $8 a day.

Hamburgers à la Russe

WITH PIERRE FRANEY

As we have noted on numerous occasions, the history of the hamburger in America is long, involved and almost if not all of its origins can be disputed. Wouldn't it be interesting if it were the Russians really who originated the dish under another name. To wit, bitoke, a well-known Russian creation (date of origin unknown) is really nothing more than ground beef cooked in butter and, generally, served with chopped fried onions and potatoes. The French word bifteck, incidentally, applies to both steaks (slabs of meat) and to hamburgers. The manner of making bitokes is virtually without end, if various meats are substituted for the ground beef. Thus the recipes on this page—bitokes of pork, chicken and veal with various sauces and seasonings.

Bitokes de Porc au Karvi

(Pork patties with caraway)

2   pounds ground pork
1   cup fine, fresh bread crumbs
    Salt and freshly ground
    pepper
1   teaspoon crushed caraway
    seeds or ½ teaspoon ground
    caraway
5   tablespoons butter
2   cups chopped onion
1   clove garlic, finely minced
6   fresh basil leaves or 1
    teaspoon crushed dried leaves
1   bay leaf
1   sprig fresh thyme or ½
    teaspoon dried
2   pounds fresh tomatoes,
    peeled, cored, and cubed,
    about 4 cups, or use an equal
    amount of crushed, canned
    imported tomatoes
3   tablespoons peanut, vegetable
    or corn oil

1. Place the pork in a mixing bowl and add the bread crumbs, salt and pepper to taste and the caraway. Blend well with the fingers.

2. Divide the mixture into 12 portions of approximately the same weight. Using the fingers, shape the portions into neat, round, flat patties. Arrange on a baking dish and refrigerate until ready to cook.

3. Heat 2 tablespoons butter and add the onion and garlic. Cook, stirring, until wilted and add the basil, bay leaf, thyme and tomatoes. Bring to the boil and add salt to taste. Simmer about 20 minutes and stir in 2 more tablespoons of butter.

4. When ready to cook, heat the oil and remaining tablespoon butter in a skillet. Brown the patties on one side, about 3 minutes. Turn and brown on the other. Continue cooking until done.

5. Serve hot with the tomato sauce spooned over.

Yield: 12 patties.

Bitokes de Volaille au Persil

(Chicken patties with parsley)

2 *pounds skinned, boneless chicken breasts*
2 *tablespoons finely chopped shallots*
1 *cup fine, fresh bread crumbs, plus bread crumbs for dredging*
½ *cup heavy cream*
   Salt and freshly ground pepper
3 *tablespoons finely chopped parsley*
3 *tablespoons peanut, vegetable or corn oil*
5 *tablespoons butter*

1. Finely grind or have ground the chicken breasts. This is easily done with a food processor.

2. Put the chicken in a mixing bowl and add the shallots, 1 cup bread crumbs, cream, salt and pepper to taste and the parsley. Blend well with the fingers.

3. Divide the mixture into 12 portions of approximately the same weight. Using the fingers, shape the portions into neat, round, flat patties. Arrange on a baking dish and refrigerate until ready to cook.

4. Dredge the patties evenly on all sides with bread crumbs, patting lightly so that the crumbs adhere.

5. When ready to cook, heat 3 tablespoons of oil and 1 tablespoon butter. Brown the patties on one side, about 3 minutes. Turn and brown on the other. Continue cooking to the desired degree of doneness (alternatively, after browning, the patties may be partly cooked and transferred to an oven preheated to 250 degrees to finish cooking, about 10 minutes).

6. Transfer the patties to a platter. Heat the remaining butter in a skillet until it comes light brown (noisette) and pour this over the patties.

Yield: 12 patties.

Bitokes de Veau Smitane

(Veal patties with pepper and sour
cream sauce)

2   pounds ground veal
2   cups sour cream
1   cup fine, fresh bread crumbs
4   teaspoons paprika
2   tablespoons finely chopped
    onion
    Salt and freshly ground
    pepper
2   tablespoons chopped dill
2   sweet peppers, preferably red
    although the green may be
    used
6   tablespoons peanut oil
2   tablespoons butter
¼   cup coarsely chopped onion
1   cup dry white wine

1. Place the veal in a mixing bowl
and add 6 tablespoons sour cream, the
bread crumbs, 3 teaspoons paprika,
the finely chopped onion, salt and
pepper to taste and the dill. Blend
well with the fingers.

2. Divide the mixture into 12
portions of approximately the same
weight. Using wet fingers, shape the
portions into neat, round, flat patties.
Arrange on a baking dish and refrigerate until ready to cook.

3. Meanwhile, prepare the sauce.
Remove the cores and seeds from the
peppers. Cut them in half lengthwise.
Slice the halves lengthwise into ½-
inch strips.

4. Heat half the oil and half the
butter in a skillet and add the pepper
strips. Cook about 4 minutes and add
the coarsely chopped onion. Cook,
stirring, until wilted and add the remaining teaspoon paprika. Add the
wine and cook, stirring, about 30 minutes. Add salt to taste.

5. When ready to cook, heat the
remaining oil and butter in a skillet
and brown the patties on one side,
about 3 minutes. Turn and brown on
the other. Continue cooking to the desired degree of doneness.

6. Reheat the pepper strips and
onions and stir in the remaining sour
cream. Stir and remove from the heat.
Add salt to taste. Heat thoroughly,
but do not boil or the sauce will
curdle.

7. Serve the patties with the
sauce spooned over.

Yield: 12 patties.

November 1976

IT IS OBVIOUS that the vast majority of articles written about gastronomy are built around the sheer pleasure of dining well. Once in a while, one is faced with a moment of daring—a new experience, a quickened emotion not unlike diving into a cold swimming pool before the sun has prepared you for it.

For six months, both in this country and in Europe, I had heard that "the world's greatest restaurant" was situated in a tiny town in Switzerland. Even some of the well-known chefs of France had hinted at the greatness of a remarkable young Swiss chef who was for the most part an experimenter and who had mastered in a brilliant fashion what is known and celebrated in France as la nouvelle cuisine. One is obviously hesitant about going out on a limb and labeling anything as the "greatest," leaving the observer open to hoots and jeers. Nonetheless, we ventured forth to the town of Crissier and Restaurant Girardet, and the experience was unforgettable. We dined on fantastic lobster stew, chicken with a splendid sauce of leeks and cream, an incomparable dish of sautéed duck liver, slightly crusty on the outside and melting within, and duly reported our find. Since that meal, and especially since our account of it, I have often been asked if I really do think Girardet is the greatest chef in Europe or the world for that matter. The fact is there are several chefs who can compete on the same level with Girardet. I can also say that that one meal is perhaps the single dinner I have ever eaten where I could not fault in any sense the food or wine.

The World's Greatest New Chef

Where people talk knowledgeably about great cooking today, forty-year-old Freddy Girardet of Crissier, Switzerland, is said to be the most illustrious thing to come along since Mrs. Escoffier gave birth to Georges Auguste 130 years ago. Even Paul Bocuse has hinted at it. And Pierre Troisgros is so impressed with the young man's talents he dispatched his young son, Michel, to serve his apprenticeship in the Girardet kitchen.

The professional restaurant critics of France are downright breathless when they mention his name. The man from *L'Express* describes Girardet's kitchen as "extraordinary, unforgettable." The scrivener of *Jours de France* says, "Sublime." There are even those who argue that what Mr. Girardet has put together is conceivably the greatest French restaurant on the European continent.

Then who is this new genius, this sorcerer of the European cookstove so recently catapulted into international eminence?

He has a modest background. He never served a day's apprenticeship in any of the great and established kitchens of France. To the contrary. In his early youth, he was a jock, and when he wasn't playing tackle with the local football team, he was working in his father's modest kitchen, here in Crissier, a town of 4,000 inhabitants. That plus a three-year stint at a popular but scarcely celebrated establishment, the Brasserie du Grand Chêne in Lausanne.

Mr. Girardet vows that his entire inspiration in cooking began with a routine visit—years ago—to a vineyard in Burgundy on a buying tour.

"I had never dined in any of the greatest restaurants in France. On this particular occasion, one of the vineyard owners suggested we drive to Roanne for lunch. He took me to the Troisgros restaurant." It was, Mr. Girardet recalled, an almost spiritual experience. In one single meal, he declared, his vision, his entire concept of what cooking was all about, was altered—irrevocably.

The thing that astonishes the young man's peers is that—following this experience—he has, solely on his own native talent, become one of the greatest creative forces in the world of chefs today. And there is no one who will declare that he is second to Bocuse, Guérard, Vergé or any of the other titans on the European scene. His cooking is also universally conceded to fit the mold of the much-publicized nouvelle cuisine of France.

"La nouvelle cuisine," Mr. Girardet noted, "is nothing more than good taste. It is to prepare dishes to preserve their natural flavors and with the simplest of sauce."

Freddy Girardet is said to be the most illustrious young chef in decades

La nouvelle cuisine is not, incidentally, what many people mistakenly presume it to be—calorie free but nonetheless delectable. To the contrary, the vast majority of the Girardet sauces—just as in the kitchen of Bocuse, Vergé, et al.—are based primarily on cream.

"I don't love cream like those Lyonnaise chefs," Mr. Girardet observed but added that he does use 100 liters (100 quarts) each week and 80 kilograms (160 pounds) of butter each week.

Although he is very much his own man and his inspirations are pure Girardet, his thinking follows closely the precepts of la nouvelle cuisine.

Flour, except in pastry-making, is never used in his sauces. Instead, he relies on long-cooked reductions of foods in liquid—veal, fish, chicken, beef and so on. The end result of the cooking is a natural gelatin base that, when strained, is used in place of starches.

On the night that we dined on an elaborate succession of dishes at Restaurant Girardet—the original name was Restaurant de l'Hotel de Ville—the meal was bliss, not a dish to be faulted, a genuine feast for the season, a repas luxueux.

The proceedings began with a fragile hors d'oeuvre, bite-size pastry tarts filled with small crawfish tails in a delicate Nantua sauce with sorrel, this accompanied by a light, dry, nicely chilled white wine bottled last autumn at a local vineyard. We were richly regaled with Girardet's much-talked-about cassolette of duck livers, the slices of liver quickly sautéed so that they are crisp on the outside, melting within, and with a hot vinegar and shallot sauce.

There was a glorious fish dish, slices of loup de mer (a fish not found in American waters although striped bass would be an admirable substitute) with oysters and a fine julienne of vegetables in a cream sauce. That plus a celestial lobster dish with basil, the lobster famous not only for its flavor but its texture. Then a poularde de Bresse, a juicy, plump chicken from the Bresse region of France, with truffles studded beneath the skin, roasted and served on a bed of finely chopped leeks and truffles in a cream sauce. And an exceptional, high-standing soufflé made with a purée of fresh passion fruit.

The wines were equal to the occasion. In addition to the Swiss wine, there were three French wines, a stately pouilly fuissé, 1972; a Chateau Pape Clement, 1961, fantastic in its round quality and lack of tannin, generally so pronounced in Bordeaux; plus a positvely silken burgundy, a chambertin, Clos de Beze, also 1961.

In an attempt to analyze his own talents, Mr. Girardet inevitably begins by talking about Girardet père.

"My father," he stated, "might not have been what you call a great chef. He

The chef, who never wears the tall hat of his profession, with some of his staff

was what you call a cuisine toute simple in a small village café. And yet he gave me a solid foundation in cooking. My ideas, my principles were laid down for me by my father. Of course, I suppose I was born with a talent. But after that first visit to Troisgros, I also learned to turn that talent in many directions, to improvise." You are, he adds, born to pursue what you like.

Life wasn't easy going in the beginning after Mr. Girardet's father died. In the first place, there wasn't a great deal of money when he decided to take on the entire burden of the restaurant.

"I remember the first year after we had decided to give up the bistro kitchen and do more ambitious things," he said. "In the beginning we had what you'd call a 'jolie petite cave.'" Things were so tough financially, he added, "If you needed anything in addition to that, I would go out and buy twelve bottles at a time." Eventually he was able to buy a healthy and sizable supply of French wines, particularly Bordeaux in the recent years when prices of those wines became depressed. His present "cave" is still "jolie" but far from "petite."

Mr. Girardet, who has soft features, auburn hair, grey eyes and large, well-manicured, unblemished hands that might belong to a sculptor, has retired from all kinds of participation in sports. But he gets his exercise by riding a bicycle on his days off up and down the banks of Lake Geneva from Lausanne to Montreux and Vevey. As he rides, he says, his mind is not on the scenery. During these sessions he creates imaginary new dishes that he later transforms into reality in his kitchen. Things like a pot au feu with pigeon; rabbit livers with leeks in puff pastry; a cassolette of turbot with lobster and cucumbers; a daube of scallops with langostine tails; and fillets of salmon baked in paper with lime.

Those cycling expeditions also give him time to think thoughts like: "You can't be a great chef if your mind is preoccupied with making money. This kind of cooking costs money and you must forget the cost." He adds, in fact, that his profit is much less on dishes with the most expensive ingredients—foie gras, for instance.

"Your markup on these dishes must be less than on more available ingredients, otherwise your public can't afford them and you will have no chance to cook them and show your best talent," he explained.

"It took me a year to find suppliers of ingredients for the kinds of dishes I wanted to create," he said. "Fresh oysters, langoustes and St. Pierre (a kind of fish) from Brittany, chickens from the Bresse region of France, ducks from the Vendée region of France, fresh shrimp from the waters around Greece, and salmon from Scotland."

There were, of course, numerous kitchen treasures in abundant supply locally—his superb assortment of thirty kinds of Swiss cheeses; butter, cream and cheese from the Jura Mountains; and marvelous fresh vegetables from local farmers. His excellent breads are also baked by a local boulanger.

His insistence on fresh ingredients today borders on the manic. He will not, for example, keep fish or lobsters (as many restaurants do) for more than a day. "After that they start to suffer and the texture of the flesh changes, I swear it."

Discussing traditional French cooking, he states simply, "I have nothing against Escoffier, Edouard Nignon and the chefs of that epoch. I hate pretentious composed dishes. Things like coquilles St. Jacques with a border of duchesse potatoes, and things like fish dishes garnished with puff pastry crescents. I like classic cooking when it is simple but would never serve traditional dishes like tournedos Rossini [topped with foie gras and sliced truffle] and lobster Thermidor."

He also spoke of what many people consider the ultimate sculptured dish in the French repertory, the classic chartreuse of pheasant, in which hundreds of vegetable cutouts are used to line a mold for a filling of pheasant and cabbage.

"It is fascinating to look at, but I ask myself, is it really worth all that labor?"

Mr. Girardet said he considered giving motivation to young, would-be chefs one of his most important roles. He most certainly does not despair that there will always be a league of young people who want to dedicate their careers to cooking. He predicts that one of his staff, a 27-year-old young man named Michel Colin, will some day be one of the great chefs of Europe. "He will," he said, "perhaps succeed me. Or he will come into his own elsewhere."

One of the more interesting problems the chef faced when he decided to convert from bistro to a more elegant ambiance was the negotiation of a new lease. The town's loss at that time was his gain.

"The town fathers had decided they had no funds to maintain the Hotel de Ville," he said. "They were forced to sell so my family bought it. Now we lease office space to them."

There isn't a great deal to be said about the décor of the restaurant. It is comfortable but decidedly not grand: white walls, a few modern paintings—simple, unpretentious and pleasant. The napery and tableware are something else: crisply starched tablecloths and napkins; handsome, commendable dinner plates of large dimensions, the better to display the good things from the kitchen. One of the chief adornments is the cassolettes, small silver dishes with handles in which numerous of the dishes are served. A Girardet design. And roses on the tables.

There are seating accommodations for only sixty guests, and there is a staff of thirty. At the present time there is a four-to-six-week wait for a reservation in the evening. Reservations at midday are occasionally available. Mr. Girardet boasts that he would never rush his clientele and there is only one service for each meal.

The last time we dined with Mr. Girardet (on his day off we had lunch at a small bistro-type placed called Chez Louis in the nearby hamlet of Tiex; choice traditional Swiss country cooking, sausages primarily) he sounded almost plaintive as he talked about his newfound success:

"I'm afraid of fame," he said. "The thing I want most is to lead life with a certain simplicity. I want to spend most of my time in the kitchen and with my family."

The following dishes were served to us when we dined at Restaurant Girardet. Pierre Franey then recreated them in our kitchen.

Volaille au Coulis de Poireaux et de Truffes

(Roast truffled chicken on a bed of leeks in cream)

1 3½-pound chicken
10 thin slices black truffles, optional
 Salt and freshly ground pepper to taste
7 tablespoons butter
½ cup water
4 leeks
¼ cup black truffles cut into ½-inch cubes, optional
½ cup heavy cream

1. Preheat the oven to 375 degrees.

2. Using the fingers and hands, separate the skin from the main body of the chicken, which is to say the breast and thighs. This is easy to do. Starting at the open neck, insert the fingers gradually between the neck and body, pushing forward with fingers, working around the breast meat and thigh meat while loosening the skin.

3. Insert the truffle slices between the skin and meat, 2 on each leg and thigh and the remainder over the breast meat. Sprinkle the chicken

inside and out with salt and pepper. Truss the chicken neatly.

4. Grease a baking dish with 3 tablespoons of butter. Rub the chicken all over with 2 tablespoons of butter. Place the chicken on its side on the dish and place in the oven. Roast, basting often, 15 minutes.

5. Turn the chicken on its other side and continue roasting and basting 15 minutes longer.

6. Turn the chicken onto its back and roast 15 minutes, basting. Reduce the oven heat and continue roasting 15 minutes, a total of 1 hour. Add the water to the baking dish.

7. Using a two-pronged fork, lift up the chicken and let the cavity juices flow into the dish.

8. As the chicken cooks, trim the leeks and split them in half. Rinse well under cold running water to remove all dirt and sand between the leaves. Cut and chop the leeks into ½-inch pieces.

9. Heat the remaining butter in a Dutch oven or casserole and add the leeks, salt and pepper to taste. Cover and cook 15 minutes. Stir in the cubed truffles. Add the cream, stir and heat thoroughly. Arrange a ring of leeks on a serving dish and place the roast chicken in the center. Carve the chicken and serve with the pan liquid and the leeks as a side dish.

Yield: 6 or more servings.

On the menu of the Girardet Restaurant, the following dish is listed as escalopes de loup de mer aux huitres or scallops of loup de mer with oysters. Loup de mer is not available in American waters and striped bass makes an admirable substitute.

Escalopes de Bar Rayé aux Huitres

(Striped bass scallops with oysters)

1 1½-pound skinless, boneless
  fillet of striped bass
1 tablespoon butter
  Salt and freshly ground
  pepper to taste
½ cup carrot cut into very fine
  julienne strips (approximately
  the thinness of toothpicks but
  about 2 inches long)
¼ cup leeks cut into very fine
  julienne strips
½ cup celery root (or use stalk
  celery) cut into very fine
  julienne strips
1 cup dry white wine
1 cup fish stock (see recipe)
24 shucked oysters with their
  liquor
1 cup heavy cream
1 tablespoon finely chopped
  chives

1. Cut the fillet into 6 portions of approximately equal weight, slicing slightly on a diagonal. Place the pieces on a flat surface and pound lightly with a flat mallet.

2. Butter a baking dish with 1 tablespoon of butter and sprinkle with salt and pepper. Arrange the fish pieces over the bottom. Sprinkle with salt and pepper. Refrigerate until ready to cook.

3. Prepare the vegetables and drop them into boiling salted water. Simmer about 5 minutes and drain.

4. Preheat the oven to 450 degrees.

5. In a casserole heat the wine and fish stock and liquid from the oysters if there is any. Bring to the boil.

6. Pour 1½ cups of the wine mixture over the fish and place in the oven. Bake 3 to 5 minutes. Do not overcook. Pour off and add the cooking liquid to the original wine mixture. Keep the fish covered with foil.

7. Add the oysters to the liquid and cook briefly, about 1 minute. Scoop out the oysters and arrange equal amounts of them over the portions of fish.

8. Meanwhile, reduce the cooking liquid to about 1 cup. Add the cream and boil over high heat about 5 minutes. Add the drained vegetables and chopped chives. Spoon the sauce over the oysters and fish and serve piping hot.

Yield: 6 servings.

Fish stock

2 pounds bones from a white-
  fleshed, non-oily fish,
  including heads if possible but
  with gills removed
6 cups water
1 cup dry white wine
1 cup coarsely chopped celery
1 cup coarsely chopped onions
3 sprigs fresh thyme or 1
  teaspoon dried
1 bay leaf
10 peppercorns
  Salt to taste
1 medium-size tomato, cored,
  optional

1. If the fish heads are used, the gills must be removed. Run the bones under cold running water.

2. Place the bones in a kettle or deep saucepan and add the remaining ingredients. Bring to the boil and simmer 20 minutes. Strain.

Yield: About 6 cups.

Note: Leftover stock can be frozen for use in other dishes.

Escalopes de Foie Frais de Canard à la Vinaigrette

(Fresh scallops of duck liver with hot vinaigrette sauce)

12	*duck livers*
	Salt and freshly ground pepper to taste
4	*tablespoons butter*
4	*tablespoons walnut oil or 4 additional tablespoons of butter*
2	*tablespoons finely chopped shallots*
¼	*cup red wine vinegar, preferably imported sherry wine vinegar*
¼	*teaspoon finely chopped parsley*
2	*tablespoons finely chopped chives*
1	*tablespoon finely chopped chervil, optional*

1. Duck livers in France are much larger than those sold in this country. In Europe they may weigh about 1½ pounds. Thus they must be sliced into scallops. If using American duck livers, there should be about 2 livers per person. Cut each liver into 2 neat, flat scallops. Sprinkle with salt and pepper.

2. Heat the 4 tablespoons of butter in a skillet and when quite hot, but not brown, add the livers. Cook about 2 minutes to a side over high heat.

3. Transfer equal portions of liver to each of 6 hot plates.

4. Quickly add the oil (or the other 4 tablespoons of butter) to the skillet and, when sizzling, add the shallots, shaking the skillet. Add the vinegar and cook over high heat about 1 minute. Spoon the pan liquid over the livers and garnish with parsley, chives and chervil. Serve immediately.

Yield: 6 servings.

Ragout de Homard aux Primeurs

(Lobster in cream sauce with vegetables)

2	*1½-pound live lobsters, preferably female*
	Salt to taste
1	*carrot, trimmed and scraped*
1	*small turnip, peeled*
6	*to 8 small green beans, the smaller the better, ends trimmed*
2	*tablespoons butter*
1	*tablespoon finely chopped shallots*
1	*cup dry white wine*
½	*cup finely shredded fresh basil, loosely packed*
2	*cups heavy cream*

1. Plunge the lobsters head first into a large quantity of boiling salted water. Cook 5 minutes and drain. Pierce the lobsters between the eyes and suspend the lobsters head down so that they drain further. Let cool.

2. Quarter the carrot lengthwise. Cut the quarters into 1½-inch lengths. There should be about ½ cup. Set aside.

3. Cut the turnip into ½-inch slices. Stack the slices. Cut the slices into ½-inch strips. Cut the strips into ½-inch lengths. There should be about 18 "battonets" thus prepared, about ⅔ cup.

4. Slice the green beans in half lengthwise. Cut the strips into ½-inch lengths. There should be about ½ cup.

5. Drop the carrot and turnip pieces into boiling salted water and cook until crisp tender, about 5 minutes. Drain and set aside.

6. Separately, drop the beans into boiling salted water and cook until crisp tender, 2 to 3 minutes. Drain and combine with the carrots and turnips.

7. Meanwhile, cut or tear off the claws and tail sections of the lobster. Crack them and pull out the meat. Set the meat aside in a bowl. Reserve the shell.

8. Split the body section in half and remove the coral and liver of the lobster. Set aside.

9. Coarsely chop and set aside all the pieces of lobster shell. In our own case we prefer to do this using a food processor. We find it in no way damages the blades or motor.

10. Heat the butter in a kettle and add the shallots and chopped carcass. Cook, stirring, and add the wine and half the basil. Add salt and pepper to taste and cook about 15 minutes. Add the reserved coral and liver and cook 1 minute, no longer.

11. As the carcass cooks, slice the lobster meat into large bite-size morsels. Place in a saucepan and add the vegetable mixture. Do not cook.

12. When ready, add the cream to the simmering carcass. Let boil about 5 minutes. Put the mixture, carcass and all, through a food mill and into a saucepan, extracting as much liquid as possible. Discard the solids. Cook the sauce, uncovered, over high heat about 2 minutes. Strain it through a sieve with the finest mesh possible, preferably the kind known as a chinois. Add salt and pepper to taste.

13. Pour the sauce over the lobster and vegetables and add the remaining shredded basil. Bring just to the boil until bubbling and hot. Do not cook but a moment or two or the lobster will toughen. Serve immediately with hot rice.

Yield: 4 servings.

That Great American Drink—Bloody Mary

To our taste, the greatest preprandial, midday drink ever created in America is a bloody Mary. We have no earthly idea where the cocktail originated, although we have heard numerous claims in that direction. As far as we can date the drink, it came about shortly after the end of the last World War. Before that—and this may be difficult for anyone under the age of thirty to believe, vodka was virtually unknown in this country and Tabasco was something that southerners added to soups and stews and sprinkled on breakfast eggs.

In any event, we have often mentioned bloody Marys in one context or another, most recently in stating that we find most canned bloody Mary mixes absolutely vile, adding that we long ago learned not to order a bloody Mary on an airline, knowing what we would be served. We stated that we carry our own Tabasco sauce and Worcestershire and order simply tomato juice, lime, vodka and ice and add the other ingredients to our own taste.

We also stated that the only well-made bloody Mary mix in a can bears the Tabasco name, but it was not, to our knowledge, available in the Northeast. Well, as of this writing we have received news from the McIlhenny Company of New Iberia, Louisiana, informing us that that mix is now available in Daitch-Shopwell stores. Another reader, Susanne Peterson of Darien, Connecticut, tells us that "the Darien Liquor Shop, Tokeneke Road in Darien, sells it at forty cents a can."

We also have advance knowledge of another excellent product that may be used in making the drink. This is produced by the Angostura bitters people. It is called the Angostura Bloody Merry Maker. It is a bottled blend of Worcestershire and lime and spices and is to be added in small quantities to tomato juice and vodka in lieu of the usual Worcestershire, lime or lemon and hot sauce. It is commendable and will be worth testing once it arrives in the markets hereabouts. At present, the company plans to introduce it locally in mid-January. The cost per bottle is $1.60 and, according to the label, one bottle is sufficient for up to fifty drinks.

While we're on the subject, numerous readers have asked us for our own favored recipe for a bloody Mary. That we are pleased to offer plus the admission that we learned one of the key elements for the great libation from our favorite bartender, Jimmy Fox, who works the day shift at that tiny, inimitable hideaway, the Blue Bar of the Algonquin Hotel.

Jimmy makes the best bloody Marys in town, and one reason is that they are quickly made and ice cold. Jimmy uses a cocktail shaker full of ice, shakes the preparation briefly but thoroughly, and pours.

Bloody Mary

1½   ounces vodka
½   cup tomato juice
     Salt and freshly ground black
     pepper to taste
     Juice of half a lime
1   teaspoon Worcestershire sauce
4   to 6 dashes Tabasco sauce
1   lime wedge

1. Ideally, a bloody Mary should be shaken, using a barman's standard glass and metal cocktail shaker set. Add the vodka, tomato juice, and so on, to the metal container.

2. Fill the glass container with ice, the smaller the cubes the better. Invert the glass into the metal and shake quickly 9 times. If the drink is shaken excessively, the tomato juice may separate. Immediately strain the bloody Mary into a glass and serve with a lime wedge dropped in.

Yield: 1 cocktail.

Two Basic Luxuries for the Kitchen

America is living in an age of unprecedented basics and luxuries for the kitchen, catering to a nationwide involvement in cooking as a pleasure, a hobby to be ranked with other indoor sports. In that respect we are rank hobbyists and our chief new acquisitions are fantastic additions to a kitchen already loaded wall to wall, storage drawer to storage drawer with worldwide gadgets ranging from an inexpensive $1.50 knife sharpener called Zip-Zap to, of course, the essential Cuisinart food processor.

The two new additions are a formidable pasta-making machine from Italy and a sensational, if a bit bulky, machine for stuffing homemade sausages. Both of them are in the luxury category, the pasta maker costing $122.50; the sausage stuffer, $225. But what fine new dimensions they've added to our day-to-day hobbying.

The advantages of the new pasta machine, which is by Bialelli, over the widely available standard stainless steel machine include the plastic rollers and the fact that it is powered by electricity, which enormously speeds up pasta making. The machine can be used for flat sheets of dough such as ravioli and thin strands for noodles.

The sausage stuffer—the trademark is Tre Spade—satisfies our unabashed liking, if not to say insatiable appetite, for homemade sausages. It is ideal for home preparation. The cylinder that contains the filling for the sausage can accommodate as little as three pounds of meat and up to, perhaps, twenty pounds. It is manually operated and comes equipped with stuffing tubes in assorted sizes and can be used for making anything from chipolatas to large liverwurst. Expensive, of course, but so is the theater and a fine set of golf clubs.

We have long been amused by that segment of the public who will spend prodigal sums of money on their hobbies—golf, tennis, travel—and yet let their kitchens go begging. Furnishing a kitchen properly—comfortably—seems to inspire a certain guilt in some misguided souls. Not ours. Cooking is a major pastime and an endless pleasure, and we gleefully accommodate our purse to the kitchen rather than the other way around. Attempting to cook with a poor stove and a tin skillet is no more fun than trying to climb a greased pole or run a foot race with your feet in a burlap bag. Or, as we have said elsewhere, playing tennis with a loosely strung racket.

At any rate, here are recipes for the new machines.

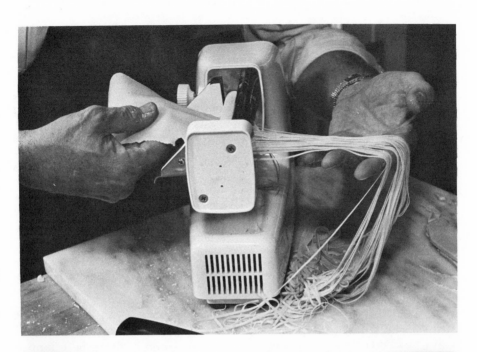

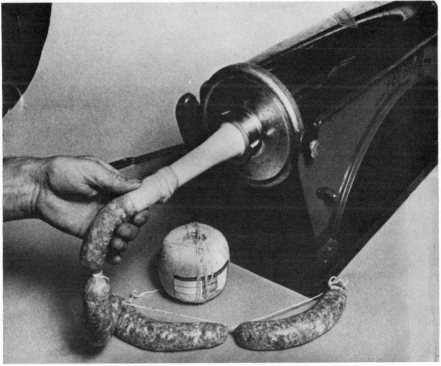

Chorizo Sausage

2   ounces guajillo or ancho
    chilies (see note), or use 2
    tablespoons chili powder
2   pounds lean pork
2   pounds pork fat
2   tablespoons finely chopped
    garlic
1   teaspoon freshly ground
    pepper
½   teaspoon oregano
½   teaspoon ground coriander
1½ teaspoons ground cumin
1   tablespoon paprika
1   tablespoon salt
½   cup white vinegar
¼   teaspoon powdered cloves
¼   teaspoon or more cayenne
    pepper
10 to 12 prepared sausage casings
    (see note and instructions for
    preparing)

1. If the whole chilies are to be used, tear off and discard the stem. Cut the chilies in half and discard the seeds. Place the chilies in a saucepan and add cold water to cover. Bring to the boil and simmer about 45 minutes. Let cool. Drain and pull off the skin or, if it does not slip off easily, scrape the pulp from the skins with a spoon. Discard the skins.

2. Put the pork and pork fat through a meat grinder outfitted with the coarsest blade. Put the meat in a mixing bowl and add the chili pulp. Add all the remaining ingredients except sausage casings and blend well. This mixture may now be fried by shaping into patties, or it may be used to prepare dried chorizos.

3. Outfit an electric grinder or a sausage-making machine—either hand-cranked or electric—with a special sausage attachment.

4. Slide 1 prepared sausage casing onto the attachment and tie the end. Grind the meat, holding the casing to permit free entry of the filling into the casing. When about 16 inches of casing has been filled, pinch the casing at the end of the sausage attachment. Pull it out to leave about 5 inches of empty casing at that end. Tie that end. Tie both ends of the sausage together. Set aside. Continue making sausage in this manner until all the stuffing has been used.

5. The sausages will keep for several days in the refrigerator. Or they may be wrapped tightly and frozen. To cook them, place a sausage ring in a heavy skillet and add 2 or 3 tablespoons of water to prevent sticking. Cook over moderate heat, turning to brown evenly on all sides. Serve with mashed potatoes, lentils and so on.

Yield: 6 to 10 sausage rings weighing ¾ to 1 pound each.

Note: Guajillo and ancho chilies are available at Casa Moneo, 210 West 14th Street.

Sausage casings are available in pork stores in metropolitan areas. There are a number of places in Manhattan, among them G. Esposito, 500 Ninth Avenue (at 38th Street).

Saucissons à l'Ail

(Garlic sausages)

3   pounds lean pork, cut into
    cubes
1½ pounds pork fat, cut into
    cubes
    Salt to taste

1   teaspoon freshly ground
    pepper
½   teaspoon saltpeter, available
    in drug stores
¼   teaspoon ground nutmeg
½   cup port wine
1   tablespoon finely chopped
    garlic
10 to 12 prepared sausage casings
    (see note and instructions for
    preparing)

1. Put the pork and pork fat through a meat grinder outfitted with the coarsest blade. Put the meat in a mixing bowl and add all the remaining ingredients except the sausage casings. Put it once more through the grinder using the coarsest blade.

2. Outfit an electric grinder or a sausage-making machine—either hand-cranked or electric—with a special sausage attachment.

3. Slide 1 prepared sausage casing onto the attachment and tie the end. Grind the meat, holding the casing to permit free entry of the filling into the casing. When about 16 inches of casing has been filled, pinch the casing at the end of the sausage attachment. Pull it out to leave about 5 inches of empty casing at that end. Tie that end. Tie both ends of the sausage together. Set aside. Continue making sausage in this manner until all the stuffing has been used.

4. The sausages will keep for several days in the refrigerator. Or they may be wrapped tightly and frozen. To cook them, place a sausage ring in a heavy skillet and add 2 to 3 tablespoons of water to prevent sticking. Cook over moderate heat, turning to brown evenly on all sides. Serve with mashed potatoes, lentils and so on.

Yield: 6 to 10 sausage rings weighing ¾ to 1 pound each.

Note: Sausage casings are available in pork stores in metropolitan areas. There are a number of places in Manhattan, among them G. Esposito, 500 Ninth Avenue (at 38th Street).

How to prepare sausage casings

1. Sausage casings are normally preserved in salt. When ready to use, put them in a basin of cold water and let stand.

2. Drain and return to a basin of cold water.

3. Lift up one end of a casing and blow into it. It will expand, balloonlike. This is how you determine if the casings have holes in them. Discard casings with holes or cut the casing at the hole and use the partial casing.

Egi Maccioni's Spinach Ravioli

The dough

4   cups flour
5   large eggs or 1¼ cups, plus 2
    egg yolks
    Salt to taste
½   to 2 tablespoons cold water

The filling

¾   pound bulk spinach or 1 10-
    ounce package fresh spinach
1   large egg, beaten
2   tablespoons finely chopped
    parsley
1   cup ricotta cheese
¼   teaspoon grated nutmeg

¾   *cup grated Parmesan cheese*
¼   *teaspoon finely minced garlic*
    Salt and freshly ground
    pepper to taste

The service

¼   *pound butter*
5   *leaves fresh or dried sage,*
    snipped in half
    Grated Parmesan cheese

1. Place the flour in a mixing bowl and make a well in the center. Beat the eggs lightly and add them to the well. Sprinkle with salt to taste. Add the water. Work well with the fingers until the dough can be handled easily. Wrap in wax paper and refrigerate.

2. Drop the spinach into boiling water to cover and cook about 1 minute. Drain immediately. When cool enough to handle, squeeze the spinach until most of the moisture is pressed out. There should be about ¾ cup of spinach. Add this to a mixing bowl.

3. Add the egg, parsley, ricotta, nutmeg and the ¾ cup Parmesan cheese. Add the garlic, salt and pepper to taste and blend well with the fingers.

4. Divide dough into 4 pieces. Roll out the dough by hand, if you are expert in pasta-making, or use a pasta machine and roll out the dough according to the manufacturer's instructions.

5. There are numerous techniques for filling pasta for ravioli. The simplest is to use a ravioli-maker that can be purchased in stores where first-class cooking equipment is sold. The commonest has 12 metal indentations. The surface should be lightly floured. As the dough is rolled out, a rectangle of dough is laid over the surface and a small amount of filling, about 1½ teaspoons, is spooned into the dough-covered indentations. Another rectangle of dough is laid over, stretching the dough gently if necessary to cover the entire pan, and a small rolling pin is run over this to seal the filling while simultaneously cutting out patterns of ravioli, which may be separated. Or, the dough can be rolled out, small mounds of filling added at intervals. This can be covered with another sheet of dough and a ravioli cutter used to outline the dumplings.

6. As the ravioli are made, arrange them in one layer on a dry floured kitchen towel.

7. When ready to serve, drop the ravioli into rapidly boiling salted water. Cook until ravioli rise to the top, stirring gently on occasion. Partly cover and continue to cook 10 to 15 minutes. Cooking time will depend on thickness of dough. Drain well and serve piping hot.

8. As the ravioli cook, heat the butter in a saucepan. Pour off about 3 tablespoons into another saucepan and add the sage. Cook about 30 seconds. Add the remaining butter and pour hot over the ravioli. Serve Parmesan cheese on the side.

Yield: 8 dozen ravioli or 6 to 8 servings.

Spinach ravioli dough using the pasta machine

1. To prepare the dough for spinach ravioli (see recipe), knead it to the point where it holds together. Or blend the mixture in the food processor.

2. Flatten the dough a bit and put it through the pasta machine using the flat roller, the roller set at the maximum opening.

3. The dough will be a bit raggedy.

4. Fold the ends—overlapping— toward the center.

5. Put the dough through the machine again.

6. Fold it as before. Continue putting the dough through—using both hands, one to put through, the other to receive—and folding until it is smooth.

7. Gradually decrease the roller opening, putting the strips of dough through the roller each time the opening is decreased. When the opening is at its minimum, the dough is ready to be used in preparing ravioli.

8. Or replace the flat roller with one of cutting rollers. Put the dough through the rollers to produce strands of pasta.

Modern Mousse

WITH PIERRE FRANEY

It is scarcely news at this late date to state that the food processor is the greatest thing to happen to the well-equipped American kitchen since refrigeration. Only a few short years ago, the dishes outlined here would scarcely have been possible for the home cook. A mousse (and a pain de poisson, which is a kind of mousse) was something reserved for professional kitchens, laboriously prepared by beating and pounding and sieving by hand. The scallop mousse is a gossamer affair with a fine, creamy tomato sauce; the French fish loaf—pain de poisson—is an equally delectable delicacy and may be served hot or cold. Either of these dishes can be prepared by using an electric blender, but it is more time-consuming and the end product will be a trifle less elegant.

Mousse de Coquilles St. Jacques

(Scallop mousse)

1   *pound scallops*
    Salt and freshly ground
    pepper
2   *large egg yolks*
20 *medium-size shrimp, peeled*
    and deveined
1   *cup heavy cream*
    Cream of tomato sauce (see
    recipe)

1. Preheat oven to 375 degrees.

2. Remove and set aside ½ cup of scallops. Place the remaining scallops in the container of a food processor (or use an electric blender and do this in as many steps as necessary). Add salt and pepper to taste and blend about 20 seconds.

3. While blending add the yolks and half the shrimp. Add the cream and blend until thoroughly smooth.

4. Butter a 5- or 6-cup ring mold and spoon half the scallop mixture into it. Cut the reserved shrimp into ½-inch pieces and sprinkle these over the mixture in the mold. Scatter the reserved scallops over this. Cover with the remaining mousse mixture and smooth it over. Cover closely with a ring of wax paper, pressing down to get out air bubbles. Place the mold in a basin of water and bake 30 minutes or until set. Unmold and serve with cream of tomato sauce.

Yield: 8 or more servings.

Cream of tomato sauce

1   *cup peeled, seeded, cubed*
    fresh tomatoes
1½ *tablespoons butter*
1   *tablespoon chopped onion*
1   *teaspoon finely chopped*
    shallots
    Salt and freshly ground
    pepper to taste
½   *cup fish broth or bottled clam*
    juice

1   *cup heavy cream*
2   *tablespoons finely chopped*
    parsley

1. Prepare the tomatoes and set aside.

2. Heat the butter in a saucepan and add the onion, shallots, salt and pepper to taste. Cook until wilted and add the tomato. Stir and simmer 5 minutes. Add the fish broth.

3. Cook until the mixture is reduced almost by half and add the cream. Simmer, stirring often, about 10 minutes and add the parsley, salt and pepper to taste.

Yield: About 2 cups.

Pain de Poisson

(A French fish loaf to be served hot or cold)

1¾   *pounds white-fleshed, nonoily*
     fish fillets such as fluke,
     flounder or black fish
2   *egg yolks*
     Salt and freshly ground
     pepper
¼   *teaspoon freshly grated*
     nutmeg
     Tabasco sauce
1½   *cups heavy cream*
3   *small green peppers, cored*
     and seeded and cut into 1-inch
     cubes
¼   *pound carrots, trimmed and*
     scraped and cut into 1-inch
     lengths
     Tomato sauce or mayonnaise
     sauce (see recipes)

1. Preheat oven to 400 degrees.

2. It is best to prepare this dish in 2 batches, using a food processor if

available. If an electric blender is used, it will have to be done in several batches.

3. Cut the fish into cubes and add half of it to the container of a food processor. Add 1 yolk, salt and pepper to taste, nutmeg, Tabasco to taste and blend. Continue blending while adding gradually half the cream. Repeat this step. As the fish mixture is prepared transfer it to a mixing bowl.

4. Blend the green peppers coarse-fine. Blend the carrots similarly. Squeeze out and discard excess liquid from the vegetables. Add the pulp to the fish mixture.

5. Spoon the mixture into a 7- or 8-cup ring mold. Smooth over the surface and cover with a round of wax paper cut to fit directly over the fish. Place the mold in a baking dish and pour boiling water around it.

6. ·Bake about 35 minutes or until set. The inner temperature should register between 150 and 160 degrees. Serve hot with a tomato sauce, lightly flavored with pernod (see recipe), if desired; or chill and serve cold with a mayonnaise sauce (see recipe).

Yield: 8 or 12 servings.

Tomato sauce with Pernod

1¼   *pounds fresh, red, ripe*
     tomatoes or use 3 cups
     imported canned tomatoes
2   *tablespoons butter*
2   *tablespoons finely diced*
     shallots
¼   *cup finely diced onion*
1   *tablespoon flour*
     Salt and freshly ground
     pepper
¼   *cup dry white wine*

½   cup fresh fish broth or use
     canned clam juice
1   cup heavy cream
1   tablespoon Pernod, Ricard or
     anise-flavored liqueur

1. Core, peel and chop the tomatoes. There should be about 3 cups.

2. Heat the butter in a saucepan and add the shallots and onion. Cook until wilted and sprinkle with flour. Add the tomatoes, salt and pepper to taste. Cook, uncovered, about 15 minutes. Add the wine and fish stock and continue cooking about 10 minutes.

3. Add the cream and bring to the boil. Stir in the Pernod and serve piping hot.

Yield: About 3½ cups.

Mayonnaise

1   egg yolk
     Salt and freshly ground
     pepper

1   teaspoon imported mustard,
     such as Dijon or Düsseldorf
1   teaspoon vinegar or lemon
     juice
1   cup peanut, vegetable, corn or
     olive oil
1   tablespoon finely chopped
     fresh tarragon or 1 teaspoon
     dried

1. Place the yolk in a mixing bowl and add salt and pepper to taste, mustard and vinegar. Beat vigorously for a second or 2 with a wire whisk or electric beater.

2. Start adding the oil gradually, beating continuously with the whisk or electric beater. Continue beating and adding oil until all of it is used. Add more salt to taste, and the tarragon. If the mayonnaise is not to be used immediately, beat in a tablespoon of water. This will help stabilize the mayonnaise and retard its turning when stored in the refrigerator.

Yield: About 1 cup.

December 1976

AS THIS YEAR ENDED, our brain and typing machine seemed heady with superlatives of the season. Last month, we explored the possibility of the world's greatest chef, and in this month we came forth with what I consider to be—and without equivocation—the world's greatest dish. It is a dish that makes me hunger in retrospect and there was the vast consolation and enjoyment of the letters received, letters something like Valentines as the old year ended, from readers who had dared to make it. (It is, in truth, an intricate dish to prepare.) Those who wrote used words like sublime and divine and blessings ever.

Added to this in December, I proposed a large listing of some of the greatest appetizers on earth, but best of all, perhaps, I was able to find in print two essays with my byline in defense of eating rich food. R.I.P.

From an Ambassador's Kitchen

It was Thursday, shortly after high noon, and we were drinking pea soup in the kitchen with Gunter Kraftner. We had not come to Washington to drink pea soup, but we were drinking it because, our host in the kitchen told us, it is an old Swedish custom to drink pea soup cooked with smoked pork on Thursday. The potage was the color of golden maize and ingeniously seasoned with a slight but pungent touch of dried marjoram. We sipped the soup between bites of smoked pork, each morsel judiciously smeared with a touch of mustard, and it was splendid fare, utterly splendid.

The real reason we had come to the nation's capital was to dine that evening at the Swedish ambassador's residence and to meet the chef whose talents we'd heard extolled at length at some function in Manhattan.

"Most of the food served in the Washington embassies," a friend told us, a fin bec who has surveyed the social scene in the capital for a number of years, "is catered by outside firms. But not the food served by the Swedish ambassador and his wife, the Count and Countess Wilhelm Wachtmeister. They have a fine European chef who does all the cooking. In Sweden, he's often cooked for young King Carl XVI Gustaf."

As we dined on the soup, we sipped a warming and mildly intoxicating glass of warm Swedish punch (made with a base of arrack). Chef Kraftner told us he was not Swedish by birth, but had lived and worked there for sixteen years. He was born in Vienna and had actually planned to come to America after a temporary stopover in Stockholm.

In Stockholm he worked in a catering firm for a number of years, and for special functions he was often asked to cook for the royal family.

One of the most incisively remembered of these occasions, he recalled, came about last March when he was asked to cook a special menu for the young monarch. The menu was modest but well-tailored: crème hongroise, a cream soup made with green and red peppers; selle d'agneau roti or roast saddle of lamb; légumes assorties or assorted vegetables; and petits choux or cream puff pastries with butter cream. At the end of the lunch, the king announced to the chef before the rest of the world heard the news that his highness was engaged to Silvia Renate Sommerlath, the daughter of the German businessman.

It goes without saying that a good deal of entertaining occurs each year at the embassy residence and, added to that the fact that some "typical" dinners actually involve two menus, young Kraftner is certainly one of the busiest chefs in

Countess Ulla Wachtmeister entertains extensively, with the assistance of chef Gunter Kraftner

town. The evening I was there, for example, the first order of eating for the twenty-one guests would be an extensive smorgasbord served on a table burgeoning with the likes of herring in assorted flavors: with leeks and onions and sour cream; with tomato sauce and marinated mustard seeds; matjes herring and so on; Swedish anchovies; a mussel salad; eggs Gripsholm; gravlax, the celebrated Scandinavian cold, cured salmon dish with mustard sauce; specially cured cold goose in aspic; and thinly sliced smoked reindeer, flown in from Lapland, with horseradish butter. One of the most memorable of the dishes was a liver pâté in aspic.

That would be for openers. The main dinner served in the embassy's grand and elegant dining room would begin with rich consommé of wild hare, followed by a mousseline of chicken with morels (woodland mushrooms) in cream sauce, steamed cucumbers with hollandaise sauce and an assortment of desserts. The liquid accompaniments for the evening—three sorts of Swedish aquavit, Dry Sack sherry (with the consommé), Chateau Haut-Brion, 1961, and Cuvée Dom Perignon, 1969.

The mistress of the embassy, Ulla Wachtmeister, a slender, soft-spoken, handsome woman, is impressively qualified to direct that many-roomed mansion. Like most young Swedish women, she was taught at an early age the requisites of "running a proper home." She is a skilled seamstress and is said to be a first-class cook in her own right. In fact, numerous dishes handed down to her from her own and her husband's families appear frequently on the embassy's menus. One of these we sampled, called eggs Gripsholm, is her creation. It was so named because her mother was married to the curator of the Gripsholm castle.

Mrs. Wachtmeister is also a professional artist whose oil paintings have been exhibited both in this country and abroad. The Wachtmeisters are the parents of three children ranging in age from 28 to 20. They plan to celebrate their thirtieth anniversary next year, perhaps with a "midsummer night in Sweden" affair or with an opera ball at the embassy next June.

Some of their most recently remembered guests are King Carl during his visits to this country and Carlton Gajdusek, winner of the Nobel Prize in Medicine (and the father of sixteen adopted children). The largest affair at the embassy was a buffet supper for Ingrid Bergman this year. There were 250 guests. When they entertain Americans, they almost invariably serve a smorgasbord and Swedish-oriented foods. When they entertain their fellow Scandinavians, the food is almost invariably American—generally steaks in one form or another and assorted native seafoods.

Mrs. Wachtmeister told us that both Vice President Rockefeller and Secretary of State Kissinger have dined at their table but never President Ford. She hopes, she said, to have President Carter to dine next year when the new Swedish ambassador arrives for a visit. "Our new prime minister, Thorbjorn Falldin, is a sheep farmer," she said with some admiration. "I think it would be nice for him to meet a peanut farmer."

Somehow, Scandinavian food lends itself to festive occasions, and it is probably the ultimate, in its variety of colors, flavors and textures, for buffet entertaining. Here is a sample of some dishes served recently in the Swedish ambassador's residence in Washington. Any or all of them would be good for the forthcoming holidays. The liver pâté, in particular, is a standout. The Swedish pea soup, perhaps not in the buffet category, is a splendid and easily made dish for Thursday or any other day in the week.

Swedish Pea Soup

2 cups fancy whole, yellow peas, preferably imported from Sweden (see note)
5 cups water
Salt to taste
1 1¼-pound smoked pork shoulder butt (porkette), available in supermarkets
1 teaspoon dried marjoram

1. Place the peas in a bowl and add cold water to cover, about 2 inches above the top of the peas. Let stand overnight.

2. Drain the peas and place them in a kettle. Add the 5 cups of water, salt and pork butt. Bring to the boil and skim the surface occasionally to remove any pea hulls that float to the top. Simmer about 1 hour or until the peas are quite tender.

3. Serve the pea soup in individ-

ual hot bowls with a light sprinkling of marjoram on top. Slice the pork butt and serve separately to be added to the soup as desired. Mustard is frequently served on the side for the pork butt slices.

Yield: 6 or more servings.

Note: Imported whole yellow peas are available at Nyborg & Nelson, 937 Second Avenue (between 49th and 50th Streets).

Swedish Liver Pâté

½   *pound liver*
½   *cup chopped onions*
2   *flat anchovies*
2   *tablespoons bread crumbs*
1   *tablespoon flour*
     Salt and freshly ground
     pepper to taste
2   *large eggs*
1   *cup heavy cream*
¼   *teaspoon nutmeg*
2   *tablespoons melted butter*
     Quick aspic (see recipe)
     Cutouts of olives, truffles,
     pimento or hard-cooked egg
     whites, optional

1. Preheat the oven to 375 degrees.

2. Combine the liver, onions and anchovies in the container of a food processor or electric blender. If a blender is used, it may be necessary to prepare the mixture in two stages.

3. Add the bread crumbs, flour, salt, pepper and eggs and continue beating. Pour in the cream while beating. Add the nutmeg and butter.

4. Generously butter the bottom and sides of a 4-cup mold, preferably a timbale mold. Chill it briefly in the freezer. Line the bottom with a round of wax paper and butter it. Pour the liver mixture into the mold. Cover with a round of wax paper. Place the mold in a basin of water and bring to the boil on top of the stove.

5. Place the mold and water bath in the oven and bake 35 to 40 minutes. Let stand until cool. Refrigerate.

6. Unmold the pâté and keep it chilled. Scrub the mold and pat it dry. Place it in the freezer.

7. Pour ½ cup or so of the chilled but still liquid aspic into the mold and turn the mold this way and that so the bottom and sides are coated lightly with aspic. Pour out excess aspic from the mold. Chill the mold so that the light coating of aspic sets. Add more liquid aspic and repeat the motion to coat the mold and chill. Continue this 4 or 5 times, chilling after each addition of aspic. Spoon about ⅓ inch of aspic into the bottom of the mold and chill to set.

8. Add, if desired, the cutouts of olives or truffles, pimento or hard-cooked egg whites, using a fancy cutter. Dip the shapes into liquid aspic and arrange them neatly over the set layer of aspic in the bottom of the mold.

9. Return the pâté to the mold, handling it gently to get it back into place over the aspic. Pour more liquid aspic down between the pâté and the interior of the mold, adding enough aspic to coat the top of the pâté with a light layer. Let stand until set. Unmold and serve cut into wedges.

Yield: 12 or more servings at a buffet.

Quick aspic

3 cups chicken broth
1 cup tomato juice
4 envelopes unflavored gelatin
  Salt and freshly ground
  pepper to taste
1 teaspoon sugar
2 egg shells, crushed
2 egg whites, lightly beaten
2 tablespoons cognac

1. In a saucepan, combine the chicken broth with the tomato juice, gelatin, salt, pepper, sugar, egg shells and egg whites and heat slowly, stirring constantly, until the mixture boils up in the pan.

2. Remove the pan from the heat and stir in the cognac.

3. Strain the mixture through a sieve lined with a flannel cloth that has been rinsed in cold water and wrung out. If the aspic starts to set or become too firm, it may be reheated, then brought to any desired temperature.

Yield: About 1 quart.

Gripsholm Eggs

10 large hard-cooked eggs
1 pound lean bacon
8 tablespoons butter
¾ cup flour
5 cups milk
1 cup Parmesan cheese
  Salt and freshly ground
  pepper to taste
½ teaspoon nutmeg
1 cup chopped parsley

1. Cook the eggs and let them cool. Peel them and cut them in half. Press enough egg yolks through a fine sieve to make 1 cup. Cover and set aside for garnish.

2. Chop the remaining whites and yolks. Cover and set aside.

3. Cook the bacon until browned and quite crisp. Drain on absorbent toweling. Let cool. Chop the bacon finely. There should be about 1 cup.

4. Melt the butter in a large saucepan and add the flour, stirring with a wire whisk. Add the milk, stirring vigorously with the whisk. Cook until the mixture is thickened and smooth. Add the Parmesan cheese. Cook 5 minutes longer, stirring often. Add salt and pepper to taste and the nutmeg.

5. When ready to serve, fold the chopped whites and yolks into the sauce. Spoon the mixture onto an oval platter. Garnish with alternating diagonal rows of sieved egg yolk, chopped bacon and chopped parsley, about ¼ of each to each row. Serve immediately.

Yield: 12 buffet servings.

Matjes Herring with Dill and Sour Cream

8 matjes herring fillets, available
  in tins where fine Swedish
  foods are sold
¼ cup chopped fresh dill
½ cup finely chopped onion
2 bay leaves for garnish
  Sour cream

1. Drain the fillets and cut them into 1-inch pieces. Arrange them neatly on a dish and sprinkle with chopped dill and onion. Garnish with bay leaves.

2. Serve with sour cream on the side.

Yield: 12 servings for a buffet.

Herring Tidbits with Leeks and Onions

36   herring tidbits, available in
     jars
⅓   cup finely chopped leeks,
     green part and all
⅓   cup finely chopped onion
1   cup sour cream

1. Drain the tidbits and arrange them on a dish in a neat pattern.

2. Blend the leeks and onion. Spoon the mixture to one side of the tidbits. Spoon the sour cream down the other side.

Yield: 12 servings for a buffet.

Herring with Mustard Seeds and Tomato Sauce

The herring

2   salt herring, soaked overnight
     in cold water

The mustard seeds

2   tablespoons mustard seeds,
     soaked overnight in cold water
     to cover
1   tablespoon peanut, vegetable
     or corn oil
1   teaspoon red wine vinegar
     Salt and freshly ground
     pepper to taste

The tomato sauce

½   cup tomato catchup
2   tablespoons red wine vinegar
4   teaspoons sugar
     Salt and freshly ground
     pepper to taste

2   tablespoons peanut, vegetable
     or corn oil

1. Soak the herring and mustard seeds overnight as indicated.

2. Drain the herring and fillet them (see instructions).

3. Drain the mustard seeds and combine with the tablespoon oil, 1 teaspoon vinegar, salt and pepper to taste. Blend and set aside.

4. Combine the ingredients for the tomato sauce.

5. Cut the herring fillets into 1-inch crosswise slices and arrange in one layer in a dish. Spoon tomato sauce over the herring. Spoon the mustard seeds down a line over the center of the dish. Serve.

Yield: 12 servings for a buffet.

How to Fillet Schmaltz Herring

Using a pair of scissors, cut off the fins from the herring. Using a sharp knife, slit open the stomach and remove the roe or milch. Discard it or set aside for another use. The roe is sometimes blended, put through a sieve and added to marinades for herring fillets but not in the recipes printed here.

Turn the herring and, using the knife, slit the fish down the back, cutting off first one fillet, then the other, inserting the knife at the tail and slicing through as close to the bone as possible. When the fillets have been cut off, skin them by pulling with the fingers, starting with the tail ends. Discard the skins. Rinse the fillets and pat them dry on paper towels.

In Defense of Eating
Rich Food

Paranoia, thy name is the American diet! Butter, eggs and cream—the absolute essentials of haute cuisine—have become the dreaded Gorgons, the absolute no-nos, the menace foods of the century.

And, lo, the poor Americans! The poor devils given to gluttony, covetous of eternal youth and simultaneously beset on all sides by merchants of fright and hysteria, quake at the thought of them.

If I were to write a diet cookbook for people who wish to eat well, lose weight and live in robust good health, it would contain exactly two words: Eat less. Or, perhaps, seven words: Savor your food but eat in moderation.

Under no circumstances would my sane and serious but short volume succumb to the idea that those foods that have nourished this nation for a couple of hundred years must be banished from the diet in the name of eternal youth or theories about health that remain matters of debate among scientists.

But Americans have become a nation of culinary schizophrenics, living in mortal dread of high-calorie foods and shunning some of the greatest pleasures of the table while mindlessly gorging themselves on all sorts of plain and junk foods in quantity and without apology.

Who would dare remonstrate if the average American goes to a ball game and downs six or more hot dogs along with a matching number of cold beers?

Or if the palate is placated with two or three hamburgers or a whole pizza downed with a Coke and followed with a banana split? It's only the sign of a happy husband or a boy or girl with a healthy all-American appetite. Tradition. The American way.

But deep-seated feelings of guilt blossom in the Yankee breast at the sight of cream soups, hollandaise and béarnaise sauces, creamed main dishes, maître d'hôtel butters for steak; anchovy butter for broiled fish; pastry creams and whipped cream if it is to be spooned over a foreign dessert such as a gâteau St. Honoré or a Viennese torte.

Dining in this country is a bewildering Everest of paradoxes and to my mind one of the biggest revolves around the American use—and nonuse—of butter.

I am constantly flabbergasted when I visit a steak house and the meat is served without melted butter. The paralogism is this: The management, at the same meal, unhesitantly serves limitless butter on the side and the patron, almost equally unhesitatingly, spreads this on bread, consumes it and then frequently asks for more, more bread, more butter.

But if just a fraction of this amount of butter were melted and poured over the steak it would enormously enhance the meat's flavor and general palatability.

As I see it, "the little foxes, that spoil the vines"—the chief culprits who give a bad name to the pleasures of the table—are two.

Chief among them are the fright merchants, both large and small, who sell substitutes—egg substitutes, sugar substitutes, cream substitutes—ad infinitum.

Second in line are the manufacturers who zero in on America's obsessive desire for eternal youth. No matter how old you are, a slender physique is equated with youth. Thus, Americans will buy any product, practice any ritual that promises that image. Via Madison Avenue, the public psyche is bombarded with advertisements promoting products that promise to arrest or suspend or, at the very least, cover up the encroachment of age.

Thus the masses are brainwashed into loading their shopping carts with the latest in egg substitutes and butter substitutes and milk substitutes and cream substitutes and artificial sweeteners and diet colas.

In this atmosphere, almost no food consumed today has escaped suspicion. Highest on the list, of course, are animal fats including, of course, butter and cream. Then there are eggs; charcoal grilled foods; drinking water; supermarket flour; sugar; salt; canned goods (they might contain botulism); and various spices including cardamom.

That is to say nothing whatever of the produce from oceans and rivers, including clams, oysters and swordfish; smoked foods in general, including ham and bacon and presumably Scotch whisky; bean paste of Chinese cookery, mono-sodium glutamate and so on.

A person susceptible to suggestions of disaster is impelled to go on a diet of pale toast and forget it.

Most Americans do something else. Filled with their fears and yearning for endless youth, they turn against what they regard as "fancy dishes"—mostly of European origin and particularly those of French origin.

They react with aversion to the thought of a spoonful of béarnaise sauce on a steak, even a very small filet mignon. And yet they will consume a large porterhouse; because of its size, it is infinitely more fattening.

They will drink two or three sugar-laden aperitifs at a cocktail party, followed after dinner by a sweet liqueur, only to arise the next morning and piously drop a sugar-substitute in their coffee.

And what of those vacuous, irresistible, high-calorie cocktail companions—roasted salted peanuts; cheese dips with their attendant scoops in the form of crisp wafers, crackers, toast, cheese-flavored crackers sculptured into the shape of fish; popcorn soggy with oil and butter; and potato chips?

To my mind, there are few things more vulgar and deplorable in this country, and which contribute more to obesity, than the thoughtless quantities of food that restaurants pile on the plates of a people raised to "finish everything."

When I have broached the subject of this swill-before-swine largess to responsible restaurateurs, they have contended that they are simply catering to their customers' desires.

It is my feeling that they are catering to a maw of gluttons rather than a clientele with discriminating palates.

Apropos of this, about fifteen years ago, Pierre Franey, then the chef at the fabled Le Pavillon Restaurant and now my collaborator and this newspaper's 60-Minute Gourmet, drove through France with me on an eating tour of two, and often three, large meals a day.

After three days, I found such immense quantities of food burdensome, and thereafter I became a taster of foods, leaving large portions uneaten on my plate. Pierre was humiliated. Quelle horreur! What would his colleagues feel upon seeing so much food return to the kitchen? So he would eat not only all the food on his plate but all on mine that had gone untasted!

But now, many years later, he, too, has learned the wisdom of moderation; on occasion, out of the corner of my eye, I have seen him leave a few morsels, even at the risk of embarrassing his colleagues behind those swinging doors.

It is my conviction that the chief causes of obesity in this country are anxiety, tension, fear, frustration and related emotional conditions. It is only natural that anyone at odds with the world yearns for creature comfort. Since the cradle, the mind has known that the body will respond with signals of reassurance when liquids and solids are taken into the mouth.

The food or drink that will reassure is peculiar to the individual. For every person who can be sated by a glass of cold milk and a candy bar (or several glasses of cold milk and several candy bars), there are others (compounding the crime to the body) who may be soothed only by double martinis or a steak the size of the Manhattan telephone directory.

Great magnitude need not characterize the anxiety and frustration that ignites an eating binge. Dinner delayed by an hour causes me to drink more and eat more. Woe be unto the host or hostess who schedules dinner at eight and sits me down (or props me up) for dinner at midnight.

Unfortunately, the average American has very little appreciation for the food that is placed before him three times a day. Great cooking is a high art, on the same plane with music and dance. The experience of dining well—the knowledgeable and sensual enjoyment of food—should be the same fine art. It can be compared to the connoisseurship of listening to music with a keen ear or watching dance with an educated eye.

The enjoyment of eating should be an attentive thing, free of impediments and distractions. There should be as little conversation as possible, barring a few murmured words of approval, an approving nod here and there and a brief sigh or two to indicate shared ecstasy.

Grievously, few people are aware of this. To them the only true, convincing medium of approval is talk, talk, talk. And more talk.

The reason for such a commonplace absence of civility is simple enough. Most people respond almost solely to surface tastes. They are not aware of, do not understand, the myriad nuances of dining well that have to do not only with flavors and temperatures and textures (and visual stimuli) but with the highly complex sensory perceptions of the tongue, the throat, the salivary glands.

Most people are aware that food—where temperature is concerned—is hot, cold or lukewarm. That it possesses one of the four basic tastes: sour, sweet, bitter or salty. That it is highly spiced or bland. But they do not appraise these factors in a natural and detached manner, and thus they are reduced to gluttony. Small wonder then that so many thousands of Americans can watch television while dining.

I am appalled that the teenagers and young adults of today have no notion of the basics of a proper diet. A diet is, of course, purely and simply the varieties of foods eaten on a fairly steady basis. But to most Americans in 1976 a diet means avoiding any foods that tend to be fattening.

This, of course, is not to say that avoiding fattening foods or simply following the rule of eating all things in moderation is the panacea for all problems of health and weight. We all know that diabetics and those with seriously high cholesterol must shun certain things at the risk of life itself. And that gout sufferers—a group to which I formerly belonged—and others know, too, that they must avoid certain foods or risk frightening setbacks to their well-being. But at this point I am addressing myself essentially to those who are in general good health.

I am convinced that the good state of my own health is without doubt attributable to my early schooling in Mississippi. We were taught in elementary school the basics of good nutrition. The rules were simple and few.

The body should be fed three times a day. The diet should contain, each day, some form of meat or poultry and, on occasion, fish; a starch such as potatoes or rice; some form of dairy products, including milk, cream and/or cheese; eggs in any of various forms, including desserts; greens in the form of vegetables and salads; and a sweet, including, perhaps, fruits and melons. And all of this done always in moderation.

I have spent the bulk of my adult life in writing about dining well and great cooking, and by great cooking I do not mean the haute cuisine of France to the exclusion of all others.

I love hamburgers and chili con carne and hot dogs. And foie gras and sauternes and those small birds known as ortolans. I like the wines of Spain and Italy and of California and the Rhine Valley as well as I do burgundies and bordeaux. I love barquettes of quail eggs with hollandaise sauce and clambakes with lobsters dipped in so much butter it dribbles down the chin. I like cheesecake and crêpes filled with cream sauces and strawberries with crème fraîche.

And I try to love the people who deplore these enthusiasms.

I do not sit at table, my mind poisoned with anxieties about foods I am about to put in my mouth, be it cream sauces or clear consommés. I approach a meal with the blissful knowledge that I will not overeat and will, therefore, enjoy the blessings that the good Lord has seen fit to provide my table with.

And if I am abbreviating my stay on this earth for an hour or so, I say only that I have no desire to be a Methuselah, a hundred or more years old and still alive, grace be to something that plugs into an electric outlet.

In that I work in the field of food, experiment with it, write about it and certainly think about it more than twelve hours a day, I am often asked how I maintain a fairly constant weight.

Such an inquiry is understandably if lamentably born of the panic in the kitchen that has resulted from the bombardment of advertisements implying that the basics of haute cuisine—butter, cream and eggs—are consumed only at one's peril. But the panic is unreasonable. Although I have sampled virtually every one of the dishes for which recipes have been printed under my name, my weight remains generally at 158 pounds in the morning, 162 pounds before retiring, and my health good.

Yet the sad (but somehow amusing) assumption remains that those recipes that call for a cup or two of heavy cream and a couple of egg yolks and are designed, let us say, for six to eight people, are deadly. In the first place, these recipes are intended for special, festive occasions. In the second place, one cup of cream in a recipe designed for eight apportions out to two tablespoons per person. The proportion of egg—on the basis of two eggs for the dish—is negligible. And if eight tablespoons of butter are called for, it still amounts to one tablespoon per person.

One of the most glorious recipes I know—and one that I have been reluctant to print—is for a magnificent caramel flan flavored with cognac and a coffee liqueur. It calls for twelve egg yolks and serves eight. The very idea would probably send some readers to an early grave. And yet it figures out to one and one-half egg yolks per person.

Hardly a witches' brew to cause one to quake in terror and shudder at intimations of mortality. Yet many do. In their fear they have lost sight of a thought as basic as hunger itself: the profoundest, most elemental reason for eating is to sustain life. And beyond that, it is possible to dine purely and simply for the pleasure of dining. I do. And why not?

Arnold Bennett, the English author who died in 1931, once estimated that a man of 60 had spent more than three years of his life in eating. And long before him, Samuel Johnson observed, "I look upon it, that he who does not mind his belly will hardly mind anything else."

When I mind my belly most literally—before my mirror—I do not behold the lithe and supple physique of a Baryshnikov, a Charles Atlas or a young Douglas Fairbanks. Nor do I see an embarrassment of flesh. The mirror may not reflect a shapely Adonis, but I am advised by my doctor and friends that the proportions are modest, age and height considered.

What is the formula? It is empirical and involves many things that have become routine.

The essentials would begin with a fairly accurate scale to check my weight at least once a day, preferably on arising in the morning. I adjust the intake of food day by day to keep the weight in balance.

In that I am convinced that most overeating is attributable to anxiety, tension, stress, frustrations and all the related emotions, I think that the body should be fed three times a day. If I skip breakfast, a nagging sensation, no matter how vague, occurs in my being. It may persist even after lunch.

Breakfast is modest and almost invariably begins with grapefruit juice—preferably freshly squeezed and never out of a can—which I am convinced is one of the finest foods for preventing head colds.

Dining patterns throughout the world are based on tradition. In Japan, rice, seaweed, fish and pickles are the basis for a proper breakfast; in France, croissants or brioche or a good crusty loaf with coffee are traditional; and in America, of course, bacon or ham and eggs with toast and coffee have been staples for a couple of centuries.

I take pleasure in breakfast and plot it according to whim. It might embrace fruits and melons in season, a hot thin soup with unbuttered toast, plus tea or black coffee.

An excellent breakfast "soup" is a combination of equal parts clam broth (preferably fresh, but bottled will do) and tomato juice with lemon juice and freshly ground pepper added to taste. Half a tomato cut into cubes and added at the last moment just to heat through is excellent.

On occasion, grapefruit followed by half a scrambled egg and a strip or two of bacon plus half a slice of lightly buttered toast and tea or coffee is, in my own diet, reasonable.

If I am alone for the midday meal, I dine simply—perhaps on a small sandwich made with a small can of tuna fish, or a tin of sardines plus a few celery ribs or carrot sticks. Or perhaps I will dine on a salad alone, lightly seasoned with a little vinegar plus a touch of oil plus the tinned fish in modest quantities.

If I dine alone in the evening, I will content myself with one grilled lamb chop, a baked potato with a small pat of butter, a mixed salad and fruit for dessert.

Meals taken with friends in, let us say, a Manhattan restaurant, are also taken in moderation. I do find that Japanese food, properly chosen, is the one least likely to cause overweight, followed closely by Chinese food taken in moderation.

In French restaurants, I frequently insist on small portions, although that goal is not easily achieved. Thus I eat as much of what is put before me as I consider discreet, whether it is fish in magnificent cream sauce or irresistible custardlike desserts. (Les oeufs sur la neige—poached meringues in a vanilla custard—is, incidentally, one of the few desserts on earth the last drop of which I must consume and wish for more.)

Although I am a passionate defender of butter and heavy cream, I generally eat it in far smaller quantities than most of my acquaintances. But there is at least one occasion on which I tend to eat butter, per se, with glorious disregard of consequences. And that is when the first crop of corn arrives on Long Island. When the cobs are taken hot and steaming from the kettle and brought to the table, I become downright lustful and slather on the butter and attack the corn while the golden rich liquid fairly dribbles down my cheeks, clambake style.

But, as I have said, occasions like these call for subsequent adjustment to keep the weight in balance. Losing weight and maintaining a constant, moderate weight require a certain amount of self-control. It seems reasonable and valid to say that the stomach cavity expands and contracts in accordance with volume eaten. Once this capacity is reduced—over a period of days—the desire for food will decrease. I also exercise in a modest manner, compatible with my age.

When it comes to excess, the fault lies not with the glories of our foods, but in ourselves. To the gluttons of the world I wish punishment in the form of signs worn around the neck, stating: "It is I who have gluttonized, who have eaten to abominable excess and, therefore, given a bad name to butter and cream and the other good things in life."

As for my own final motto, it is this: "All things in moderation; except happiness."

Crowd Pleasers

WITH PIERRE FRANEY

As the season to be jolly fast approaches, to be swiftly followed by the time for ringing the old out and the new in, there follows a flurry of requests for quantity cookery; recipes, that is, to serve a crowd. A crowd, as we reckon it, is almost any gathering that numbers more than twelve. On this page we offer three long-time favorites—two of them typically American, the other borrowed from Mexico or Peru or other parts South—designed to serve a crowd.

Jambalaya

¼ pound salt pork, cut into small cubes
¾ pound hot link sausages such as chorizos or hot Italian sausages
4 cups finely chopped onions
3 cups finely chopped celery
3 tablespoons finely minced garlic
4 cups chopped sweet green peppers
1 cup chopped sweet red peppers or use an additional cup of chopped green peppers in substitution
3 pounds porkette, available in supermarkets, or a cooked ham in one thick slice
3 bay leaves
3 sprigs fresh thyme or 1 teaspoon dried
1 35-ounce can tomatoes, preferably Italian imported tomatoes
1 cup finely chopped parsley
  Salt and freshly ground pepper
  Tabasco sauce

1 quart oysters with their liquor
4 cups, approximately, fish broth or use fresh or canned clam broth
4 cups water
3 cups raw rice
5 pounds raw shrimp, shelled and deveined
1½ pounds fresh bay scallops

1. Using a large kettle or Dutch oven, cook the salt pork cubes, stirring often, until rendered of fat.

2. Cut the sausages into ½-inch thick slices and add them. Cook about 8 minutes, stirring occasionally, and add the onions. Cook, stirring often, until wilted and add the celery, garlic, green pepper and red pepper.

3. Cut the porkette or ham into 1-inch cubes and add it. Add the bay leaves, thyme, tomatoes, parsley, salt and pepper to taste and Tabasco sauce to taste. Continue cooking. Drain the oysters and add the liquid. There may be from about ½ cup to 1 cup. Set the oysters aside.

4. Add half the fish broth and half the water. Cook, stirring once or twice from the bottom, about 10 minutes.

5. Add the rice and stir gently. Cover and cook about 15 minutes. If necessary, add a little more broth and water to prevent sticking.

6. Add the remaining broth and water, the shrimp, scallops and oysters. Cook, stirring often from the bottom, 15 to 20 minutes. If necessary, add more liquid to prevent scorching and drying out.

7. Serve with a bottle of Tabasco sauce on the side.

Yield: 24 or more servings.

Brunswick Stew

1   9-to-10-pound capon or use 2 or 3 chickens with 10 pounds total weight, cut into serving pieces.
    Salt and freshly ground pepper

¼   cup butter
3   cups thinly sliced onions
2   cups diced sweet green peppers, seeded
2   cups diced celery
1   tablespoon finely minced garlic
2   dried, hot, red pepper pods
3   bay leaves
1   cup coarsely chopped parsley
8   cups water
4   cups peeled, chopped tomatoes
10 or more ears fresh corn on the cob or use 3 10-ounce packages frozen whole kernel corn
5   cups potatoes, peeled and cut into ½-inch cubes
4   cups freshly shelled baby lima beans or use 3 10-ounce packages frozen baby lima beans
1   tablespoon Worcestershire sauce

1. Sprinkle the chicken pieces with salt and pepper. Heat the butter in 2 large skillets and brown the chicken pieces on all sides. Or use 1 skillet and do this in several steps.

2. Remove the chicken and add the onions, peppers, celery and garlic. Cook until the vegetables give up their liquid. Cook until liquid evaporates and the vegetables start to brown.

3. Return the chicken to the skillet or skillets and add the hot pepper pods, bay leaves, parsley, water and tomatoes. Cover and cook 15 minutes.

4. Meanwhile, drop the corn into boiling water and cover. When the water returns to the boil, remove it from the heat. Let stand, covered, 5 minutes. Drain and let cool.

5. Add the potatoes to the stew and cook 5 minutes. Add the lima beans and continue cooking 15 minutes. Uncover and continue cooking 10 minutes or until potatoes and beans are tender.

6. Cut and scrape the kernels off the cob. There should be about 6 cups. Add this to the stew. Add salt and pepper to taste. Stir in the Worcestershire sauce and serve piping hot.

Yield: 18 or more servings.

Picadillo

(A meat stew with olives and capers)

1   *cup dried currants*
4   *tablespoons peanut, vegetable, corn or olive oil*
3   *cups finely chopped onion*
2   *to 4 tablespoons finely chopped garlic*
3   *cups chopped green peppers*
1   *10-ounce jar stuffed green olives*
3   *3½-ounce jars capers, drained*
½   *cup white vinegar*
    Salt
1   *tablespoon freshly ground pepper*
¾   *teaspoon cinnamon*
1   *teaspoon ground cloves*
2   *bay leaves*
    Tabasco sauce
6   *pounds ground round or chuck steak*
12   *cups peeled chopped tomatoes*
    Freshly cooked rice

1. Place the currants in a bowl and add warm water to cover. Let stand until they "plump," about ½ hour.

2. Meanwhile, heat half the oil in a very large kettle and add the onion, garlic and green peppers. Cook, stirring, until wilted. Add the green olives, capers, vinegar, salt to taste, pepper, cinnamon, cloves, bay leaves and Tabasco sauce to taste. Cook, stirring, about 10 minutes.

3. In a large casserole or Dutch oven heat the remaining oil and add the meat. Cook, stirring with the side of a metal kitchen spoon to break up all lumps. Cook only until the meat loses its red color.

4. Add the green olive mixture and stir to blend.

5. Drain the currants and add them.

6. Add the tomatoes and cook, stirring often, about 1 hour. Skim off the fat as it rises to the surface. Serve hot with rice.

Yield: 18 or more servings.

To Whet the Appetite

The Greeks have a word for them and so do the Spanish and French. There is, in fact, no civilized society on earth that does not accord a special place to the assortment of dishes known as appetizers or hors d'oeuvre. What would the Italian table be without its antipasti; the Greeks without mezedaki; the Spanish without their entremeses and the Germans without vorspeise. The Swedes call them cocktail tilltugg and the Mexicans antojitos.

There's a reason for this. A well-made appetizer is as irresistible as sin, yet marvelously lawful. And thus, an offering for the season: nearly a score of appetizers international in scope, ranging from the taramosalata of the Greeks to that delectable provençale specialty, brandade de morue poorly translated into English as a mousse of salt cod. Some of the dishes can be prepared in minutes, others require a certain amount of detail, the jambon persillé, for example. But, as the saying goes, the game is worth the candle.

Any or all of these dishes would fare well for a holiday buffet. Some of them will have a familiar guise; others, perhaps, are trifles unknown. Whatever else, it is a highly personal selection of dishes we have admired and enjoyed over the years.

Liver Pâté with Hazelnuts

1 pound coarsely ground pork
1 pound coarsely ground veal
⅛ pound salt pork cut into ¼-inch cubes
¼ cup thinly sliced shallots
¼ pound mushrooms thinly sliced
1½ bay leaves
1 teaspoon dried thyme
1 pound chicken livers, picked over to remove veins and connecting tissues
Salt and freshly ground pepper to taste
½ teaspoon ground nutmeg
¼ teaspoon allspice
2 tablespoons cognac
1 egg, lightly beaten
½ cup broken hazelnuts or pistachios
3 to 4 very thin slices unsalted pork fat or lean bacon
1 cup flour
3 tablespoons water
Quick aspic (see recipe)

1. Preheat the oven to 375 degrees.

2. Place the pork and veal in a mixing bowl.

3. Add the salt pork to a saucepan and, when it is rendered of its fat, add the shallots, mushrooms, half a bay leaf and thyme. Cook, stirring oc-

casionally, about 5 minutes and add the chicken livers, salt, pepper, nutmeg and allspice. Cook, stirring, until livers lose their red color. Add the cognac and remove from the heat.

4. Spoon and scrape the mixture into the container of a food processor or electric blender. Add the egg, and blend. Spoon out and add to the meats in the mixing bowl. Add the hazelnuts, salt and pepper and blend well. You may fry a little of the mixture to test for seasonings and add more as desired.

5. Spoon the mixture into a 6-cup pâté mold and place the remaining bay leaf in the center. Cover the top with the salt pork or bacon. Cover with a round or oval of wax paper cut to fit.

6. Blend the flour and water well, kneading. Shape it into a round or oval, to fit over the wax paper. Cover with another oval of wax paper and cover with the mold's lid.

7. Place the mold in a basin of water and bring to the boil on top of the stove. Place in the oven and bake 2 hours. Remove. Add a 3-pound weight to the top of the pâté and let cool at room temperature. Refrigerate.

8. Scoop out and discard the untidy natural gelatin and liquid around the pâté. Clean the mold with a sponge to make it neat.

9. Pour quick-aspic around the pâté and on top. Let cool and spoon more aspic on top and around. Chill and repeat as often as necessary to give a nice aspic coating to the pâté.

Yield: 20 or more servings with other buffet dishes.

Quick aspic

3   *cups chicken broth*
1   *cup tomato juice*
4   *envelopes unflavored gelatin*
    Salt and freshly ground black
    pepper
1   *teaspoon sugar*
2   *egg shells, crushed*
2   *egg whites, lightly beaten*
2   *tablespoons cognac*

1. In a saucepan combine the chicken broth with the tomato juice, gelatin, salt, pepper, sugar, egg shells and egg whites and heat slowly, stirring constantly, until the mixture boils up in the pan.

2. Remove the pan from the heat and stir in the cognac.

3. Strain the mixture through a sieve lined with a flannel cloth that has been rinsed in cold water and wrung out. If the aspic starts to set or becomes too firm, it may be reheated, then brought to any desired temperature.

Yield: About 1 quart.

Taramosalata

(A carp roe spread)

1   *English muffin, preferably*
    onion-flavored
10 *tablespoons tarama (available*
    in the refrigerator section of
    stores that specialize in Greek
    and Turkish delicacies)
1   *clove garlic, finely minced*
5   *tablespoons lemon juice, more*
    or less, to taste
⅔   *cup olive oil*
2   *tablespoons water*
½   *cup chopped green onion*

1. Place the English muffin in a small bowl and add water to cover. Let stand until thoroughly saturated with water; then squeeze the muffin to extract most of the excess moisture. Add the squeezed muffin to the container of a food processor or electric blender.

2. Add the tarama, garlic, lemon juice, olive oil and water and blend to a mayonnaise-type consistency. Spoon the taramosalata into a bowl and fold in the green onion.

Yield: 20 or more servings with other buffet dishes.

Melitzanosalata

(Eggplant salad)

2 eggplants, about 1 pound each
½ cup sesame seed paste (not sesame oil), available in shops that specialize in Middle Eastern and Chinese foods
6 tablespoons lemon juice
½ cup olive oil
⅓ cup water
3 cloves garlic, finely minced
Salt and freshly ground pepper to taste
¾ teaspoon crushed dried oregano
½ cup chopped scallions
1 cup peeled, seeded, cubed tomato
¼ cup finely chopped parsley

1. Place the unpeeled eggplants over a gas flame, turning them as they cook and adjusting the flame as necessary. Cook until the eggplants are somewhat charred. The skin will no doubt burst during the cooking. When ready, the eggplants should be

cooked through the center. Or, prick the eggplants in several places and place on a baking dish in an oven preheated to about 375 degrees, about 1 hour. Let the eggplants stand until they are cool enough to handle.

2. Peel the eggplants and add the inner pulp to a mixing bowl.

3. Add the sesame seed paste, lemon juice, olive oil, water and garlic to the container of a food processor or electric blender and blend until a white paste is obtained. Add the eggplant pulp, salt, pepper and oregano and blend until smooth. Spoon the mixture into a bowl and, just before serving, fold in the remaining ingredients.

Yield: 20 or more servings with other buffet dishes.

Hummus bi Tahini

(Chick pea salad)

½ cup sesame seed paste (not sesame oil), available in shops that specialize in Middle Eastern and Chinese foods
⅓ cup water
¼ cup olive oil
6 tablespoons lemon juice
4 cloves garlic, peeled
3½ cups (two cans) well-drained chick peas or garbanzos
½ teaspoon ground cumin
1 teaspoon ground coriander seeds
5 scallions, trimmed and chopped
Salt and freshly ground pepper to taste

1. Combine the sesame seed paste, water, oil, lemon juice and gar-

lic in the container of a food processor or electric blender. Blend until smooth and light colored.

2. Add the chick peas, cumin and corianders. Blend to a puree. Fold in the scallions and add salt and pepper to taste. Serve with Middle Eastern bread.

Yield: 20 or more servings with other buffet dishes.

Roast Peppers with Anchovies

4 large, sweet peppers (bell peppers) preferably red, although green may be used
16 anchovy fillets, see note
2 tablespoons red wine vinegar
½ cup olive oil
1 clove garlic, finely minced
½ teaspoon crushed oregano
¼ cup chopped parsley
   Lemon halves for garnish

1. Do not core the peppers. Preheat the broiler and arrange a square of heavy-duty aluminum foil on the bottom. Add the peppers and broil close to the source of heat until they blister. Turn them as they blister until they have been broiled on all sides including, if it can be managed, the base. Drop the hot peppers into a paper bag and seal closely. This will cause the peppers to steam and will facilitate peeling.

2. When the peppers are cool, remove and peel them. Cut away and discard the core, the interior veins and seeds. Slice the peppers into strips about ½ inch wide.

3. Arrange the strips neatly and compactly on a serving dish. Arrange the anchovies over the peppers in a lattice pattern. Sprinkle with vinegar, oil, garlic and oregano. Sprinkle with the chopped parsley and garnish with lemon.

Yield: 20 or more servings with other buffet dishes.

Note: Ideally, this dish should be made with imported salted whole anchovies purchased in bulk. These are available on Ninth Avenue in stores that specialize in Mediterranean foods. One source is Kassos Brothers, 570 Ninth Avenue (between 41st and 42d Streets). To prepare the anchovies, rinse them by hand to remove the external salt. Split in half and remove the backbone. Rub off the skin, if desired. Drain well and add olive oil to cover until ready to use.

Celeri Rémoulade

(Celery root with mustard mayonnaise)

1¾ pounds knob celery, also known as celery root
1 tablespoon imported mustard such as Dijon or Düsseldorf
1 tablespoon red wine vinegar
   Salt and freshly ground pepper to taste
1 cup mayonnaise

1. Peel the knob celery, trimming off all the dark spots. Slice the celery as thinly as possible using a food processor, hand slicer, mandolin or even a sharp knife. There should be about 8 cups.

2. Stack the slices and cut them into the finest julienne strips. Place in a mixing bowl and add the remaining

ingredients. Toss with the hands until thoroughly blended.

Yield: 20 or more servings with other buffet dishes.

Mussels with Anchovy Mayonnaise

2   quarts well-scrubbed mussels
¼   cup dry white wine
3   sprigs fresh parsley
1   bay leaf
2   sprigs fresh thyme or 1 teaspoon dried
    Anchovy mayonnaise (see recipe)

1. Place the mussels in a kettle and add the wine, parsley, bay leaf and thyme. Cover and bring to the boil, shaking the kettle to redistribute the mussels occasionally. Cook until mussels open, about 5 minutes or longer. Let cool.

2. Drain the mussels but save the cooking liquid for the mayonnaise. Open the mussels and discard the top shell of each. Leave the mussels on the half shell and spoon enough mayonnaise over each to cover the mussels.

Yield: 20 or more servings with other buffet dishes.

Anchovy mayonnaise

1   cup mayonnaise (see recipe)
2   teaspoons liquid in which mussels cooked
1   tablespoon finely chopped shallots
1   tablespoon anchovy paste or chopped anchovy fillets.

Combine all the ingredients and chill until ready to serve.

Yield: About 1 cup.

Freddy Girardet's Brie and Roquefort Cheese Loaf

½   pound Brie at room temperature
½   pound Roquefort cheese at room temperature
¾   cup coarsely ground walnuts or pecans

1. Trim off and discard the "crust" of the Brie. Cut both the Brie and Roquefort into 1-inch cubes and add the pieces to the container of a food processor.

2. Blend until smooth. Remove the cheese and refrigerate until it is manageable. Shape it into a round or oval loaf.

3. Spread out a length of wax paper and sprinkle the nuts in the center. Roll the cheese loaf into them until the loaf is coated all over. Roll the loaf in plastic wrap and refrigerate. Let soften slightly before serving.

Yield: 20 or more servings with other buffet dishes.

Seviche of Scallops with Avocado

1½   pounds fresh bay scallops
5   tablespoons lime juice
½   squeezed lime shell
     Salt and freshly ground pepper to taste
1   tablespoon finely chopped fresh hot green or red pepper or 1 or 2 canned serrano chilies added according to taste

¼   teaspoon dried crushed
     oregano
1½ cups cubed, fresh, ripe but
     firm, unblemished avocado
2   tablespoons finely chopped
     fresh coriander (cilantro)
     leaves

1. Even if the scallops are small, cut them in half against the grain. Place them in a bowl and add 4 tablespoons of lime juice. Stir.

2. Cut the lime shell into tiny pieces and add them. Add salt and pepper and stir. Cover and refrigerate at least 12 hours.

3. Add the remaining ingredients. Stir well and serve with crisp leaves of romaine lettuce.

Yield: 20 or more servings with other buffet dishes.

Salade de Concombres à l'Aneth

(Cucumber and dill salad)

3   or more cucumbers
¼   cup plus 2 teaspoons superfine
     sugar
9   or 10 tablespoons white
     vinegar
     Salt to taste
3   tablespoons finely chopped
     fresh dill

1. Peel the cucumbers and slice them thinly. There should be about 4 cups. Add them to a mixing bowl and add a quarter cup of sugar and about 6 tablespoons of vinegar. Add salt to taste and mix well with the fingers. Cover and refrigerate several hours. The cucumbers will give up a good deal of liquid.

2. Drain the cucumbers and press to extract excess moisture. Add more sugar and vinegar and salt. Sprinkle with dill and toss again.

Yield: 20 or more servings with other buffet dishes.

Poached Striped Bass

1   4½-to-5-pound striped bass,
     cleaned and with head on but
     with gills removed
9   cups court bouillon (see
     recipe)

1. Rinse the fish in cold water. Wrap it in cheesecloth and tie it in several places with string.

2. Place the fish in the court bouillon. The liquid should just cover the fish. Partly cover. Bring to the boil and simmer 12 minutes.

3. Remove from the heat and let stand 20 minutes. Place it on a serving dish and carefully remove and discard the skin from the main body of the fish. Serve with any desired sauce such as sauce gribiche (see recipe).

Yield: 12 to 20 servings with other buffet dishes.

Court bouillon
(Poaching liquid for a 5-pound fish)

8   cups water
1   cup dry white wine
1   cup chopped celery
1   cup chopped carrot
1   cup chopped onion
4   sprigs fresh parsley
1   bay leaf

3 sprigs fresh thyme or 1
   teaspoon dried
2 cloves garlic, crushed
   Salt to taste
12 crushed peppercorns
⅛ teaspoon cayenne pepper

Bring all the ingredients to a boil, preferably in a fish poacher, and simmer 20 minutes. Let cool before adding fish.

Yield: Enough liquid to cook a 5-pound fish.

Sauce gribiche

1 cup mayonnaise (see recipe)
1 tablespoon finely chopped
   shallots
1 tablespoon finely chopped
   onion
1 tablespoon finely chopped
   chives
2 eggs, hard-cooked and pressed
   through a sieve
1 tablespoon water
   Salt and freshly ground
   pepper to taste
1 tablespoon chopped parsley

Combine all the ingredients in a mixing bowl and blend well. Serve with cold or lukewarm fish or meats.

Yield: About 2 cups.

Mayonnaise

1 egg yolk
1 teaspoon wine vinegar
1 to 3 teaspoons prepared
   mustard, preferably Dijon or
   Düsseldorf
   A few drops of Tabasco
   Salt and freshly ground
   pepper to taste

1 cup oil, preferably a light olive
   oil or a combination of olive
   oil and peanut, vegetable, or
   corn oil
   Lemon juice to taste, optional

1. Place the yolk in a mixing bowl and add the vinegar, mustard, Tabasco, salt and pepper to taste. Beat vigorously for a second or two with a wire whisk or electric beater.

2. Start adding the oil gradually, beating continuously with the whisk or electric beater. Continue beating and adding oil until all of it is used. Taste the mayonnaise and add more salt to taste and the lemon juice if desired. If all the mayonnaise is not to be used immediately, beat in a tablespoon of water. This will help stabilize the mayonnaise and retard its turning when stored in the refrigerator.

Yield: About 1 cup.

Dill Mayonnaise

2 cups mayonnaise made with 2
   egg yolks and 2 cups of oil
1 tablespoon imported mustard
   such as Dijon or Düsseldorf
½ cup finely chopped dill
1 cup finely chopped heart of
   celery
⅓ cup finely chopped onion
   Salt and freshly ground
   pepper to taste

Blend all the ingredients in a mixing bowl.

Yield: About 3 cups.

Poached Shrimp

4   pounds fresh shrimp in the
    shell, the smaller the better
    Cold water to cover
2   hot dried red chili peppers
    Salt to taste
12 crushed peppercorns
1   bay leaf
1   teaspoon allspice

Rinse and drain the shrimp. Place them in a kettle and add the remaining ingredients. Bring to the boil, simmer about 30 seconds and remove from the heat. Let stand until lukewarm. Peel and, if desired, devein. Serve with any desired sauce such as a dill mayonnaise (see recipe).

Yield: 20 or more servings with other buffet dishes.

Brandade de Morue

(Mousse of salt cod)

1½ pounds dried salt cod,
     preferably boneless (see note)
1   pound potatoes, about 2
2   cups milk
1   bay leaf
½   onion stuck with 2 cloves
1   cup olive oil
1   cup heavy cream
     Salt and freshly ground
     pepper to taste
¼   teaspoon nutmeg
⅛   teaspoon cayenne pepper
1   truffle cut into ¼-inch cubes,
     optional

1. Place the cod in a basin and add cold water to cover. Let soak, changing the water occasionally, about 12 hours.

2. When ready to cook, preheat the oven to 375 degrees.

3. Place the potatoes in the oven and bake 45 minutes to 1 hour or until tender. Remove.

4. Drain the soaked cod and place it in a deep skillet. Add cold water to cover, ½ cup of milk, bay leaf, onion stuck with cloves. Bring to the boil and simmer about 3 minutes. Drain. If the cod is not boneless, carefully remove any skin and bones.

5. Gently heat the remaining milk, oil and cream in separate saucepans.

6. Split the potatoes in half. Scoop the hot flesh into the bowl of an electric mixer. Discard the potato skins. Start the beater on low speed and add the cod. Continue beating, gradually increasing the speed.

7. Alternately and gradually, beat in the hot milk, cream and oil. Beat in the nutmeg and cayenne. If used, stir in the truffle.

8. Serve with triangles of French bread fried in olive oil or with sliced French bread.

Yield: 12 to 20 servings with other buffet dishes.

Note: Dried salt cod is available in many markets in Manhattan on Ninth Avenue that specialize in Italian and Mediterranean specialties and at Casa Moneo, 210 West 14th Street.

Mushrooms à la Grecque

1   teaspoon coriander seeds
½   teaspoon oregano
½   teaspoon dried marjoram

½ teaspoon dried fennel seeds
1 teaspoon dried sage leaves, crushed
½ teaspoon dried thyme
1 bay leaf, broken
1 large garlic clove, crushed but unpeeled
¼ cup water
2 tablespoons lemon juice
3 tablespoons olive oil
1 tablespoon distilled white vinegar
Salt and freshly ground pepper to taste
1 pound mushrooms, the smaller the better
Lemon wedges or parsley for garnish

1. Crush the coriander seeds and add them to a saucepan large enough to hold the mushrooms. Add the oregano. Place the marjoram, fennel, sage, thyme, bay leaf and garlic in a small square of cheesecloth. Bring up the edges and tie with string.

2. Add the cheesecloth bag to the saucepan and add the water, lemon juice, olive oil, vinegar, salt and pepper to taste. Bring to the boil and cover over high heat 5 minutes.

3. Meanwhile, rinse the mushrooms in cold water and drain them well. If the mushrooms are very small, leave them whole. Otherwise, cut them in half or quarter them, depending on size.

4. Add the mushrooms to the saucepan and return to the boil. Cover and cook over high heat 7 to 8 minutes, shaking the saucepan to redistribute the mushrooms so that they cook evenly. Uncover and cook about 5 minutes longer over high heat.

5. Spoon the mushrooms, cooking liquid and cheesecloth bag into a mixing bowl and cover. Let cool. Chill overnight. Remove and discard the cheesecloth bag. Serve cold or at room temperature. Garnish, if desired, with lemon wedges or parsley. Serve, if desired, with other vegetables à la grecque.

Yield: 6 to 8 servings.

Fresh Fennel à la Grecque

Follow the instructions for mushrooms à la grecque but substitute 2 pounds (about 3 or 4 bulbs) of fresh fennel for the mushrooms. Trim off the tough stalks and the bottoms of the vegetable. Cut the vegetable into quarters or sixths. Increase the water to 1 cup and cook for a total of 12 to 15 minutes or until the fennel is tender but not mushy. If there is too much liquid, remove the fennel and let the sauce cook down to the desired consistency.

Jambon Persillé

(Parsleyed ham, Burgundy-style)

1 5-pound canned ham
2 pounds fresh pigs' knuckles or 3 pounds fresh pig's feet
1 1-pound section fresh pork skin (optional)
6 cups fresh or canned chicken broth
1 cup dry white wine
3 small ribs celery tied in a bundle
1 carrot, trimmed and scraped
1 turnip, trimmed, peeled and quartered
3 large cloves garlic, unpeeled

1   *onion, peeled and quartered*
2   *sprigs fresh thyme or 1*
    teaspoon dried
1   *bay leaf*
12 *crushed peppercorns*
1   *or 2 large bunches fresh*
    parsley
¼   *cup red wine vinegar*
    Freshly ground pepper
    Imported Dijon mustard
    Cornichons (small sour French
    pickles)

1. Open the can and remove the ham. Spoon out any gelatin remaining in the can into a bowl. Reserve it separately. Scrape off any gelatin from the ham into the bowl. Place the ham on its side and slice it into 3 equal, flat slices. Set aside.

2. Place the pig's knuckles or pig's feet and pork skin in a kettle and add cold water to cover. Bring to the boil and drain. Return the meat to a clean kettle and add the chicken broth, wine, celery, carrot, turnip, garlic, onion, thyme, bay leaf and peppercorns. Add the reserved gelatin from the canned ham. Cover and cook 2 hours.

3. Remove the pig's knuckles and let cool.

4. Add the flat slices of ham in one layer to the kettle and cook about 15 minutes. Turn the slices and continue cooking about 15 minutes. Remove the ham and set aside.

5. Continue cooking the liquid in the kettle until it is reduced to about 4 cups. As the liquid cooks, take care to skim the surface to discard all scum that rises to the top. Discard the pork skin.

6. Remove the meat and skin from the pig's knuckles. Discard the bones. Combine the meat and skin in

the container of an electric blender and add 1 cup of the cooking liquid. Blend. Return this to the kettle.

7. Cut the ham pieces into ¾-inch slices. Cut these slices into ¾-inch strips. Set aside.

8. Cut off the tough stems from the parsley. Wash the parsley thoroughly and dry it. Chop it. There should be 3 or more cups of chopped parsley.

9. Select a round-bottom mixing bowl with a 2-quart capacity. The object now is to fill the bowl compactly with layers of ham, parsley, cooking liquid and a little vinegar.

10. Make a layer of about 6 tablespoons of parsley. Arrange over this a parallel layer of ham strips, close together but not too close to block the liquid when added. Add enough liquid to nearly cover the strips, while simultaneously flowing between the strips. Add a light layer of parsley and a sprinkle of vinegar and freshly ground black pepper. Add more strips, more liquid, more parsley and so on until the bowl is almost filled. Cover with a round of wax paper and a weight such as a round pie plate filled with a metal mallet. Refrigerate overnight.

11. Dip the bowl in hot water, wipe it off and invert it to unmold the ham. Serve cut into slices, starting at the center. Serve with imported Dijon mustard and cornichons.

Yield: 1 parsleyed ham.

Snow Crab Claws with Pernod

2   pounds (20 to 25) fresh or
    frozen crab claws
    Salt and freshly ground
    pepper to taste
2   tablespoons, approximately,
    Pernod or Ricard

1. If the snow crab claws are frozen, allow them to defrost, preferably
in the refrigerator.

2. Arrange the claws in one layer
on a flat surface. Sprinkle with salt
and pepper. Using a small spoon,
pour equal amounts of Pernod over
the exposed portion of each claw.
Chill until ready to serve.

3. Serve with celery mayonnaise
and tarragon mayonnaise (see recipes)
on the side.

Yield: 6 or more appetizer servings.

Tarragon Mayonnaise

1   cup mayonnaise, preferably
    freshly made (see recipe)

1   tablespoon finely chopped
    fresh tarragon or half the
    amount dried
    Salt and freshly ground
    pepper to taste
    Lemon juice to taste.

Combine all the ingredients and
chill until ready to serve.

Yield: About 1 cup.

Celery Mayonnaise

4   or more tender ribs of celery,
    trimmed
½   cup mayonnaise, preferably
    freshly made (see recipe)
    Salt and freshly ground
    pepper to taste
1   teaspoon white vinegar
¼   cup heavy cream

1. If the celery ribs are a bit
tough, scrape them with a swivel-
bladed vegetable knife. Using a sharp,
heavy knife, cut the celery into thin
crosswise pieces. There should be
about 3½ cups.

2. Combine the celery with the
remaining ingredients and blend well.
Let chill until ready to serve.

Yield: About 4½ cups.

The World's Greatest Dish

List-making is something that critics do to make their spirits soar as each year sags, Christmas approaches and December slouches to a close. This year I shall uncharacteristically rise to the occasion—let my own spirits levitate—and list what is to my mind the world's greatest dish. There are those, of course, who will disagree with me, but it's my spirits that need the bellows as of this writing.

The dish, the world's greatest, is purely and simply that excelling and sublime creation known in French as coulibiac de saumon, and sometimes koulibiak de saumon.

It is not easy to explain to the uninitiated precisely what a coulibiac de saumon is. The easiest way out would be to define it, as it frequently is in dictionaries of gastronomy, as a "pâté of salmon." Such a definition is woefully inapt. It is no mere trifle, no ordinary pâté, something to be dabbled with while awaiting a second course or third or fourth. A coulibiac is a celestial creation, manna for the culinary gods and a main course unto itself. I'm not at all convinced that anything should precede such a sublime invention, except perhaps a spoonful or two of caviar. And I am less convinced that anything should follow it. Who can improve on paradisiacal bliss?

A coulibiac admittedly demands patience, time, talent and enthusiasm, and if you are possessed of these, what a magnificent offering to those invited to your table for the holidays. Fie on goose, fie on turkey, fie on game and all the rest. Blessed be the holiday table graced with coulibiac. And blessed be any cook who can master it. And almost any cook can; any cook that is skilled enough to prepare a brioche dough, a standard French crêpe and make a cream sauce. If you can do these, you are equal to the task.

One of the bonuses of a coulibiac: almost all the components can be made the day or night before. The brioche and crêpe are the externals, the outer trappings of the dish. The filling is a well-seasoned but easily made compendium of textures and flavors that include fresh salmon, hard-cooked eggs, rice, dill, mushrooms and shallots. And, classically but by no means essential, chopped, cooked vesiga, the spinal marrow of sturgeon that is, indeed, available in New York.

One of the greatest and most celebrated titans of French cooking shared in his day an unabashed enthusiasm for the dish.

Edouard Nignon by name, who lived around the turn of the century, wrote quite lyrically about food and dining well. In his book, *Eloges de la Cuisine Française,* a compilation of essays and recipes, he relates quite rhapsodically the fact that he served a coulibiac (made with perch; salmon is better) to Tsar Nicolas at the Kremlin Palace and the tsar was equally unstinting in his praise for the chef's sorcery and, one presumes, his coulibiac.

Although the name coulibiac or koulibiak is of Russian origin, one French food dictionary states that it derives from a German word, kohlgeback, a dish brought to Russia many years ago by German immigrants. Kohlgeback, apparently, was a pastry filled with chopped cooked cabbage, a pastry similar, one suspects, to a pirog or piroshki.

Oddly and unfortunately there are very few restaurants in New York where one may dine on coulibiac, an unhappy circumstance that may depend on the public's unawareness of the glory of the dish as well as of the time required to make it.

It can be yours for the making. Read on. We'll show you how.

The Assembly and Baking of a Coulibiac of Salmon

Brioche dough (see recipe)
Salmon and mushrooms with
   velouté (see recipe)
14 7-inch crêpes (see recipe)
Rice and egg filling (see recipe)

Ingredients used in assembly

2   egg yolks
2   tablespoons cold water
2   tablespoons butter at room
    temperature
¾   pound plus 4 tablespoons hot
    melted butter

For instructions on assembling the coulibiac, see steps 7–12 on pages 294–296.

Brioche dough

¾   cup milk
¼   teaspoon sugar
3   tablespoons (packages) dry
     yeast
4   to 4½ cups flour
     Salt to taste
1   cup egg yolks (about 12)
8   tablespoons (one stick) butter
     at room temperature

1. Pour the milk into a saucepan and heat it gradually to lukewarm. Remove from the heat. If the milk has become too hot, let it cool to lukewarm.

2. Sprinkle the milk with sugar and yeast and stir to dissolve. Cover with a towel. Let stand about 5 minutes and place the mixture in a warm place (the natural warmth of a turned-off oven is good for this) about 5 minutes. It should ferment during the period and increase in volume.

3. Place 4 cups of flour with salt to taste in the bowl of an electric mixer fitted with a dough hook, or use a mixing bowl and wooden spoon. Make a well in the center and pour in the yeast mixture, the cup of yolks and butter. With the dough hook or wooden spoon gradually work in flour until well blended. Then beat vigorously until dough is quite smooth and can be shaped into a ball.

4. Turn the dough out onto a lightly floured board and knead until it is smooth and satiny, about 10 to 15 minutes. As you work the dough, continue to add flour to the kneading surface as necessary to prevent sticking, but take care not to add an excess or the finished product will be tough.

5. Lightly butter a clean mixing bowl and add the ball of dough. Cover with clean towel and let stand in warm place about 1 hour or until double in bulk. Punch the dough down. Turn it out once more onto a lightly floured board. Knead it about 1 minute and return it to the clean bowl. Cover closely with plastic wrap and refrigerate overnight.

6. The next morning, punch the dough down again and continue to refrigerate, covered, until ready to use.

Salmon and mushrooms with velouté

The salmon and mushrooms

2   skinless, boneless salmon
     fillets, preferably center-cut,
     each weighing about 1½
     pounds
2   tablespoons butter
2   tablespoons finely chopped
     onion
2   tablespoons finely chopped
     shallots
     Salt and freshly ground
     pepper to taste
¾   pound fresh mushrooms,
     thinly sliced
¼   cup finely chopped fresh dill
2   cups dry white wine

The velouté

2   tablespoons butter
3   tablespoons flour
⅛   teaspoon cayenne pepper
3   tablespoons lemon juice
5   egg yolks

1. Preheat the oven to 400 degrees. Using a sharp carving knife, cut each fillet, one at a time, on the bias into slices about ⅓ inch thick. Each fillet should produce about 12 slices. Select a heatproof rectangular baking dish. It should be just large enough to

hold two rows of slightly overlapping slices (a dish measuring 13½ by 8½ by 2 inches was used in testing this recipe). Rub the bottom of the dish with the 2 tablespoons butter and sprinkle with onion, shallots, salt and pepper. Arrange two parallel rows of salmon slices, the slices slightly overlapping over the onion and shallots. Sprinkle with salt to taste. Sprinkle somewhat liberally with black pepper. Scatter the mushrooms over the salmon.

2. Sprinkle the mushrooms with fresh dill and pour the wine over all. Cover with aluminum foil and bring to

to the boil over high heat. Tilt the dish containing the salmon. More liquid will accumulate as it stands. Spoon or pour this liquid into the saucepan containing the cooking liquid.

4. For the velouté, melt the 2 tablespoons butter in a saucepan and stir in the flour, using a wire whisk. When blended, add the cooking liquid, stirring rapidly with the whisk. Cook about 5 minutes, stirring often. Add the mushrooms and continue cooking about 20 minutes, adding any liquid that accumulates around the salmon. Add the cayenne pepper and lemon juice. Beat the yolks with a whisk and scrape them into the mushrooms, stirring vigorously. Cook about 30 seconds, stirring, and remove from the heat. Add salt and a generous amount of pepper to taste.

the boil on top of the stove. Place the dish in the oven and bake 15 minutes.

3. Remove the dish, uncover and pour the accumulated liquid into a saucepan. Carefully spoon off most of the mushrooms and transfer them to another dish. Bring the cooking liquid

5. Spoon and scrape this sauce—it should be quite thick—over the salmon. Blanket the salmon all over

with an even layer of the sauce but try to avoid having it spill over the sides of the salmon.

6. Smooth the sauce over. Let cool. Grease a neat rectangle of wax paper with butter. Arrange this, but-

tered side down, on the sauce-covered salmon and refrigerate until thoroughly cold.

The assembly

7. Remove the salmon from the refrigerator. Using a knife, cut it in half lengthwise down the center.

8. Remove the brioche dough from the bowl and with floured fingers shape it into a thick, flat pillow shape. Place the brioche dough on a lightly floured board and roll it into a rectangle measuring about 21 by 18 inches. The rectangle, of course, will

have slightly rounded corners. Arrange 8 crêpes, edges overlapping in a neat pattern, over the center of the rectangle, leaving a border of brioche dough.

9. Sprinkle the crêpes down the center with a rectangle of about one-third of the rice mixture. Pick up half the chilled salmon and carefully arrange it, mushroom side down, over the rice mixture. Sprinkle with another third of the rice mixture.

10. Top this, sandwich fashion, with another layer of the chilled salmon filling, mushroom side up.

Sprinkle with remaining rice. Cover with 6 overlapping crêpes.

11. Bring up one side of the brioche. Brush it liberally with a mixture of 2 beaten yolks and 2 tablespoons cold water. Bring up the opposite side of the brioche dough to enclose the filling, overlapping the two sides of dough. Brush all over with egg yolk. Trim off the ends of the dough to make them neat. Brush with yolk and bring up the ends, pinching as necessary to enclose the filling. Butter a baking dish with 2 tablespoons of butter. Carefully turn the coulibiac upside down onto the baking dish. This will keep the seams intact.

Brush the coulibiac all over with yolk. Using a small, round, decorative cookie cutter, cut a hole in the center of the coulibiac. This will allow steam to escape. Brush around the hole with yolk. Cut out another slightly larger

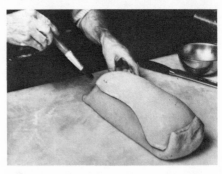

ring of dough to surround and outline the hole neatly. Roll out a scrap of dough and cut off strips of dough to decorate the coulibiac. Always brush with beaten yolk before and after applying pastry cutouts.

12. Roll out a 6-foot length of aluminum foil. Fold it over into thirds to make one long band about 4½ inches in height. Brush the band with 4 tablespoons of melted butter. Arrange the band neatly and snugly around the loaf, buttered side against the brioche. The purpose of the band is to prevent the sides of the loaf from collapsing before the dough has a chance to firm up while baking. Fasten the top of the band with a jumbo paper clip. Run a cord around the center of the foil band to secure it in place. Run the cord around three times and tie the ends. Make certain the bottom of the loaf is securely enclosed with foil. Set the pan in a warm, draft-free place for about 30 minutes. Meanwhile, preheat the oven to 400 degrees. Place the loaf in the oven and bake 15 minutes. Reduce the oven heat to 375 degrees and bake 10 minutes longer.

Cover with a sheet of aluminum foil to prevent excess browning. Continue baking 20 minutes (a total baking time at this point of 45 minutes). Remove foil and continue baking 15 minutes more. Remove the coulibiac from the oven. Pour ½ cup of the melted butter through the steam hole into the filling. Serve cut into 1-inch slices with remaining hot melted butter on the side.

Yield: 16 or more servings.

Crêpes

1½　cups flour
3　large eggs
　　Salt and freshly ground
　　pepper to taste
1¾　cups milk
2　tablespoons melted butter
1　tablespoon finely chopped
　　parsley
1　tablespoon finely chopped dill

1. Place the flour in a mixing bowl and make a well in the center. Add the eggs, salt, and pepper and, stirring, gradually add the milk.

2. Put the mixture through a sieve, running the whisk around inside of the sieve to remove lumps. Add the melted butter, the parsley and dill. Use to make crêpes.

Yield: About 14 7-inch crêpes.

Note: Leftover crêpes may be frozen. Interlayer them with rounds of wax paper, wrap in foil and freeze.

Rice and egg filling

3　hard-cooked eggs
1¾　cups firmly cooked rice
¼　cup finely chopped parsley
1　tablespoon finely chopped dill
　　Salt and freshly ground
　　pepper to taste
1½　cups chopped cooked vesiga
　　(see recipe below)

1. Chop the eggs and add them to a mixing bowl.

2. Add the remaining ingredients and blend well.

Vesiga for coulibiac

One of the classic—but optional—ingredients for a coulibiac of salmon is called vesiga. It is a ropelike, gelatinous substance, actually the spinal marrow of sturgeon. The vesiga, after cleaning, must be simmered for several hours until tender. It is then chopped and looks like chopped aspic. It has a very mild, bland flavor and its principal contribution to the dish is its slightly tender but chewy texture.

Vesiga is by no means a staple item, but it is often available from certain sources in Manhattan. They include Iron Gate Products, 424 West 54th Street (757-2670) and at F. Rozzo and Sons, a fish market, at 159 Ninth

Avenue, near 20th Street (242-6100). It is best to telephone in advance to make certain of the product's availability. Prices of vesiga vary.

½   *pound vesiga*
    Salt to taste

1. Wash the vesiga in cold water.

Split it as necessary for thorough cleaning. Drain the vesiga and place it in a saucepan. Add water to cover and salt to taste. Bring to the boil.

2. Simmer 4 hours, replacing the liquid as it evaporates. Drain the vesiga and chop it. It will be translucent and look like chopped aspic.

Yield: 1½ cups.

Index